3RD EDITION

EFFECTIVE
Police
Leadership

Moving Beyond
Management

THOMAS E. BAKER

Looseleaf
Law Publications, Inc.

43-08 162nd Street
Flushing, NY 11358
www.LooseleafLaw.com
800-647-5547

This publication is not intended to replace nor be a substitute for any official procedural material issued by your agency of employment or other official source. Looseleaf Law Publications, Inc., the author and any associated advisors have made all possible efforts to ensure the accuracy and thoroughness of the information provided herein but accept no liability whatsoever for injury, legal action or other adverse results following the application or adoption of the information contained in this book.

Library of Congress Cataloging-in-Publication Data

Baker, Thomas E., 1941-
  Effective police leadership : moving beyond management / Thomas E. Baker. -- 3rd ed.
      p. cm.
  Includes bibliographical references and index.
  ISBN 978-1-60885-020-4
  1. Police administration--United States. 2. Police--Supervision of--United States. I. Title.
   HV8141.B28 2010
   363.2068'4--dc22

1st Printing: 2010
2nd Printing: 2011

2010020309

Cover by *Sans Serif, Inc.*, Saline, Michigan

```
┌─────────────────────────────────────────┐
│                                           │
│            DEDICATED TO                   │
│            MY WIFE, JANE                   │
│         DAUGHTER, SHANNON                  │
│               and                          │
│         THE MEN AND WOMEN                  │
│         OF LAW ENFORCEMENT                 │
│                                           │
└─────────────────────────────────────────┘
```

ACKNOWLEDGMENTS

Jane Piland-Baker, B.S. Virginia Commonwealth University; M.S. University of Scranton. I would like to thank my wife, Jane, my partner in life for the last 35 years. Her encouragement has been essential to the completion of this book.

To the staff at Looseleaf Law Publications, Inc.: Mary Loughrey, Editorial Vice President, Maria Felten, Production Editor, Michael Loughrey, President and CEO.

Dr. Daniel V. Fraustino, Professor of English, B.A. University of Buffalo; M.A. San Diego State University; Ph.D. Binghamton State University. Dr. Fraustino is a full professor at the University of Scranton and teaches literature and writing. Dan's editing skills were essential to the development of the First Edition of this book.

Quotes noted in this text are used with the permission of:
The National Association of Chiefs of Police, Washington, D.C.
The International Association of Chiefs of Police
The Houston Police Department

Law Enforcement Oath of Honor

"On my honor, I will never betray my badge, my integrity, my character, or the public trust. I will always have the courage to hold myself and others accountable for our actions. I will always uphold the Constitution and community I serve."

Used with permission of
International Association of Chiefs of Police

ABOUT THE AUTHOR

Thomas E. Baker is an associate professor of criminal justice at the University of Scranton and Lt. Col. United States Army Reserve Military Police Corps (Ret.). In addition, Lt. Col. Baker has served as a police officer with Henrico County, Virginia and as an investigator with the Organized Crime, Vice Intelligence Unit, Montgomery County Police Department, Maryland.

Lt. Col. Baker's military assignments include: special agent, detachment commander, battalion level commander and a Command Headquarters assignment with the United States Army Criminal Investigation Command. Additional assignments include: provost marshal, military police investigations, staff officer for Training and Doctrine Command and instructor for the United States Army Command and General Staff College. He has earned over ten military and national police awards, including the Meritorious Service Medal.

Lt. Col. Baker is a graduate of the Basic Military Police Officer's Course, Advanced Infantry Officer's Course, Advanced Military Police Officer's Course, Criminal Investigation Course, Advanced Criminal Investigation Management Course, Psychological Operations Course, Field Grade Infantry Course, and the United States Army Command and General Staff College.

His academic degrees include: A.A. Law Enforcement, B.S. Sociology/Social Welfare and M.S. Counseling from Virginia Commonwealth University; M.Ed. Physical Education, M.S. Health Education, East Stroudsburg University; CAGS Psychology and Counseling, Marywood College; and Advanced Study Adult Education, Pennsylvania State University and Temple University.

Prof. Baker has been teaching courses in police administration, public safety administration, criminal investigation, and crime prevention for over 38 years.

He is the author of 5 books and 150 articles that have appeared in professional journals and has presented research at national meetings. Professor Baker is the author of *Intelligence-Led Policing: Leadership, Strategies and Tactics,* a Looseleaf Law publication.

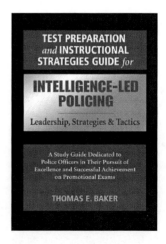

TABLE OF CONTENTS

PREFACE

What lies behind us and what lies before us are tiny matters compared to what lies within us.

- OLIVER WENDELL HOLMES

The purpose of this book is to identify what leaders must BE, KNOW and DO to gain followship. A number of prominent authors have developed their own definitions of leadership. For example, Warren Bennis has defined management and leadership as the manager doing the right things and the leader doing things right. Ken Blanchard defines management as goal setting and showing approval. Steven Covey portrays the leader as one who decides on which one of the many walls to place a ladder, whereas the manager decides on how to climb it most successfully. Peter Drucker has written that management equates with efficiency, whereas leadership is effectiveness. After reading these texts, one understands that the leadership process is more important than basic definitions.

Defining leadership is a difficult task. However, the application of leadership principles is even more complex. Leadership is a process that fluctuates; however, its basic fundamentals remain constant. This book discusses "can do" leadership fundamentals essential to influencing police officers.

WHAT SHOULD A LEADER BE? Leaders implement the process by possessing three leadership attributes: (1) character, (2) knowledge, and (3) skills.

WHAT SHOULD A LEADER KNOW? Leaders consider four major areas of concern: (1) the leader, (2) the follower, (3) communication and (4) the situation. These four factors have a significant impact on leadership behaviors and timing.

i

WHAT SHOULD A LEADER DO? Leaders provide vision and direction. In addition, they instill trust and confidence. (Adapted from FM 22-100 Military Leadership) Refer to the "Can Do" interview with Sergeant Raymond T. Hayes on page 235 for additional information. For a more detailed description of this process read CHAPTER 12 EFFECTIVE LEADERSHIP: 10 "CAN DO" APPLIED FOCUSING POINTS.

Excellent leadership is a quality that transcends all organizational, police, military, or civilian sectors. Effective leaders are in demand, especially "can do" leaders, who accept responsibility and accountability. While the book emphasizes "can do" leadership skills, management is considered an important support function. One must not underestimate the value of excellent management skills. Managers require efficiency, while leaders point the way. Both management and leadership skills provide a total quality police service.

Managers with a reputation for getting things done become known as "can-do" leaders. Dependability in getting the job done is worthy of recognition and promotion. An appropriate evaluation process helps assess if an officer has the ability to become a "can do" leader.

Potential leaders often make two mistakes that impact on advancement: (1) they fail to keep pace with their contemporaries; and (2) they become over specialized. Proper preparation increases readiness for leadership responsibilities and sets the foundation for success. The failure to prepare insures that someone else will be selected.

Adequate leadership preparation has no substitute. Knowledge is power and serves as the foundation for leadership excellence. To gain the appropriate expertise, one must pursue knowledge vigorously. "Can do" leaders constantly evaluate and cultivate leadership skills.

Successful leadership requires the determination to overcome obstacles and plan for the future. Alert leadership candidates prepare for promotion and advancement. Dedicated officers assume initiative and responsibility. Above all, prospective leaders persist in the accomplishment of personal goals and pursuit of excellence. They never tire in their struggle to achieve.

A leader's expertise is essential to being respected. Leaders with expert power will be respected and sought out for advice and assistance. Officers will have confidence in leaders who have the ability to perform, the end result being the cooperation and support from others. Preparation for leadership includes understanding the leadership process. Self-improvement requires that study time be dedicated to personal growth and development. Enjoy leisure time and life; however, invest in the future.

Remaining in one specialized position often results in non-advancement in police agencies. Spending too much time in narcotics or other specialized task force responsibilities does not prepare officers for leadership. The security of a well-known job must be traded for professional risk taking and new opportunities. Failure to take risks can stunt a promising career. Confining oneself to one's specialty leads to stagnation and a truncated career track. However, rotating assignments may broaden career potential. New assignments expand capabilities and therefore opportunities.

Those who prepare for leadership study the position, rather than memorize promotional examination questions. Potential leaders with knowledge and expertise achieve success on the examination. Awareness of professional requirements allows candidates to reason examination questions. Preparing for the role assures success on the examination, interview and police assessment process.

Effective Police Leadership will help you develop "can do" leadership skills. Keep this book and reread it for understanding rather than memorization. Continue to read and prepare for leadership roles during the course of your career. *Effective Police Leadership* will help you focus on your career as a police leader and arrive at your professional destination.

Preface

Those who desire to be successful "can do" leaders in the twenty-first century must prepare now. "Can do" leaders read leadership materials such as those contained in this and other books, and take every opportunity to keep pace with the future. They anticipate and prepare for leadership positions that may become available in the future.

HOW TO GET PROMOTED

Officer Jack Jones	Strategic Goals and Objectives
Officer Jack Jones is an excellent officer. He assesses his career and realizes that the first promotion to sergeant is important. The competition is intense and there are few positions for many candidates. Officer Jones appreciates that outstanding leaders plan their careers. Jack's positive professional attitude places him in an excellent position for selection. Peers admire his professional expertise, skills and maturity. Officer Jones outlines the following strategic goals and objectives:	**General Goals:** • Outline the "big picture" for promotional opportunities • Place yourself strategically by engaging in professional development and training • Identify key staff officers who have decision making responsibilities • Express to leadership your interest in the position • Develop a reputation for being an excellent leader in your present capacity **Specific Objectives:** • Prepare for the rank by developing an understanding of the expertise necessary for success • Study for promotional examinations early • Study for understanding, rather than memorization • Identify criteria for promotion and assessment procedures

INTRODUCTION: THIS BOOK IS ABOUT POLICE LEADERSHIP

Leadership is not a spectator sport.

- KOUZES AND POSNER

This book suggests that police leadership directly impacts on the quality of life and delivery of services. At their best, leaders inspire officers; at their worst, they sabotage the community. Superior leaders provide excellence in police service to their community.

This book describes the essentials of leadership that foster a "can do" attitude. However, leadership has no simple recipe. The literature establishes leadership as both a social science and art form. Moreover, leadership has no one correct style but depends on the officer's readiness to perform the mission in a given situation.

This book encourages its readers to focus on leadership issues and organizational structure. Improvements in both areas enhance the delivery of services to a community. "Can do" leadership encourages positive change and professional advancement. Once readers address leadership issues, they may apply problem-solving approaches to community concerns.

STRATEGIC LEADERSHIP

Strategic leadership anticipates problems by applying strategic and tactical methods. Successful strategic leaders plan and assess changing situations, an approach that serves as the foundation for problem-solving policing.

Strategic leadership does not wait for problems to develop but targets individual problems and executes effective solutions.

This kind of leadership anticipates possible courses of action that address unique problems. It also permits leaders to respond in a timely manner without being driven by events. In other words, it opposes the crisis management approach. Responding to individual emergencies without looking at the complete situation leads to frustration and failure.

Communication is the essential ingredient that enables leaders to integrate the command effort. Police leaders plan strategy together to maintain a unified approach. With everyone included in planning, consensus and support intensifies.

Strategic leadership and planning are essential responses to rapidly changing social conditions. In recent years, it has become critical because of shifting police strategies. The change from the "past" to the "future" creates the need for reform and conceptual thinking.

SHIFTING STRATEGIES

One advantage of the community-oriented policing philosophy is that it frames policy and defines the department's relationship with citizens. It also offers direction for police decision-making and provides guidance in the absence of the Chief or other leaders. The philosophy provides police officers the navigational system for developing a "can do" attitude.

Police efficiency closely relates to structure and function. Police agencies are beginning to modernize and restructure to achieve new strategies. Reorganization will be necessary to develop the community-oriented and problem-solving approach.

Bureaucracies are characterized by control and hierarchies that resist change. Autocratic leadership stifles initiative and creativity. This approach was accepted under the traditional model of policing, but not under the new community-oriented philosophy.

Unfortunately, in many departments, the old organizational structure and bureaucratic style of leadership remains in place. Implementation of problem-solving policing will require a change in organizational structure. Police leaders are rapidly shifting strategies from a reactive to a proactive approach.

Police leaders and officers need flexibility in decision-making. The emphasis is no longer on command and control, but on decentralization. Police management is in transition to a participatory style of leadership. The strategic shift from management to leadership will not take place without creativity and innovation.

MANAGEMENT TO LEADERSHIP

The old bureaucratic model requires managers to control and manage all departmental resources, which results in micro-management of competent officers and a lack of trust. Effective leadership moves beyond control but focuses on motivating people toward the successful accomplishment of a department's mission.

Community policing requires creativity and ingenuity. Police leadership is changing to meet the new requirements. The transition is from centralized control to participative leadership. Strategic and situational leadership are essential to effective policing. The combination of both approaches can be applied to a variety of unique problems and situations.

STRATEGIC AND SITUATIONAL LEADERSHIP

Strategic and situational leadership addresses the needs of both officers and the community. The combination of strategic and situational leadership provides a framework for long-term and short-term decision-making. Both approaches provide a flexible foundation that offers police leaders a road map for effective leadership. It also enhances the possibility of successful problem-solving policing.

Strategic leadership and situational leadership are ideally suited to (1) community-oriented policing, (2) neighborhood-oriented policing, (3) problem-solving policing and (4) Neighborhood Watch programs. This focus helps facilitate and plan the "can do" attitude.

ASSESSMENT OF THE SITUATION

Effective leaders fully understand the situation and their subordinates' readiness to perform. They have the ability to influence and develop their officers. However, followers have considerable influence on the successful completion of the mission.

The assessment of the department's readiness to change is essential to moving forward. The starting point for developing a "can do" leadership process is to identify existing problems. Once problems have been identified, efforts must be directed at eliminating them. Police leaders organize problem-solving teams that plan together to resolve problems. Teams can accomplish more than individuals striving independently.

THE POLICE EXECUTIVE: THE CHIEF

The chief forecasts well into the future. He or she is responsible for developing the department's vision and mission statement. The chief sets clear priorities and standards. This is followed by allowing leaders to concentrate on priorities and provide support. Generally, the method for accomplishing specific tasks is left to the discretion of subordinates.

The Chief of Police is ultimately responsible for everything that goes right or wrong. The final decision is always the responsibility of the chief. The chief shares power with two or three senior leaders in functional areas, for example, operations and administration. They share their power with middle managers. Finally, power is allocated to sergeants and police officers. At every level, power is exercised with responsibility and accountability for the mission.

The chief personally evaluates how the department responds and what corrective actions are needed. This includes having face-to-face contact with officers. On-site contacts are essential when delegating and empowering others. "Leading from the front" is an essential leadership concept of the "can do" approach.

SENIOR LEADERSHIP: VISION

Senior leadership provides vision and a sense of mission. Leadership requires critical thinking and strategic planning. Problem-solving and effective decision-making skills are all necessary to pursue excellence and chart the journey. An emphasis on vision requires leaders to ask three questions before implementing the "can do" approach: (1) Where is the department going? (2) How will the department get there? and (3) How will arrival be evaluated?

Senior leaders establish strategic objectives and share their vision with department members. Senior leaders work primarily through indirect leadership, emphasizing delegation and collaboration with staff and middle managers. Clearly, the chief and senior leaders rely on the informal use of power, rather than the abuse of formal power.

MIDDLE MANAGERS

Middle managers act as liaison between the chief and senior leaders, and have a responsibility to relate to sergeants. Middle managers assist with planning and training, and support administratively and logistically. These administrative responsibilities are essential but represent a small segment of the middle manager's role.

Managers are leaders, and leading includes mentoring and coaching. Managers build teams, empower officers and reward effort. When the leadership role is neglected, subordinates feel abandoned, which results in a lack of direction and incohesiveness.

SERGEANTS LEADING THE WAY

A police sergeant's influence can be strategic and dynamic. Sergeants "lead the way" by implementing tactical planning strategies and they direct and empower their officers. Sergeants apply direct leadership skills by supervising and training teams. They have great influence over the success of their officers.

The "power down" and "can do" leadership approach requires a shifting of influence "down" to sergeants and police officers. This does not mean a loss of power for commanders. It places decision-making where it belongs. This encourages community operations and participation rather than "command and control."

CHARACTER AND VALUES

Character remains the moral test of leadership. Superior leaders possess exceptional character. Personal traits and values have a great influence over police officers and the moral climate in which they work. Effective leadership provides officers values and guidance.

Values lay the foundation for beliefs. They determine what action is taken in a moment of crisis. Values define what officers can and cannot do, and set standards for acceptable performance. Values provide the moral foundation. They offer direction, hope, inspiration and guidance for leaders, as well as police officers. A police leader's character, values and ethics remain crucial to the leadership process. Leaders with superior character and values have the potential to build a positive organizational climate.

BUILDING THE CLIMATE

A critical component of a "can do" attitude is the establishment of a healthy police climate. This attitude will help foster a total team effort. A positive climate exists when trust and confidence is shared by competent police leaders and officers. Police leaders must cooperate and establish rapport with their officers. They must strive for open communication down the chain of command and encourage feedback from lower organizational levels. Upward communication must be emphasized.

Leaders create a "can do" climate by setting attainable and clearly defined standards. Because prudent risks are encouraged and rewarded, mistakes must be accepted as part of the learning process. The emphasis is on learning from mistakes. This spirit is communicated throughout the department.

The best leaders create a climate free of punishment when necessary mistakes are made in accomplishing the mission. This does not include tolerating incompetence or illegal acts. A stifling climate encourages unethical misbehavior; therefore, freedom and discipline must be balanced.

Empowering police leaders and officers does not mean abdicating responsibility and accountability but sharing power, which helps create a "can do" attitude among subordinates. In fact, if the chief and senior leaders do not share power, they will fail in their mission, and officers will be unmotivated.

BUILDING MORALE

Participatory management enables officers to contribute. Through participation officers feel connected to the department, not alienated from the decision-making. When officers participate in the process, morale and productivity increase.

What makes morale plummet in police organizations? The failure to accomplish the mission is directly related to poor morale. When officers receive unfair criticism and a lack of recognition for a job well done, attitudes change. Leaders who build a "can do" organizational climate provide incentives and recognition for outstanding performers.

What improves morale? Leaders cannot force morale upon their officers, but they can monitor for morale problems. Moreover, they resolve conflict and enhance morale through action, not rhetoric. Corrective action demonstrates concern for their officers.

What are the indicators of success? Motivation, self-esteem and the desire to win. Police officers feel valued when providing excellent services to the community. Police officers take pride in their work and the department when they are successful.

EMPOWERING OTHERS

Empowering officers does not mean abdicating authority and power. "Powering Down" places responsibility and accountability at the appropriate level of execution. It permits police officers to perform the mission.

The failure to delegate power and trust subordinates results in a "cannot" or "will not" attitude. This attitude fosters a social climate of distrust and poor morale. Officers will fear seizing initiative because they lack support and the necessary experience to assume responsibility.

Participatory management does not require every decision to have consensus, but allows input concerning common problems and working conditions. The one advantage to this approach is that officers tend to support what they have helped develop. This outcome leads to increased morale and acceptance.

TRAINING AND READINESS

Recently, the trend toward empowering police officers has served as the basis for problem-solving policing. This has not been without problems, most notably among the unwilling and unable. Empowerment can be a frightening experience for those who have been restrained and inadequately trained.

Preparation empowers officers and ensures readiness and performance. Police leaders assess individual and group readiness to perform the task. Only when police officers feel the "can do" attitude will they pursue the mission with purposeful behavior.

Training enables successful policing. The training experience enables the improbable to become possible by showing officers that they "can do." Therefore, training empowers officers and breeds success.

CONCLUSION

Leadership combines conceptual, human relations, and technical skills. "Can do" leadership is based on strategic leadership concepts and situational leadership principles. The foundation is focused on strategic and tactical planning.

There must be common agreement on top priorities and strategic issues in order to move forward. This approach offers a consistent leadership framework for problem-solving policing. With this foundation, all is possible; without it, little will be accomplished. The scope and organization of the following chapters will help describe the essentials of leadership excellence.

SCOPE AND ORGANIZATION

The book is divided into four parts. Part I describes shaping the social climate. Part II addresses effective leadership. Part III examines the issues of direction, excellence and performance. Part IV describes charting the course, planning and evaluation.

PART I
SHAPING THE SOCIAL CLIMATE

CHAPTER 1, COMMUNITY POLICING, describes establishing an effective community climate through: (1) Community-Oriented Policing, (2) Problem-Oriented Policing and (3) Neighborhood-Policing and the Leadership Challenge.

CHAPTER 2, PROFESSIONAL ETHICS, describes establishing an effective police ethical climate by: (1) Assessing the Ethical Climate, (2) Teaching Values and Ethics, (3) Role Modeling the Behaviors and (4) Inspiring Your Officers.

PART II
EFFECTIVE LEADERSHIP

CHAPTER 3, POLICE SENIOR LEADERSHIP, describes the role of senior leadership as: (1) Developing and Sharing the Vision, (2) Charting The Journey, (3) Establishing Strategic Objectives and (4) Collaboration and Delegation.

CHAPTER 4, MIDDLE MANAGERS AND LEADERSHIP, describes the role of middle managers as: (1) Coordinating and Planning, (2) Mentoring, (3) Coaching, (4) Building Teams, (5) Empowering and (6) Rewarding.

CHAPTER 5, SERGEANTS AND POLICE OFFICERS, describes the role of first-line supervisors as: (1) Sergeants Leading the Way, (2) Leadership by Example, (3) Supervising and Training Teams and (4) Evaluating Performance.

PART III
DIRECTION AND EXCELLENCE

CHAPTER 6, MOTIVATION AND POLICE PERSONNEL, discusses: (1) Defining Excellence, (2) Defining the Goals and Objectives, (3) Evaluating Performance and (4) Rewarding Performance.

CHAPTER 7, POLICE TRAINING, describes the essentials of police training programs: (1) Defining the Strategic Training Program, (2) Training That Builds Performance, Morale, and Confidence.

CHAPTER 8, HUMAN RESOURCES, describes the management of human resources: (1) Identifying Strategic Human Resources, (2) Character Foundations, (3) Excellent Mentorship (4) Coaching Police Officers.

CHAPTER 9, CONFLICT MANAGEMENT, describes police conflict issues: (1) Developing Conflict Plans, (2) Managing Internal Conflict and (3) Managing Community Conflict.

PART IV
CHARTING THE COURSE

CHAPTER 10, CRITICAL THINKING, PLANNING AND PROBLEM-SOLVING, describes the critical thinking, planning and decision-making process: (1) Identifying the Mandates and Present State, (2) The Desired Future State and (3) Implementing Strategic and Tactical Plans.

CHAPTER 11, EVALUATION: HOW DO WE KNOW WHEN WE HAVE ARRIVED? describes the evaluation process: (1) Identifying Goals and Objectives, (2) Selecting the Evaluation Process, (3) Determining Results, and (4) New Destinations.

CHAPTER 12, EFFECTIVE LEADERSHIP: WHAT DID WE LEARN? describes the elements of effective leadership: (1) Developing a Sense of Mission, (2) Encouraging

Positive Relationships, (3) Encouraging Prudent Risk Taking and (4) Praising the Correct Behaviors.

CHAPTER 13, INTELLIGENCE-LED POLICING: PULLING IT ALL TOGETHER, describes the elements of Intelligence-Led Policing: (1) Strategic Leadership, United Kingdom Model, (3) National Intelligence Model, and (4) Johari Window Feedback.

CHAPTER 14, EPILOGUE, describes tomorrow's strategies for successful leadership.

Part I

SHAPING THE SOCIAL CLIMATE

ESTABLISHING AN EFFECTIVE COMMUNITY CLIMATE

* COMMUNITY-ORIENTED POLICING

* PROBLEM-ORIENTED POLICING

* NEIGHBORHOOD POLICING

* NEIGHBORHOOD WATCH PROGRAMS

ESTABLISHING AN EFFECTIVE POLICE ETHICAL CLIMATE

* POLICE VALUES AND ETHICS

* TEACHING VALUES AND ETHICS

* MODELING BEHAVIORS

* INSPIRING OFFICERS

PART I

LEADERSHIP FOUNDATIONS	GUIDEPOST BEHAVIORS
Develop a community-oriented policing philosophy	Articulate the community-oriented philosophy inside and outside the department
Develop problem solving policing	Apply the SARA planning model and strategies
Develop Neighborhood Watch programs	Organize and train Neighborhood Watch participants
Develop a department mission statement	Publish the mission, values and principles statement
Establish ethical training and accountability programs	Assess and inspect ethical behaviors
Define the values and principles statement	Build the social and ethical climate
Role model appropriate law enforcement behaviors	Demonstrate positive examples for loyalty, integrity, courage and competence

Chapter 1
COMMUNITY-ORIENTED POLICING

*In this rapidly changing environment...
the concept of community policing is
taking hold.*
- BUREAU OF JUSTICE ASSISTANCE

P olice leaders search for more effective ways to improve police services. The movement toward community policing is gaining momentum, and police officers are feeling excitement and interest in its application. However, traditional and professional policing remain the foundation for community policing, transition to which requires cooperation and patience from police officers as well as the community.

TRADITIONAL POLICING

Traditional policing has been portrayed as a simplistic approach to policing. This stereotype describes officers who wait in their police cars and exclusively respond to "calls for service." Traditional policing is often described as resulting in inefficiency and disrespect.

Research has exaggerated the disadvantages of traditional policing, which has provided compassionate service to communities. Traditional policing does more than respond to calls; it effectively acts to help citizens. Indeed exaggerated criticism and inflated rhetoric has interfered with the implementation of community-oriented police (COP) philosophy.

DEVELOPING A PHILOSOPHY

Many police administrators underestimate the practical value of a sound police philosophy. However, an executive's philosophy that includes guidelines for appropriate police officer conduct can have a dramatic impact on the entire department.

A police philosophy is an assessment of beliefs, attitudes, and values that determine police action and its rationale. If "Where are you going?" is a valid question, then a sound police philosophy helps determine "How you will get there?" Community-oriented policing offers that kind of direction. Policing without a sound philosophy is like a ship without a navigator.

THE ADVANTAGES OF COMMUNITY POLICING

A COP philosophy when properly administered has many advantages, among which is a valuable reference point for problem-solving. But police need to work closely with the community to identify concerns and implement solutions. This is the essence of community policing: the provision of guidance for police behavior and police action.[1]

The foundation for COP policing is the neighborhood-oriented approach, for crime prevention must be implemented block by block, neighborhood by neighborhood. This, in turn, acknowledges that the police mission is broader than "law enforcement," for the police are part of a larger social web. "Neighborhood-oriented policing has promise not because it is a nicer or kinder approach, but because it marshals greater resources, implements tailored solutions and addresses real and perceived problems."[2]

Police officers and citizens cooperating in the problem-solving process may develop a better understanding of each other. Community policing and Watch Programs have the potential for fostering interaction. The core components of the COP partnership is the application of the problem-solving approach to community crime prevention. Establishing trust is the essential goal of a successful community partnership, for cooperative partnership is the key to successful crime prevention and mutual respect.

COMMUNITY POLICING DEFINED

One major problem concerning COP policing is the lack of a clear definition. Some of the terminology has been used interchangeably and incorporated into the general philosophy of COP policing. For example, the general philosophy of COP policing can be found in neighborhood-oriented policing, Neighborhood Watch programs and problem-oriented policing. COP policing represents a broad philosophical position. Neighborhood policing and Neighborhood Watch programs apply the philosophy block by block through proactive citizen participation. Problem-oriented policing is the strategic and tactical means of achieving those ends.

"The phrase 'community policing' is an all-encompassing idea that focuses on a single goal: reducing crime and public fear....Community policing is an imperceptible term that has no concrete definition."[3] "Community-oriented policing is many different things to many different people. Community policing is an elastic term that is often used to give superficial coherence to a wide and disparate set of policing activities and various forms of police community dialogue."[4]

Community policing has different levels of meaning, which must be distinguished. "At one level, community policing is about developing a set of programs or activities for police: foot patrol, community-based crime prevention, ways of consulting communities about the kinds of problems they have and the kind of policing they want. The emphasis tends to be on the pragmatic and small-scale....[On the second level] community policing is about promoting better police-public relations and a better police image....It is undertaken because community policing activities are seen as good in themselves.... Community policing is also about changing the ethos of policing to emphasize notions of service, flexibility, consumer responsiveness, conciliation, consultation, and negotiation."[5]

Community policing involves the community in an active partnership with the police. This is not new; it dates back to the "Hue and Cry" community system. Sir Robert Peel, 1829, and Arthur Woods, Police Commissioner, 1914, New York City, both advocated community policing. [6] "The power surge is derived from police and community working together. Victory depends on a team effort. This philosophical and organizational strategy allows the police and community to work together in new ways. Together, they solve the problems of crime and disorder." [7]

"....Police officers and citizens working together in creative ways can help solve contemporary community problems related to the fear of crime, physical disorder, and neighborhood decay. The philosophy is predicated on the belief that achieving these goals requires that police departments develop a new relationship with law-abiding people in the community, allowing them greater voice in setting local police priorities and involving them in efforts to improve the overall quality of life in their neighborhoods. It shifts the focus of police work from handling random calls to solving community problems." [8] Viewed from one perspective, it is not a new concept for the principles have evolved from policing's oldest traditions.... "What is new is the idea that community policing is not a particular program within a department, but instead should become the dominant philosophy throughout the department." [9] COP is not a program but a police philosophy.

THE NINE "P's" THAT HELP DEFINE COMMUNITY POLICING

Trojanowicz and Bucqueroux describe nine "P's" that help to define community policing:

Community policing is a philosophy of full-service personalized policing, where one officer patrols and works in the one area permanently in a proactive partnership with citizens to identify and solve problems.

PHILOSOPHY. The community policing philosophy rests on the belief that contemporary challenges require the police to provide full-service policing, proactive and reactive, by involving the community directly as partners in the process of identifying, prioritizing, and solving problems. These problems include crime, fear of crime, illegal drugs, social and physical disorder, and neighborhood decay. A department-wide commitment implies changes in policies and procedures.

PERSONALIZED. By providing the community its own community policing officer, community policing breaks down the anonymity on both sides – community policing officers and community residents know each other on a first-name basis.

POLICING. Community policing maintains a strong law enforcement focus. Community policing officers answer calls and make arrests like any other officer, but they also focus on proactive problem-solving.

PATROLS. Community policing officers must walk and patrol their communities. To free them from the isolation of the patrol car, they walk beats or use other modes of transportation, such as bicycles, scooters, or horses.

PERMANENT. Community policing requires assigning community policing officers permanently to beats so that they have the time, opportunity, and continuity to develop the new partnership. Permanence means that community policing officers would not be rotated in and out of their beats.

PLACE. All jurisdictions, no matter how large, ultimately break down into distinct neighborhoods. Community policing decentralizes police officers, often including investigators. Community policing officers benefit from "owning" their neighborhood beats, for they can tailor their responses to the area's needs and resources. Moreover, community policing decentralizes decision making. It allows officers the autonomy and freedom to act, and empowers officers to participate in community-based problem-solving.

PROACTIVE. In providing full-service policing, community policing balances police responses to crime incidents and emergencies. Community policing also helps prevent problems before they occur.

PARTNERSHIP. Community policing encourages a new partnership between people and their police, based on mutual respect and support.

PROBLEM SOLVING. Community policing redefines the mission of the police to focus on solving problems, so that success or failure depends on qualitative outcomes (problems solved) rather than just on quantitative results (arrests made, citations issued—so-called "numbers policing"). Both quantitative and qualitative measures are necessary.

SOURCE: Robert Trojanowicz and Bonnie Bucqueroux,
            Community Policing: A Contemporary Perspective
            (Cincinnati: Anderson Publishing Company, 1994): 3-4.

APPLICATION: PROBLEM-ORIENTED POLICING

The community-oriented philosophy offers general guidance, not the specifics, in accomplishing missions. Herman Goldstein developed the concept of problem-oriented policing which helps answer the question: How will we get there? His problem-solving and evaluation approach focuses on causes.

Traditional policing is incident driven, and response oriented, not problem oriented. "In the vast majority of police departments, the telephone, more than any policy decision by the community or by management, continues to dictate how resources will be used." [10]

"The primary work unit in the professional model is the incident, that is, an isolated event which requires a police response. The institution of 911 has greatly increased the demand for police services and the public's expectation that the police will respond quickly." [11]

"Most policing is limited to ameliorating the overt, offensive symptoms of a problem. He suggests that police are more productive if they respond to incidents as symptoms of underlying community problems. A problem is a cluster of similar, related, or recurring incidents rather than a single incident, a substantive community concern, and a unit of police business. Once the problems in a community are identified, police efforts can focus on addressing the possible causes of such problems.

"A problem-oriented (POP) approach relies heavily upon citizen involvement. The police must do more than they have done in the past to engage the citizenry in the overall task of policing....A community must police itself. The police can, at best, only assist in that task." [12]

POP policing attempts to formalize what many law enforcement officers have been doing for years. It uses crime analysis, critical thinking, traditional and non-traditional techniques to solve crimes and address related problems. Police officers must apply the problem-solving and decision-making process to determine the underlying causes of crime in their community. They analyze the problem, develop a response, and evaluate the response.

POP officers attempt to discover root-causes of crimes. The modus operandi system was developed in an attempt to locate serial offenses, linked to recurring violations. For example, drug offenses may be related to a burglary trend in a particular neighborhood.

Armed with this basic knowledge of the underlying problem, the information can be used to gain the support of community agencies, and enlist citizen cooperation. The emphasis is not on reacting to a series of events but rather on crime POP methods. The focus is on analysis of the underlying causes of criminal behavior, to prevent those incidents from repeating.

The POP or problem-solving policing strategy consists of four distinct SARA parts: scanning, analysis, response, and assessment. [13] The information is collected and analyzed to develop innovative problem-solving techniques. Crime patterns may require non-traditional approaches based on community policing strategies, i.e., dispute resolution, crime prevention and cooperation with other public and private agencies.

The following case studies are compared and contrasted to illustrate the differences between the traditional policing and POP approach.

CASE STUDY
TRADITIONAL POLICING APPROACH

At 1:32 A.M. a man we will call Fred Snyder dials 911 from a downtown corner phone booth. The dispatcher notes his location and calls the nearest patrol unit. Officer Knox arrives 4 minutes later. Snyder says he was beaten and robbed 20 minutes earlier and didn't see the robber. Under persistent questioning, Snyder admits he was with a prostitute he had picked up in a bar. Later, in a hotel room, he discovered the prostitute was actually a man, who then beat Snyder and took his wallet.

Snyder wants to let the whole matter drop. He refuses medical treatment for his injuries. Knox finishes his report and lets Snyder go home. Later that day Knox's report reaches Detective Alexander's desk. She knows from experience the case will go nowhere, but she calls Snyder at work.

Snyder confirms the report but refuses to cooperate further. Knox and Alexander go on to other cases. Months later, reviewing crime statistics, the city council deplores the difficulty of attracting businesses or people downtown.

CASE STUDY
PROBLEM-ORIENTED POLICING APPROACH

Midnight-watch patrol officers are tired of taking calls like Snyder's. Sergeant James Hogan decides to reduce prostitution-related robberies, and Officer James Boswell volunteers to lead the effort. First, Boswell interviews 28 prostitutes who work the downtown area to learn how they solicit, what happens when they get caught, and why they are not deterred.

They work downtown bars, they tell him, because customers are easy to find and police patrols don't spot them soliciting. Arrests, the prostitutes tell Boswell, are just an inconvenience. Judges routinely sentence them to probation, and probation conditions are not enforced.

Based on what he has learned from the interviews, and his previous experience, Boswell devises a response. He works with the Alcoholic Beverage Control Board and local bar owners to move the prostitutes into the street. At police request, the commonwealth's attorney agrees to ask the judges to put stiffer conditions on probation. Convicted prostitutes are given a map of the city and told to stay out of the downtown area or go to jail for three months.

Boswell then works with the vice unit to make sure downtown prostitutes are arrested and convicted, and that patrol officers know which prostitutes are on probation. Probation violators are sent to jail, and within weeks, all but a few prostitutes have left downtown.

Then Boswell talks to the prostitutes' customers, most of whom don't know that almost half of the prostitutes working the street are actually men posing as women. He intervenes in street transactions, formally introducing the customers to their male dates. The U.S. Navy arranges talks for him with incoming sailors to tell them about the male prostitutes and the associated safety and health risks.

In three months, the number of prostitutes working downtown drops from 28 to 6 and robbery rates are cut in

half. After 18 months, neither robbery nor prostitution
violations show signs of returning to their earlier levels.

SOURCE: Adapted from William Spellman and John E. Eck,
           Problem-Oriented Policing (Washington, DC:
           National Institute of Justice, 1987).

DEVELOPING PROACTIVE STRATEGIES

Many police departments, with diverse populations, may
find the COP philosophy an acceptable solution for their
community. Can you adopt both community-policing and
problem-oriented policing approaches? The answer is "yes."
Each approach reinforces the other's desired outcomes and
goals. COP and POP are complementary components.

While community policing is an umbrella concept, problem-oriented policing involves specific strategies and tactics.
The best system combines the community-policing philosophy and problem-solving approach (COPPS). The foundation for problem-solving is based on the Neighborhood
Watch programs.

NEIGHBORHOOD WATCH: A LEADERSHIP CHALLENGE!

"Experience and research reveal that 'community institutions are the first line of defense against disorder and
crime....' Thus, it is essential that the police work closely
with all facets of the community to identify concerns and
find the most effective solutions. This is the essence of
community policing." [14]

Frequently implemented under community-oriented
policing plans, Neighborhood Watch programs have received
much attention over the past years. However, experts rarely
discuss the steps that lead to their successes. Many police
departments have implemented Neighborhood Watch
programs with much success; however, some have difficulty
initiating and sustaining the groups. Unfortunately, this
proves particularly true in those communities that most need

assistance. Middle-class communities, with the least to fear, seem to sustain the effort. On the other hand, low-income communities have a difficult time maintaining community-based groups, even in the presence of severe crime rates. [15]

Indeed, developing programs and maintaining community participation in Neighborhood Watch programs remain difficult leadership challenges. The average life expectancy of a Neighborhood Watch group is rather short, and the program itself, problematic. The most successful watches recruit new members a few times a year. Ongoing recruitment nurtures the program by involving new, motivated members. These fresh individuals replace those who feel they no longer need to participate because they either have become disenchanted with the program or feel their concerns have been addressed.

Despite the difficulties associated with establishing a successful community program, experts rarely discuss the steps that lead to success. Although police agencies interested in obtaining specific details on starting a group can do so easily, material on broad leadership issues, such as group dynamics and maintenance techniques, remain undeveloped areas. Such information would help organizers facilitate and maintain these successful supporting programs. In short, communities need information on how to maintain Neighborhood Watch programs, not just on how to start them.

Without citizen trust and cooperation, police officers work in an information vacuum and lack the criminal intelligence needed to perform their basic duties. Identifying the fundamental causes of crime depends, to a great extent, on citizens who make observations and report illegal activity. Police executives must reward these efforts and take appropriate steps to encourage continued citizen support and cooperation.

The philosophy of shared community crime prevention holds great promise but requires a great deal of leadership on the part of both the citizens and the police. Some administrators approach those programs involving citizen participation with apprehension and caution. Those police leaders, concerned with power and control, may be the most reluctant to support citizen involvement. They may fear loss of control over their departments more then they fear the actual level of crime.

FIVE STEPS FOR SUCCESS

Adequate preparation, planning, and training for citizen involvement can reduce confusion and create opportunities for better communication and increased cooperation. To achieve some degree of success, departments need to consider five steps during the development and maintenance of Neighborhood Watch programs. Without the proper foundation, the programs become disorganized. These steps set the stage for enhanced participation, cooperation, and retention of Neighborhood Watch members.

First Step: Plan Strategies

In the first step toward community involvement, organizers should develop strategies for dealing with crime patterns and form appropriate community and police intervention strategies. A well-constructed strategic plan may ease some of the anxiety and fear associated with community participation. Problem-oriented policing and crime-specific planning remain essential to the tactical planning process. These also will help minimize costly mistakes and enhance the opportunity for a successful collaboration between citizens and police departments.

In many cases, police departments blame citizen apathy for the failure of Neighborhood Watch programs. However, more often than not, the lack of appropriate planning, group maintenance, and support activities cause the failure. Crime prevention initiatives tend to disintegrate when police leaders fail to provide timely, ongoing guidance and support to citizens.

Second Step: Train Officers

Neighborhood Watch programs require well-trained crime prevention officers to assist citizens. These officers must possess the expertise, training, and personal qualities to successfully initiate and maintain a crime prevention program. Departments must carefully select these officers, who will provide specialized training to citizens. Crime prevention officers need motivation, perseverance, creativity, and enthusiasm in their assignments. They will become role models for the department's crime prevention initiatives and have considerable impact on the success of Neighborhood Watch programs.

Third Step: Assess Community Needs

The third step involves an effective assessment of community attitudes and opinions concerning police services and specific Neighborhood Watch programs. All too often, officers assume that they are performing effectively without surveying citizens. Fortunately, many progressive departments attempt to measure, evaluate, and improve their quality of service by seeking input from the community.

At the same time, needs assessments lay the foundation for defining goals, setting objectives, and developing work plans. More important, needs assessments rally citizen interest and focus on crime prevention initiatives. For example, the community may identify significantly different issues from those of the police. The police may be concerned with the drug problem while citizens may focus on the possibility of child abduction and molestation. Because citizens tend to perceive or fear crimes that may not, in reality, present a problem, providing local crime statistics may help determine community needs. In addition, addressing overlapping areas of interest may enhance rapport and citizen support.

Fourth Step: Select and Train Volunteers

The identification and selection of an appropriate watch coordinator remains one of the most important initial decisions. Although all neighborhood participants usually volunteer for the positions, watch leaders need to possess excellent leadership, organizational, and time-management skills because they will have an enormous impact on the enthusiasm for, and success of, the program.

Police leaders should provide thorough training for Neighborhood Watch program participants. Departments should offer training periods more than once and at convenient times to provide all block leaders an opportunity to attend. In return, the block leaders ultimately will become primary trainers of the Neighborhood Watch members. Clearly, watch administrators should not underestimate the necessity of an adequate training program for volunteers. The training process strengthens the program and helps guard against confusion, poor decisions, and costly mistakes.

Fifth Step: Develop Meaningful Projects

Unfortunately, members often lose interest after a crisis ends or the Neighborhood Watch has addressed their primary concerns. Citizens need involvement that satisfies and rewards. Moreover, they possess unique skills, interests, and material resources—such as home computers, cellular phones, or citizen band radios—that may be used by the group. Others may express an interest in repairing playground equipment, painting over graffiti, or perhaps developing a picnic area for children or elderly residents. Leaders should survey the members' interests and abilities, encourage creativity, and allow them to create opportunities for involvement. This approach will help maintain interest, motivation, and community pride.

One activity that leaders might encourage is publishing an anti-crime newsletter, which can provide crime prevention tips, local crime news, citizen recognition, and information on community events. A Neighborhood Watch newsletter becomes an excellent way to inform the neighborhood about crime trends that may affect them. Keeping citizens informed of accurate information may reduce their fear of crime.

ESTABLISHING THE TONE

Neighborhood Watch leaders should not underestimate how the tone of the meetings will impact the participation and retention of group members. Leaders must ensure that everyone gets treated with respect and that inappropriate behavior will not be tolerated.

Some individuals can dominate meetings by talking incessantly and interrupting others. Leaders must ensure that everyone has an opportunity to speak without interruption and should not tolerate inappropriate remarks or sarcasm. The meeting tone should encourage positive interaction, respect for diverse opinions, and active listening. Establishing a positive, respectful tone will enhance interaction and the possibility of accomplishing goals.

Meetings must not linger on discussions that do not lead to problem-solving solutions. Productive meetings encourage those in attendance to participate further. Neighborhood Watch leaders and members should leave meetings pleased they attended and feeling inspired to continue their participation.

Credibility Gap and Retention

Police officers must actively listen to community concerns, suggestions, and complaints. Departments then must be prepared to intervene appropriately. Failure to do so creates a credibility gap for those community members who have voiced concerns. If the program does not address citizens' concerns, apathy and disintegration of the Neighborhood Watch program will follow. Moreover, group members may conclude that the police department is not concerned. Therefore, police involvement becomes especially important when the department can easily and inexpensively implement remedial action. Citizens evaluate the work accomplished by attending meetings and participating in crime prevention activities. Citizens want to see their concerns addressed and their continued participation may hinge on the accomplishments they see.

Additionally, crime prevention officers must help citizens define and set reasonable goals and then support the achievement of those goals. The accomplishment of one goal enhances mutual cooperation and progression to another one. When leaders address the concerns of citizens and treat them as partners in crime prevention, interest remains high and participation continues.

Police and Citizen Roles Defined

The relationship between citizens and crime prevention officers increases qualitatively with the clear definition of respective roles. "The motivated citizen works with, rather than for, the crime prevention officer, who is much more a resource available to the citizen than the reverse. Within lawful limits, citizen crime prevention activities are in no way directed by police. The one cannot be subservient to the other; instead, both must collaborate as partners. Thus, where citizen participation strategies are correctly developed, there is no need for conflict over the issue of program control." [16]

When watch administrators define roles in early planning stages, conflict decreases. When roles are not clearly defined, confusion and mistrust can develop, and program members may lose interest. Police officers need a specific agenda for each meeting and should encourage citizens to voice their concerns.

Group Dynamics

One of the most difficult tasks of implementing a successful neighborhood-oriented policing philosophy involves meeting the expectations of diverse community groups. Officers who participate must understand basic leadership principles and group dynamics.

Group members may attend meetings for numerous reasons. Some attend to address safety concerns, discuss crime trends, or share personal problems, while others may have a social agenda. Some come with the hope of solving specific neighborhood problems that have not been addressed through other avenues or approaches.

The amount of cohesiveness among group members determines the level of cooperation and communication within the group and ultimately helps achieve specific goals. The number of members and the leader's style influences the cohesiveness of informal groups. Small, informal work groups with strong leaders historically prove the most effective.

FOUR STAGES OF GROUP DEVELOPMENT

Police leaders tend to become discouraged in the initial stages of Neighborhood Watch programs. They often comment on group member apathy or anger, which is the most difficult part of starting a Neighborhood Watch program. Police officers need to overcome these initial feelings and listen to the group's complaints. If officers remain patient, these problems should dissipate.

Participating officers need to recognize when group members are ready to venture out into the community. It may take some time for the members to gain this confidence, but without it, they may be unwilling to participate in projects.

Some of the members' insecurities may result from inadequate training and preparation. Police leaders and the watch coordinators must continually assess group members' confidence and their ability to perform tasks and achieve objectives.

Group development has four stages: 1) forming, 2) storming, 3) norming, and 4) performing. Neighborhood groups that achieve highest productivity levels move through each of these stages. The duration of each stage depends on group leaders, group members, and task complexity. [17] Watch organizers must first form the proper foundation, or the group may not evolve beyond its initial stages. Therefore, Neighborhood Watch leaders must monitor their groups, clear up misunderstandings, and avoid rushing through developmental stages.

The Forming Stage

In the forming stage, Neighborhood Watch groups usually are disorganized. Members may demonstrate anxiety and insecurity about the structure of the group. At this point, they depend on police leadership to provide useful information and ease tensions. Organizers should use this period to get acquainted and set a positive tone for future group meetings. Because watch members are not yet ready to address community objectives, leaders should concentrate on an effective orientation and training program. These activities will help provide the basic foundation for a successful group.

The Storming Stage

The storming stage often involves a struggle for power. Conflict among members for recognition and influence still exists. As members learn to confront others constructively, they may even challenge police leaders during this stage. This early period of development establishes how members will handle conflict in the future. The group must evolve through these difficulties to achieve independence and successfully accomplish goals during this stage; however, they are not yet ready to work effectively on their own. Neighborhood Watch leaders should remain steadfast and listen to all complaints. Crime prevention officers should not become defensive because this will lead to citizen criticism and poor communication.

Officers should avoid becoming discouraged with a neighborhood group's performance. Active listening skills and patience should continue during this stage to enhance communication. Cooperation helps the members move forward in the process of group development.

Police leaders must encourage individuals to pursue a positive path and put aside personal issues in favor of community interests. This opportunity also helps members accept their share of responsibility for the direction of the group. This should move the group to the next stage.

The Norming Stage

The norming stage can be characterized by the development of team cohesion. By this point, the group members have survived a period of testing, have resolved conflicts, and have bonded enough to work together closely. Members should feel more confident and ready to accomplish modest tasks and objectives. Cohesion and confidence will greatly impact the success of the group and its work.

Watch leaders must monitor the progress of their group. Moving too quickly to the performing stage may create frustration and group incohesiveness. Patience, active listening, open communication, and understanding enhance the possibility for successful transition.

The Performing Stage

The performing stage is team-oriented; leaders should have established roles, and members should be ready for higher levels of cooperation and performance. In other words, the group, now a team, pulls together to accomplish major goals and objectives. [18] However, this stage does not end the process. Members must continue to evaluate their satisfaction and take corrective measures to keep the program successful. During this stage, members of productive Neighborhood Watch groups feel empowered and secure enough to address concerns and make meaningful changes.

The climate of trust that reduces tension, fear, or anxiety in the forming and storming stages will assist in the transition to the norming and performing stages of development. Positive communication, accurate information, and the reduction of rumors remain essential during all stages in order to encourage positive group development.

FOCUS POINTS: NEIGHBORHOOD POLICING

What will make the COPPS philosophy work? Police practitioners understand that community policing is a philosophical position, not a solution. Police officers approach the world realistically; they are rarely utopian. Community policing is neither new nor theoretical but merely a shift in traditional policing. The jargon may be new, but the practice as old as the concept of community.

Excellent leadership by senior police leaders requires that police procedures are not based on false assumptions. Police executives need to form a partnership with researchers who are free of ideological agendas. This relationship is absolutely essential to identify valid community policing policies and procedures. It will take many years of careful planning to change the status quo. Defining and implementing the community policing philosophy is neither easy nor fast.

The shift in philosophy to neighborhood-oriented policing requires mutual trust and a reliance on citizen participation. Neighborhood Watch programs can help build a bridge to the community that serves as the foundation for mutual respect and successful crime prevention initiatives. Working with Neighborhood Watch programs requires exceptional leadership skills and a great deal of patience; however, the rewards should prove considerable.

The success of a Neighborhood Watch program directly relates to the department's commitment to establish a strategic plan, train the participants, and encourage open communication within the community. Moreover, starting a Neighborhood Watch program may prove less difficult than maintaining citizen interest and participation. Leaders first must define the group's mission to establish direction. Next, by assessing and articulating community needs, they can sustain the program's direction.

Finally, they should redirect the members to new goals and objectives once they complete a specific mission. Indeed, citizens who participate in crime prevention programs must have adequate support and opportunities to help implement positive changes in their communities.

In short, to succeed, Neighborhood Watch programs require planning, dedication, and motivated leadership, coupled with enhanced citizen support of police agencies. Those departments that maintain these essential ingredients will build a solid program that combats crime and addresses citizen concerns.

Figure 1-1
Maximizing Community Support

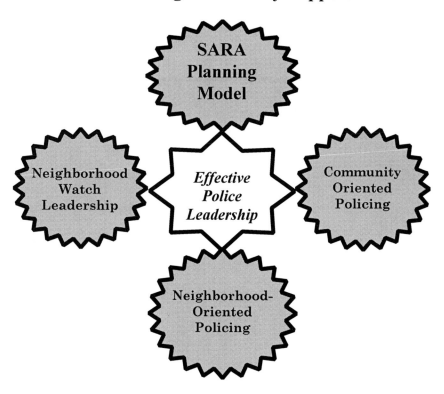

CONCLUSION

Researchers, scholars and practitioners attempted to differentiate between community-oriented, neighborhood-oriented and problem-oriented policing. Many articles were written, based on agency and individual preferences. All three approaches are founded on the common theme of police-citizen interaction and communication, inseparable concepts of policing. They are all connected by way of philosophy, practice and application.

The philosophical foundations of community-policing establish direction for the department and reflect on the underlying rationale for asking three basic questions: (1) Where are you going? (2) How will you get there? (3) How will you know when you have arrived? The latter will be determined more formally through problem-oriented policing, strategic planning, and the evaluation process. Community-oriented policing (COP) and problem-oriented policing (POP) applied together as (COPPS) will prove to be the most effective and efficient approach to policing in the future. [19]

Chapter 2
POLICE LEADERSHIP AND PROFESSIONAL ETHICS

Subordinates cannot be left to speculate as to the values of the organization. Top leadership must give forth clear and explicit signals, lest any confusion or uncertainty exist over what is and is not permissible conduct. To do otherwise allows informal and potentially subversive "Codes of Conduct" to be transmitted with a wink and a nod, and encourages an inferior ethical system based on "going along to get along" or the notion that "everybody's doing it."
- RICHARD THORNBURG

The chief and senior leaders should: (1) raise ethical questions, (2) reward ethical behavior, and (3) establish ethical purpose in the department. Tough ethical standards should be rewarded because they enhance the legitimate power of command. Certain shared values help achieve ethical behavior. "Why is a code of ethical behavior so important? Law enforcement officers are on the front lines protecting life, liberty, security and human rights. What they do matters!" [20]

The visibility of senior leaders ensures that their shortcomings will be noticed and analyzed; therefore, senior leaders must be consistent and avoid double standards. Subordinates quickly detect pretentiousness in leadership. "Can do" leaders must uphold and follow the highest standards of ethical behavior. To promote ethical standards, they must serve as appropriate role models so subordinates will identify with their professional values and standards. "Can do" leaders promote ethical behavior through personal contact and shared ethical values. Excellent leaders speak through actions as well as words. To promote ethical development in their subordinates, senior leaders must hold officers responsible for their actions.

"Can do" leaders must be consistent to develop and sustain the ethical climate. The successful senior leader will make the consequences of unethical behavior known to all members of the department. The chief and senior leaders create an appropriate ethical climate by: (1) modeling ethical behavior, and (2) teaching and enforcing the standards.

ETHICAL ACCOUNTABILITY

Police leaders ensure that everyone in their command assists in the prevention of corruption and unethical behavior. The role of leadership in maintaining ethical credibility cannot be abdicated. Commanders are responsible for their officers' actions.

Police officers tend to respond to what is inspected, supervised, and rewarded. Leaders must take corrective action and demonstrate a commitment to excellence. If police executives do not address ethical issues, their agencies lose professional credibility and community support, both directly related to violations of the Law Enforcement Code of Ethics, Police Code of Conduct, and the Canons of Police Ethics!

Deteriorating ethics, then, remain the central management issue of any law enforcement agency. The test for law enforcement leadership in the twenty-first century will be integrity, moral leadership, and ethical coaching skills. Leaders who possess those attributes and instill them in their subordinates will succeed.

Leadership is a human endeavor based on organization, cohesion, and human motivation. "Can do" police leaders apply "moral force" to police organizations. Leadership is not merely expedient; it is also moral and ethical whose essential elements of moral leadership are expert power, confidence, and competent leadership.

The chief and senior leaders are responsible for developing the moral and ethical climate of the police department. They may delegate this authority, but not the responsibility for an ethical climate. The appointment of a Commander of the Internal Affairs Unit, demonstrates this concern for a professional and ethical climate. The Commander must have a reputation for character and integrity in the department; he must be a role model for ethical behaviors. Ethical behavior is demonstrated by example, leadership values, attitudes, beliefs, and behaviors demonstrated at every opportunity. They must reinforce or instill these values in their subordinates.

Individuals who do not follow professional standards of ethical conduct must be removed from service. Ethical accountability cannot be shifted from leadership to the Internal Affairs Unit Commander. The senior leader must be aware of individuals who are willing to abandon traditional values in the pursuit of their own success and personal financial gain. The importance of ethical leadership cannot be overstated.

ASSESSMENT OF PROFESSIONAL ETHICS AND STANDARDS

The police are first-line guardians of the U.S. Constitution who swear an oath to the U.S. Constitution, State Constitution, and to the enforcement of criminal law. Police methods must support this oath, not violate laws they swore to enforce. Police officers should use sound methods of prosecution and conviction. Every officer represents the law; they are not above the law, nor should they abuse the law.

CHARACTER AND VALUES

Anyone who has held a command position understands the risks of taking a moral stand. Truth is sometimes unwelcome. People tend to "go along" and "get along," and it is sometimes expedient to make the popular, rather than the right, decision. The following points are worth noting:

* "Each step on the path to a higher standard of leadership takes courage – courage to commit to absolute values and to the universal code of conduct to treat others as ourselves.

* "Moral courage determines the standard of leadership in the practical arenas – of politics, business, academics, and the community.

* "To stand up for what you believe is right, you must have the courage to acknowledge your actions and face the consequences. [21]

Character, values, beliefs, and ethics are the foundation for competence as a leader. They influence how leaders think and how they treat the officers in their police organization, as well as the public. Values provide guidance and influence decision-making:

"Values are the beliefs that guide an organization and the behavior of its employees…. The most important beliefs are those that set forth the ultimate purposes of the organization…. They provide the organization with its raison d'etre for outsiders and insiders alike and justify the continuing investment in the organization's enterprise…. [They] influence substantive and administrative decisions facing the organization, they lend a coherence and predictability to top management's actions and the responses to the actions of employees. This helps employees make proper decisions and use their discretion with confidence that they are contributing to rather than detracting from organizational performance." [22]

The Houston Police Department Mission Statement describes the Department's values and principles. The Mission Statement in Table 2-1 provides a navigational compass for ethical decision-making. The Department's values and principles provide guidance for officers. **Chapter 3, SENIOR LEADERSHIP**, includes additional discussion concerning mission and values statements.

Table 2-1
MISSION STATEMENT
HOUSTON, TEXAS POLICE
DEPARTMENT

MISSION STATEMENT: The mission of the Houston Police Department is to enhance the quality of life in the City of Houston by working cooperatively with the public and within the framework of the U.S. Constitution to enforce the laws, preserve the peace, reduce fear and provide for a safe environment.

Values

Preserve and Advance Democratic Values

We shall uphold this country's democratic values as embodied in the Constitution and shall dedicate ourselves to the preservation of liberty and justice for all.

Improve the Quality of Community Life

We shall strive to improve the quality of community life through the provision of quality and equitable services.

Improve the Quality of Work Life

We shall strive to improve the working environment for the department's employees by engaging in open and honest communication and demonstrating a genuine concern for one another.

Demonstrate Professionalism

We shall always engage in behavior that is beyond ethical reproach and reflects the integrity of police professionals.

Principles

Life and individual freedoms are sacred.

All persons should be treated fairly and equitably.

The role of the police is to resolve problems through the enforcement of laws—not through the imposition of judgment or punishment.

The neighborhood is the basic segment of the community.

Because law enforcement and public safety reflect community wide concern, the police must actively seek the involvement of citizens in all aspects of policing.

The fundamental responsibility of the police is provision of quality services.

The department's employees are its most valuable asset.

Employee involvement in departmental activities is essential for maintaining a productive working environment.

Employees should be treated fairly and equitable in recognition of basic human dignity and as a means of enriching their work life.

> *Reprinted with permission of the Houston Police Department*

Character and values allow one to behave consistently, regardless of circumstances. Leadership behavior reflects character, and leaders must have strong character to produce positive results; weak character produces negative results. Police executives who have strong character attract followers. Leaders with weak character do not attract followers because they lack consistency and purpose. "Can do" police leaders have strong character, they emphasize duty, honor and country.

CASE STUDY IN CHARACTER

The following hypothetical case study illustrates two types of character profiles. Major Drone has weak character that is self-serving. In comparison, Captain Jackson demonstrates strong character that is moral and attracts followers. Captain Jackson has values, ethics, and is mission oriented. He has the professional drive, self-discipline and will power to accomplish the mission.

CASE STUDY: CHARACTER AND MAJOR DRONE

Major Robert Drone has been a member of his local police department for twenty years. He achieved his rank because of his skill at manipulating the Chief, fellow officers and the Mayor. Major Drone is viewed as someone who forced his way to the top at the expense of others. Subordinates believe he is power hungry and would do anything for promotion.

The Major is pragmatic and deceitful, without thought of moral consequences. He lies to and psychologically manipulates others, but demonstrates a special capacity to influence his superiors.

Major Drone uses for his own self-interests the power of his position, plus reward and coercive power. Officers who confront him about his unethical behavior, are quickly punished, their personal loyalty questioned. While Major Drone never accepts responsibility for his inappropriate actions, he is swift to blame others. His real power comes from his personal relationship with the Chief and his influence as a manager. The knowledge he gains from these relationships is another form of power that he applies.

However, Major Drone lacks personal charisma and referent power. He is considered unprofessional by line officers and their supervisors; only the Chief respects him. Major Drone's field efforts are awkward and inexpert in law enforcement. He does not understand basic police work and tactical situations. He earned his rank by running errands and tending to the Chief's business.

On one hot summer day, Major Drone made the mistake of assuming command of a police shooting incident. On that particular day, a patrol officer answering a domestic call was shot on the front porch of a suburban home. Bleeding profusely, the officer was unable to move from the area because of hostile gun-fire from Jake James, a construction worker. The wounded officer called for help for hours, eventually rescued by Captain Scott Jackson.

Major Drone took hours to respond tactically. The attempted rescue failed and two other officers were wounded. He failed as a leader at the hostage scenario, and allowed the defendant to dominate the scene. Finally, an off-duty captain responded to the scene, relieved Major Drone, and assumed command.

Captain Scott Jackson resolved the incident in less than 15 minutes. Captain Jackson was known for his character, integrity, and tactical expertise. The officers respected him and would risk their lives to support Captain Jackson. They knew that Captain Jackson would not ask them to face any danger that he would not face personally. Captain Jackson would lead from the front, not from the Command Center.

LESSONS LEARNED

During crises Major Drone is incompetent. However, Captain Jackson is a selfless leader who succeeds in situations requiring character and courage. Self-serving, high-ranking officers like Major Drone are ineffective in crises because police officers are unwilling to risk their lives to follow him.

Captain Jackson is candid and honest. He accepts full responsibility and does not blame others when the mission does not go well. Captain Jackson demonstrates loyalty to superiors and officers. He reasons that officers treated with respect, return respect. Why is Captain Jackson successful in saving the officer's life? Because he leads daily with ethics and values. His integrity and principles of selfless service are respected by everyone.

Captain Jackson emphasizes several important areas that reflect a leader's character and ethics. He never criticizes subordinates or superiors in their absence but demonstrates loyalty instead. His competence, courage and persistence earn respect. This kind of integrity and loyalty has numerous advantages in a crisis situation. Captain Jackson has a reputation as someone with high standards and commitment to duty. These attributes enable him to prevail in crises because Captain Jackson's character and expertise earn him respect. The point of this case study is to discuss the essentials of ethical leadership: honorable character and selfless service to the community, department, and officers. If leaders desire respect, they must demonstrate character and values.

PROFESSIONAL VALUES AND ETHICS

Successful leaders must understand themselves and the mission. Leaders lead by example, demonstrating character, values, and integrity. Many of these leadership principles can directly improve the ethical climate of police organizations. Some basic principles concerning those standards are listed below:

* "The standard of leadership depends not only on the qualities and beliefs of our leaders but also on the expectations we have of them.

* "We need a new heroic ideal: the brave, truthful, non-violent individual serving of humanity, resisting injustice and exploitation, and leading by appealing to our ideals and our spirit.

* "We disrespect leaders whose private and public conduct we do not approve. Leaders who do not command our respect reduce the legitimacy of their leadership and lose our trust.

* "Leaders have the greatest responsibility. Without absolute values, they cannot guide others.

* "Leaders try to do things better tomorrow than it was done today. Improvement leads to a higher standard of leadership." [23]

Police leaders and managers can engage in rationalizations that may lead to violations of the Police Code of Ethics, Police Code of Conduct, and the Canons of Police Ethics. Listed below are some of the rationalizations that can lead to misconduct by managers.

* "A belief that the activity is within reasonable ethical and legal limits, that is, it is not 'really' illegal or immoral.

* "A belief that the activity is in the individual's or the department's best interests, that the individual would somehow be expected to undertake the activity.

* "A belief that the activity is 'safe' because it will never be found out or publicized.

* "A belief that because the activity helps the company, the company will condone it and even protect the person who engages in it." [24]

VALUES AND BEHAVIOR

The question of "Who am I?" must be addressed. Having a philosophy and core universal values helps leaders provide guidance for others. A multidimensional value system should address self-assessment, the need for growth, competence, and self-esteem.

Before leaders can lead and understand others, they must understand themselves. Through self-assessments, leaders understand their own personality, values, strengths, and weaknesses. The wise leader acknowledges limitations as well as assets. Only then can leaders maximize strengths and improve weaknesses. Self-assessment is essential before moving into a key leadership position. This assessment will help identify the officer's personal values and philosophy of leadership.

We have come to accept a lower moral standard that has produced the principle of expediency and a double-standard of conduct. Leaders do not have private lives. Their public and private lives are merged into one. Violations of ethical standards and the failure to uphold basic police values will reduce the legitimacy of the leader. Leaders have a greater responsibility. Without the compass of values, how will they guide others?

"More than anything else, we are what we believe, what we dream, what we value. For the most part we try to mold our lives to make our beliefs and dreams come true. In our attempts to reach our goals, we test ourselves again and again in diverse ways, and in doing so we grow. With this growth comes change, so that new goals emerge, and in support of these new goals come new beliefs, new dreams, and new constellations of values. Some unusual people grow and change many times throughout their lives." [25]

Leaders can develop their sense of ethical behavior by examining personal values, enduring beliefs that result in a specific model of conduct. "A map and a compass are similar to values. They show us where we may want to go (a goal) and how we best can arrive there (a means). Ethics are certain, select values that serve as a moral compass. A compass has a true north that is objective and external, that reflects natural laws or ethics. We must develop (and, when necessary, change) our value system with enduring respect for 'true north' ethics." [26]

For example, if leaders believe that acting on one's beliefs is important, they may generate decisions that are not considered politically popular. Because of their values, "can do" leaders may find it difficult to survive. "Can do" leaders will excel in a problem-solving environment, not under the bureaucratic model. Leaders who value independence and the "can do" approach will differ from those who value getting along and bureaucratic values.

One cannot meet a higher standard of leadership if values are not clarified and developed. Values play an important role in relationships and group dynamics, for they influence the leader's perceptions of others and what constitutes organizational success. While values guide the way to successful leadership, they ultimately challenge leaders to treat others as themselves.

APPLIED VALUES AND ETHICS

Poor leaders seek their own comfort at the expense of others, while successful leaders place the welfare of the officers above their own. "Can do" leaders are concerned about their officers' welfare and working conditions. Leaders who abuse privileges at the expense of their officers discard ideals of selfless service.

Most leaders want to be liked, a temptation that should be avoided. Leaders who act on values and professional ethics, do not please everyone. Leaders must cultivate respect not popularity. Respect enables leaders to lead, but trying to satisfy everyone to become popular never succeeds.

Leaders should avoid several land mines: the abuse of authority and power; accepting favors from subordinates; lax discipline. Those who violate these principles compromise their opportunity to lead.

"Can do" leaders accept responsibility for their actions. They value performance and demonstrate their willingness to accept greater responsibility. Superior leaders understand that it is easy to accept the glory but difficult to accept responsibility when something does not go well. Officers follow leaders who accept responsibility; however, if leaders blame them when things go wrong, they will fail to respond to leadership.

Leaders guided by values reflect convictions. Leaders who say "yes" when they should be saying "no" lack moral responsibility. Further, while "yes people" make leaders feel good, leaders who surround themselves with "yes people" have a higher probability of failure in emergency situations, especially when the situation calls for a clear sense of values and professional ethics. Successful leaders are candid and honest and therefore, lead with integrity and honesty.

FOCUS POINTS: BUILDING THE ETHICAL CLIMATE

When senior leadership develops the proper ethical climate by encouraging ethical behavior, departments more efficiently discourage corruption. Ethical issues must be emphasized at every organizational level. Ethical police officers are found in an organizational climate, that gives a high priority to ethical behavior.

The chief must establish goals, standards, and ethical policies. The police senior leaders must view ethical behavior as an important goal of the administration and the department. The selection of personnel, promotions, rewards and discipline must be ethically based and administered, and the initial training of recruit officers should stress ethical behavior.

In-service training of all members of the department, is essential. The chief and senior leaders promote organizational ethical development through personal contact with subordinates. If senior leadership develops a shared ethical perspective at every department level, officers will have a common foundation to cope with uncertainties in field operations.

The chief and senior leaders are accountable if the organization fails to develop ethical standards; they are responsible for sustaining a healthy ethical climate. Many of the trust and confidence issues in police organizations can be related to ethical issues. Unclear ethical expectations and policies send mixed messages to officers concerning their expected behaviors.

Figure 2-1
Police Professional Ethics

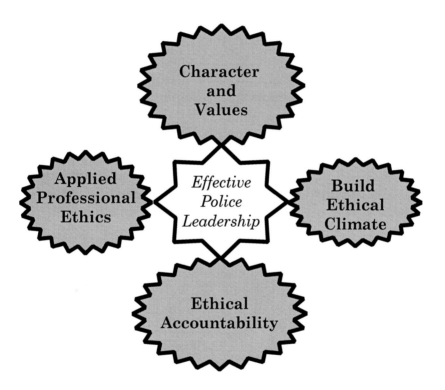

CONCLUSION

Leadership that enhances ethical behavior focuses on two points: administration and policy. Ethical behavior must be a primary and continuing goal of administrative and senior leadership. Senior leaders can develop and sustain a positive ethical climate by: (1) developing trust; (2) listening to and supporting personnel; (3) tolerating honest mistakes but punishing dishonest behavior; and finally, (4) leading by example. Leaders must role model for loyalty, integrity, courage, and competence.

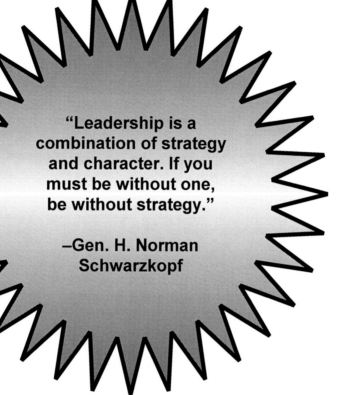

"Leadership is a combination of strategy and character. If you must be without one, be without strategy."

–Gen. H. Norman Schwarzkopf

Part II
EFFECTIVE LEADERSHIP

SENIOR LEADERSHIP

* DEVELOP AND SHARE THE VISION

* CHART THE JOURNEY

* ESTABLISH STRATEGIC OBJECTIVES

* COLLABORATE AND DELEGATE

MIDDLE MANAGERS

* COORDINATE AND PLAN

* MENTOR AND COACH

* BUILD TEAMS

* EMPOWER AND REWARD

FIRST-LINE SUPERVISORS

* SERGEANTS LEAD THE WAY

* LEADERSHIP BY EXAMPLE

* SUPERVISE AND TRAIN TEAMS

* EVALUATE PERFORMANCE

PART II

LEADERSHIP FOUNDATIONS	GUIDEPOST BEHAVIORS
The Chief and senior leaders look to the future.	Assist in establishing vision with subordinates.
The Chief and senior leaders set strategic goals and objectives.	Coordinate with middle managers and first line supervisors.
Middle leaders define and coordinate objectives with sergeants.	Empower subordinates to implement goals and objectives.
Middle leaders help build the organizational climate and delegate authority.	Coach, mentor and share power.
Sergeants are direct leaders and supervisors.	Assess, plan and evaluate objectives.
Sergeants are the most important level of supervision and leadership.	Sustain the ethical climate and proactive leadership with officers.
Sergeants are important because of their immediate contact with officers.	Follow-up to ensure mission success.

Chapter 3
POLICE SENIOR LEADERSHIP

*You do not lead by hitting people over
the head – that's assault, not leadership.*
- PRESIDENT DWIGHT D. EISENHOWER

The Chief of Police is the most important strategy initiator. The chief has the main responsibility for strategic planning and forecasting the future. However, senior leaders and middle managers have an important role in the process. The chief defines the department's vision and how to achieve the goals. In addition, senior leaders determine priorities for middle managers and sergeants.

THE CHIEF: STRATEGIC THINKING
Strategy is the chief's plan for effective management and consists of approaches that enhance police performance. The chief, senior leaders, and middle managers develop strategies that determine the department's destination. Together they develop operational procedures that prescribe the method to achieve department objectives.

INDIRECT LEADERSHIP
As one moves higher in rank, the ability to conceptualize, plan and implement future strategies becomes critical. Unlike junior leaders, senior leaders divide their attention between organizational objectives and indirect leadership, which then translates into direct action. Senior leadership

43

establishes priorities based on tasks needed to be accomplished.

The manner in which senior leaders provide motivation demonstrates the indirect influence of their command roles. While leaders can motivate some officers directly, they cannot possibly interact with every officer. The senior-level command officer provides motivation by ensuring a positive command climate and fostering a sense of unity throughout the police organization.

VISION AND FORECASTING

Police senior leaders look further into the future than their subordinates. The success of any organization depends on the ability to forecast the future. Senior leaders envision what needs to be accomplished, and influence subordinates to complete related goals. Vision is the thoughtful, future analysis and planning that enables leaders to develop a system to forecast the future.

Where does vision come from? Vision originates from the department's environment, culture, and community. The past is important, but analysis of the future is essential. Vision evolves from community expectations. It starts with the chief and senior leaders but is modified through feedback from subordinates.

How do we implement vision? Well-trained chiefs and senior leaders are responsible for inventing the right motto; leadership markets it and demonstrates the concept. The motto is repeated until incorporated into the department's culture. This message guides strategic planning and decision making.

Vision derives from analytical skills and an intuitive sense of the future. What is vision? Quite simply, it should help answer the question: Where are we going? "An organizational vision presents a clear picture of what direction the organization plans to take in the future. It should represent an achievable, challenging, and worthwhile long-range target toward which personnel can direct their energies." [27] "Vision is an ideal and unique image of the future. Vision often begins as a vague dream of what should be accomplished. The desire to achieve something then forces clarification of the dream within the mind. An image of the organization or unit then forms. As the dream becomes clearer, one's determination to work toward it grows. It takes on new intensity and is then shared. Increasing fervor forces you to enlist others to accompany you in this journey." [28]

To successfully implement their vision, police leaders must lead from the front, not the office. Through their physical presence in the field excellent leaders accurately adjust their vision. How can you lead when you don't understand what your police officers are experiencing in the field? The information leaders gather will be vital in the development of vision.

DEFINING THE ORGANIZATION'S PHILOSOPHY AND VALUES

The chief and senior leaders set the moral tone for the department through personal example, philosophy, and mission/value statements. Ultimately, the chief is responsible for the department's relationship with the community. His philosophy guides police and civilian employees in accomplishing their assignments.

THE MISSION STATEMENT

The chief and subordinates develop the mission statement to implement direction. The mission statement also demonstrates the law enforcement's agency's purpose. In recent years, law enforcement executives have acknowledged the value of a well defined mission statement integrated into decisions at every department level. The mission statement defines acceptable attitudes, conduct, and performance.

The mission statement documents department values. Simply put, a mission is a reason to work. More than just an empty platitude, a mission statement is the standard against which administrators evaluate all decisions and actions. The following mission statement is a model: "To seek and find ways to affirmatively promote, preserve and deliver a feeling of security, safety and quality services to members of the community." [29] "A clear mission statement may be an organization's most important asset. It calls attention to what management believes is important, and it sets goals that align practices with values." [30]

VALUE STATEMENT

The value statement combines with the mission statement to create an ethical climate. "The values statement declares the moral and ethical qualities to which the organization is committed. For example, values statements often clarify how much significance the organization places on honesty, customer satisfaction, ethical conduct, innovation, teamwork, community awareness, self-directed work, tolerance of dissenting views, and public relations." [31]

"While the mission statement describes where the organization is going, the values statement articulates how it will get there. It is a detailed guide of behaviors that management accepts and supports within the organization. While values statements provide guidance for officer performance, the mission statements define acceptable behaviors." [32]

PLANNING A STRATEGY

The chief's strategy-making process identifies how to achieve targeted objectives, the "ends," while strategy is the "means" for achieving them. The chief and senior leaders recognize the "big picture" when analyzing internal and external environmental factors. Basic strategies are developed to accomplish the mission.

Strategic plans must be developed to designate direction and to achieve objectives. Sometimes plans may be an informal agreement between the chief and senior leaders. However, the best way to measure progress is to formalize the process in written form. Plans act as a guide for achieving outcomes.

SETTING POLICE OBJECTIVES

The degree to which strategies are developed and executed indicates the effective use of police executive management. Progress in attaining objectives can be measured only after the chief converts the mission statement into specific target objectives. Because objective-setting establishes desired outcomes, managers have something to reach for and a means to measure progress. Objectives both challenge and reward.

Strategic planning considers both short-term and long-term objectives while short-term objectives define present priorities, long-term objectives define future priorities. Although top management establishes organizational objectives, managers participate in the process.

BUILDING A SOCIAL CLIMATE

The chief avoids isolation through communication. He or she accomplishes this by maintaining visibility and actively listening and responding appropriately. The chief establishes rapport and gathers information senior leaders may hesitate to provide.

Senior leaders develop management teams that impact on the organizational social climate. They set the stage for the achievement of objectives and are the standard bearers of professional and police traditions.

Because senior leaders role model, they must demonstrate professional values. Excellent leaders protect professional ethics and communicate them to others. The chief and senior leaders coach and instill the will to achieve, and promote organizational spirit and morale.

The chief actively listens to each messenger, though news may be unpleasant. However, to obtain accurate information, one cannot solely rely on managers, the latter may hesitate to disclose information that adversely reflects on their leadership.

Police senior leadership is the science and art of direct and indirect influence. It includes motivating subordinates to achieve desired outcomes. The chief and senior leaders concentrate on creating an organizational climate that encourages others to achieve success. They establish a clear definition of the mission to provide direction.

DELEGATION OF AUTHORITY

Senior leaders are confronted with complex issues. The Chief of Police has the power to impact on the entire organization. However, most of the decisions that impact on daily activities are made at lower organizational levels. Operational decision making remains at the level of execution. Senior leaders describe what they want to happen, rather than how to do it. The details are left to subordinates.

The chief and senior leaders cannot be everywhere simultaneously, so their leadership style is indirect except for a few chosen subordinates. The chief's span of control is normally limited to administrative services, field operations, and technical services commanders.

The Chief of Police applies direct leadership through two or three assistants, a narrow "span of control." Because five or six individuals report to first-line supervisors at lower levels of the department, the chief, through key subordinates, achieves only indirect department leadership.

The delegation of authority is essential at senior levels. The chief and senior leaders, who lead indirectly, delegate power to middle managers to act in their absence. On occasion, middle managers may delegate authority to first-line supervisors but never responsibility. The chief is responsible for the department's achievements and failures. He or she does not "pass the buck" when a situation becomes uncomfortable.

The chief or senior leaders may delegate authority to act in their absence; however, tasks need to be clearly defined. "Can do" leaders do not delegate and then ignore the performance of assigned objectives. Regardless of how the organization may be subdivided, authority and responsibility must be clearly defined.

Although responsibility exists at every organizational level, the Chief of Police does not relinquish responsibility for the mission and behavior of individual police officers, but inspects and assures accountability at all levels. This accountability may not be delegated. The authority to act is commensurate with responsibility. Leaders do not assign responsibility without giving the proper latitude to make timely decisions. Officers who do not have the authority to act are rendered ineffective and soon ignored. Effective leadership assigns responsibility and accountability to a subordinate and then encourages her to execute the functions of her office. The authority to make and execute decisions is delegated to the lowest levels of the organization. Everyone in the organization is held accountable and for their use of power and authority.

UNITY OF COMMAND

The concept of "unity of command" can be traced to the Roman Legions and adheres to the "chain of command" concept. The chain of command hierarchy begins with officers, sergeants, middle managers, senior leaders, and finally the Chief of Police.

Unity of command places officers under the direction of one leader because subordinates effectively serve only one leader. Subordinates who answer to two leaders must often follow conflicting orders, which violates the "unity of command."

This dilemma may occur when staff supervisors attempt to exercise control over line personnel and violate effective leadership principles. Staff leaders must communicate with line commanders rather than by-passing them in the chain of command. Exclusion of line commanders from the chain of command creates confusion.

DEVELOPING A CONCEPTUAL APPROACH

The four basic concepts of command, control, leadership and management are essential to implementing vision. Command is the primary means of communicating vision to members of police organizations. The senior police leader performs four major functions: (1) Communicates intent and provides direction; (2) Establishes the structure to focus effort; (3) Plans and organizes the activities necessary to achieve results; and (4) Motivates and influences subordinates to develop and sustain organizational vision.

Senior leadership requires conceptual and human relations skills. Promotion does not guarantee that officers will make the mental transition to senior-level conceptual skills. Well-trained police executives understand how they can influence the organization through indirect leadership, vision, direction and a positive organizational climate.

CASE STUDY: CHIEF SHANE PILAND

Chief Piland served as a police officer before joining the Army. He was promoted to Major after completing ten years of miliary service. However, Chief Piland was eliminated during military cutbacks because he only had two years of college.

Chief Piland made the decision to enroll in courses at a local university and soon completed his bachelor's degree in social work and criminal justice. He later completed a master's degree in leadership and policy. Chief Piland's academic achievements were completed while working as a full-time police officer.

Chief Piland's distinguished police record included rapid promotion from sergeant to major. He applied to be Chief of Police of a rapidly growing Northeast city upon completion of his twenty-second year as a former military and civilian police officer. The department had grown to its present size of approximately two hundred officers.

The new assignment would prove to be challenging. Chief Piland replaced Chief Barker who was frequently seen directing traffic at a local intersection. The gold braid on the former Chief's hat could be seen by drivers and pedestrians alike when it glistened in the sunlight. Unfortunately, directing traffic was the highlight of his leadership endeavors during his thirty year tenure. The former chief never made the mental transition to senior leadership. In addition, the department had grown ten fold during the last three decades.

After assuming command, Chief Piland interviewed key commanders and staff officers concerning the department's status. He soon learned that the reporting system and evidence room procedures were almost non-existent and in complete disarray. More importantly, officer morale was low and the staff felt incapable of making changes because the former Chief insisted on making all of the decisions. However, the former Chief's preoccupation with traffic control precluded anything from being decided or accomplished.

The new Chief realized that a senior leader could not be everywhere at the same time or make personal contact with all of the officers. Chief Piland's leadership style would emphasize indirect leadership, employing direct leadership only when necessary. His first direct leadership decision would be to empower his two primary subordinates to act in his absence.

The Chief would delegate authority and achieve accountability through the Major in charge of operations and Major responsible for staff services. He was aware that he could maintain and extend his indirect influence and leadership through them. Responsibility and accountability would be achieved through his two principle subordinates. Chief Piland praised achievements and encouraged the majors to take responsibility and make decisions. He created a climate that would enhance the possibility for personal growth, decision-making and risk taking.

Chief Piland realized that after years of being restrained, empowerment would take time, support, and coaching, but he was willing to make the commitment. Eventually, empowerment would cascade down the chain of command to middle managers and sergeants. Most importantly, the empowerment of officers would enhance problem-solving skills and morale. Improved leadership skills would be essential to the community-oriented policing philosophy.

The Chief fully understood that his function was not to direct traffic, but to provide guidance. He knew the department was in turmoil because officers did not have a shared vision, mission, and values statement. This step was given top priority, and participation at every level of the organization was encouraged. Mutual cooperation in the writing process would enhance esprit de corps and the possibility of successful completion of future projects.

The Chief would provide direction through a clearly defined vision. He would involve the department and the community in planning and implementing phases. The Chief and his staff would set realistic goals and objectives. The vision would identify timelines, fiscal needs, personnel, and accountability that would improve the present and future status of the organization. Vision provides the path for excellence and "goals" for others to follow.

The next step was to write a mission statement. The Chief quickly realized that the mission statement must evolve from the hearts and minds of his officers. Therefore, the statement cannot be taken from a book or adopted from another department. Furthermore, it must characterize the needs of the department and community. The mission statement is not owned by the Chief, it belongs to the entire Department. The accompanying values statement follows the same stages of development.

The Chief applies strategic leadership while providing a framework that guides decision making. He influences the direction of the Department by determining strategic goals and objectives. Once the Chief defines strategic goals, middle leaders can identify planning, timelines, and priorities. After the strategic planning process has been established, resources can be allocated and team strategies can be implemented. While strategic thinking seeks to anticipate problems, critical thinking enhances the problem solving process. The Chief realizes that conceptual thinking helps define the underlying reasons for problems.

The Chief's next step was to initiate strategic leadership and implement the vision and mission statement. The first step is to define the vision. The second step is to develop the mission statement, which focuses attention on the problems.

The third step, strategic planning, provides the goals for accomplishing the mission. The fourth step, tactical planning, establishes the means for accomplishing the goals and objectives for police officers.

LESSONS LEARNED

The Chief knew that an outside manager would need to wisely use his power base to influence reform. He would plan methodically and coordinate from inside and outside of the department. Winning support would involve coordination with other commanders, especially those who believe they should have had the position.

POWER COORDINATION POINTS

The Chief must be willing to pursue power and invest the effort it takes to maintain power; however, earning power requires time and dedication. Successful chiefs understand how to use power appropriately. Understanding power allows the chief to influence the: (1) Community, (2) City Manager, and (3) the local government.

EXECUTIVE MANAGEMENT: THE CHIEF

The top management title may vary from department to department, depending on the law enforcement agency. The nomenclature may read "Chief of Police," "Director of Police," "Superintendent," or "Sheriff." However, the responsibilities are similar and executive in nature.

The chief performs many roles when relating to subordinates, community, political leaders, other law enforcement executives, and government officials. The chief needs to communicate effectively with the media.

The top executive role differs from lower level managers in that the chief looks to the future and plans for the long term. The chief is able to envision the entire community, and function in an environment cloaked in internal and external politics. The successful chief is mission oriented and a positive public relations representative to other agencies. The chief's role requires visibility and frequent public appearances.

Senior and middle managers focus on the internal organization, including its politics. They are planners who program, assign tasks, and recommend to the chief executive. Staff recommendations are considered and incorporated into the planning process. The chief bases decisions on recommendations that have broad implications throughout the department.

THE CHIEF AND THE COMMUNITY

Public opinion can remove the most powerful police executive from office. The chief's tenure has limitations and an angered community can readily force a chief's resignation. The most important relationship that the chief can cultivate is community relations.

"Police leadership must commit to the following seven-step process if the department is to improve and meet community expectations:

"1.   Create and nurture a vision, and communicate this vision to all employees and the community.

2.   Live your values. In times of crisis, people look for direction.

3.   Be able to listen. Listen to people in the community and their reaction to police services. A survey may be needed.

4.   Hire for tomorrow by considering the cultural diversity of your community.

5.   'Turf,' not time, enhances policing. Community policing emphasizes neighborhoods, not time and shifts.

6.   Pay attention to perception. Open, honest relations between police and the community and between police and the media are essential to positive community perceptions. Statistics are not the only criteria for involvement.

7.   Decisions should not be made on emotion. Teams, where possible, make better decisions than individuals." [33]

THE CHIEF AND THE CITY MANAGER

Municipal government takes two basic forms: the city or county manager and the strong mayor. The professional managerial system is generally acknowledged as superior because mayors come and go with political forces, creating managerial discontinuity.

Two advantages of the professional manager system would be the advanced training and education of the candidate. While city managers almost always possess an undergraduate or graduate degree in a relevant area, the strong mayor has few or no qualifications to serve as head of government. Mayors have the advantage of greater executive control than that possessed by managers. In either case, the chief needs to communicate with the administrator.

The chief needs to develop a positive relationship with the city manager or mayor. The chief reports to the city manager or mayor through verbal and written communications because "A chief's tenure and success is very dependent upon establishing an effective relationship with the city manager of his [or her] community. To be at odds with the city manager is a form of career suicide." [34]

The chief and city manager represent a powerful coalition when they work together harmoniously. They need to support each other to meet the challenges. They should meet formally and informally. "The Chief might invite the city manager to in-service training sessions, roll calls, ride-alongs, stakeouts and the like. The Chief should also find

out just what the city manager expects from the police
department and its chief." [35]

LOCAL GOVERNMENT CONTROL: THE CHIEF

The executive function of the mayor or city manager
controls the Chief of Police; unfortunately, city ordinances
and charters on issues of control may be unclear. Council
members may issue conflicting orders to the chief, violating
the "unity of command" and confusing the chief and the
community.

Ordinances or charters need to be specific regarding control of the chief, but not so specific that they restrain. If this
happens, the chief may not be able to perform effectively. In
most cases, the chief's appointment is made by the mayor or
city manager.

The chief serves at the pleasure of the executive head of
government, with approval of a majority of council. In most
cases, the chief can be removed by the city manager, with
the approval of and a majority vote by council.

An ordinance identifies the chain of command for control
of the police department's chief executive. In addition, a
directive or memorandum is written to support the ordinance. A clear chain of command links the council, city manager or mayor, with the chief.

In most cases, the chief refrains from communicating
directly with council members. He remains politically neutral and non-partisan. Initially, partisan politics may work
in favor of the chief but may ultimately lead to her dismissal.

The appointment or dismissal of the chief is often linked
to partisan politics. In many small, local communities, the
mayor appoints the chief because of partisan politics and
political support. If the standard is power politics and "to
the victors go the spoils," the chief's tenure may be short. In
most cases, police executives have little insulation against
unjustified removal from their positions. Political pressures
on the chief executive can be burdensome and interpersonal
conflicts may lead to dismissal.

Police executives who seek power, influence, and support should consider informal leadership. In most cases, the informal power structure is hidden from public view. The chief may end up in a quandary without a clear understanding of the informal power structure.

POWER AND INFLUENCE

The chief and senior leaders rely on the informal use of power rather than its formal application. The formal use of power may be applied when necessary and is granted to chiefs and senior leaders. Informal power is earned over a period of time and develops out of long-term relationships and reputation. Informal power uses others to achieve goals. "Informal power helps bring out creativity within the individual and his or her co-workers. It also tends to foster a high degree of self-confidence. When police managers are able to mix both formal and informal power in day-to-day operations, their level of influence in relation to both subordinates and superiors seems boundless. There are three major steps in developing informal power:

1. **"Being visible.** That is, making themselves available, so that subordinates can get to know them as human beings. In short, being visible means being available. When something must be done, the leader with informal power is available and usually knows how to do it.

2. **Maintaining integrity.** Integrity is the willingness to be open and maintain one's values and principles. Leaders who strive to develop informal power have a clear idea of their strengths, limitations, and goals. They also have a clearly defined system of values. They do not appear lazy or dependent on others. When they value a principle, they have chosen it carefully, cherish it, and pursue it on a day-to day basis. Police leaders with informal power know how to trust themselves as well as others.

3. Maintaining performance. Performance is the ability to listen, to be open and honest, and to live up to one's word. This, the production side of management, is especially important in the development of informal power." [36]

THE POWER BASE: One can identify five sources of power that an individual may employ to influence others. However, the certainty that someone has power may be enough to influence others. The taxonomy of social power proves quite useful for understanding the power and influence that leaders have over followers. [37]

EXPERT POWER: Expert power is based on knowledge and expertise. An example of expert power may be found in patrol officers who have seniority in the patrol division. Peers respect their street knowledge and understanding of the informal aspects of group leadership.

Leaders who teach at the police academy have an opportunity to develop expert power through the display and demonstration of their expertise. This activity develops referent power with academy trainees who will eventually be assigned to them. Young officers will advance through the ranks and eventually influence others.

REFERENT POWER: Referent power is based on personal relationships. It can be used to offset a lack of expert power. This kind of power is based on potential influence, due to the strength of the personal relationship between the leader and subordinate.

Subordinates tend to follow leaders when they personally like them. For example, the lieutenant who shows great concern and empathy for her officers is usually more powerful than the officer who does not. However, referent power and personal relationships do not always lead to efficiency. Excessive identification with subordinates can lead to unfortunate consequences.

LEGITIMATE POWER: Legitimate power depends on the officer's position and role and can be defined as her formal power and authority. The chief and senior leaders can form compliance simply because they have legitimate power and authority.

Position power can be effective in the presence of the leader, and ineffective in his absence. The Colonel can order compliance with policy, rules, regulations and procedures; however, power alone does not create a leader.

Subordinates sometimes resist legitimate authority. "Effective leaders often intuitively realize they need more than legitimate power to be successful. Before he became president, Dwight Eisenhower commanded Allied troops in Europe during World War II. In a meeting with his staff before the Normandy invasion, Eisenhower pulled a string across a table to make a point about leadership. He was demonstrating that just as you can pull a string, not push it, officers must lead soldiers and not 'push' them from the rear." [38]

REWARD POWER: Includes the ability and potential to influence officers. The leader has control over most rewards and benefits. This includes the power to promote, award raises and make special assignments.

COERCIVE POWER: Influences officers through negative sanctions. Leaders often use fear to control officers, however, coercive power leads to resentment. An official letter of reprimand is an example of coercive power.

The leader investigates and evaluates the subordinate's position before administering discipline. Leaders who abuse coercive power soon find it comes "full-circle" in the form of resentment, which undermines a senior leader's power and authority.

FOCUS POINTS: UNDERSTANDING POWER

Leaders need to understand the basis of power in order to improve influence. Power is a two-way street. A leader influences followers and the opposite is also true. Followers influence and exert power over leaders.

Leaders who apply (1) expert power, (2) referent power, (3) legitimate power, (4) reward power and (5) coercive power in a judicious manner may generate superior leadership and influence. Effective leaders take advantage of every source of power available to them.

The chief can build a power base and relationships that provide influence by linking senior leaders, middle managers and first-line supervisors. In addition, the chief reaches outside the organization to influence and apply power throughout the community. The ability to link the power of the mayor or city manager and the council is essential to the process. The chief has rallied all of the potential power sources when this has been accomplished.

CONCLUSION

The chief and senior leaders are the department's strategic managers. Together they plan effective management. Top management formulates mission statements and goals, with the assistance of managers and officers. The chief's strategy-making process identifies goals and objectives that evolve from the mission statement. Senior leadership develops a vision for the future, which addresses the following questions: (1) Where is the Department going? (2) How will we get there? and (3) How will we know when we have arrived? Finally, the chief charts and navigates the department's course, remaining alert to the quicksands of social change that may cause a department to reduce effectiveness.

Chapter 4
MIDDLE MANAGEMENT AND LEADERSHIP

The definition of total quality is simple:
It is a leadership philosophy which
creates through-out the entire enterprise
a working environment which inspires
trust, teamwork, and the quest for
continuous, measurable improvement.
- JOHN M. LOH

Senior leaders lead with their conceptual skills and vision. Middle managers or leaders emphasize their human relations skills and understand the human side of the enterprise. Middle managers are not usually referred to as leaders. This may have a profound impact on role performance. Leadership responsibilities exist at every level of the organization. Middle managers tend to concentrate on controlling personnel and allocating funds. But the challenge for middle management is to rise above managing and aspire to leadership.

MANAGEMENT VERSUS LEADERSHIP

How does management differ from leadership? While management focuses on a task's intrinsic value, leadership focuses on people. Managers tend to support the "old way of doing things," while leaders focus on values and ethics, thus demonstrating maturity, courage, and vision.

A true leader leads from any organizational position and does not need rank. A patrol officer may have more influence than a captain or lieutenant. The informal leader powerfully influences peer behavior for or against organizational objectives.

LEADERSHIP AND MANAGEMENT DEFINED

Managing is "the process of organizing the activities of individuals in groups in efforts toward goal achievement in a given situation; working with and through individuals and groups to accomplish organizational goals. In essence, leadership is a broader concept than management. Leadership occurs any time one attempts to influence behavior."[39] Management accomplishes its work through others while leadership works with others. Optimally, both approaches should be combined.

Middle managers have traditionally been charged with basic POSDCORB functions. This acronym stands for the organizational areas of planning, organizing, staffing, directing, co-ordinating, reporting and budgeting.[40] While this acronym describes management areas, it does not address human components. New leadership watch words are coach, inspire, empower, and affirm. They also include flexibility, responsibility, self-management, power sharing, team autonomy, and unit entrepreneurialship.[41]

"The most basic difference between leaders and managers is this: Managers think it is their job to run the organization well. That is why, more often than not, managers give themselves ulcers trying to know and control everything. Leaders know it is their job to make sure the organization is run well by others. Leaders concentrate on having the right people, in the right places, doing the right things. Leaders are comfortable sharing authority and responsibility, successes and failures, with other leaders."[42] The following case study exemplifies leadership versus management approaches.

CASE STUDY: LEADERSHIP VERSUS MANAGEMENT

Captain Josh Williams was a perfectionist who over managed his sergeants and police officers. He was more concerned with following police regulations than the welfare of his officers. This obsessed shift commander demanded total adherence to the regulations without exception. In addition, his leadership style was authoritarian and demeaning.

The Captain commanded the midnight shift on a permanent basis. He was not in favor with the top commanders and served in exile. Captain Williams peaked his career at age fifty and was not competitive for another promotion. Williams was bitter and cynical because he made his last promotion twenty years earlier.

The Captain's favorite method of supervision was to follow officers in the late morning hours, enforcing minor regulations. He would cite and discipline officers for failure to wear their hats, writing adverse letters and placing them in personnel folders. Many officers considered this behavior petty and became openly hostile. Morale was at a low point under Captain William's leadership.

"Good leaders understand that being the boss does not mean bossing—it means breaking down barriers to accomplish the job in the best possible way; by providing employees the reserves, training and coaching they need, and by providing them with the information they need so they can see the organization's big picture." [43]

Power must be used legitimately and formal power should be used sparingly. "We must learn to handle power humanely and effectively so as to better motivate subordinates. An experienced, effective leader knows that the power he [or she] holds over...workers should be used minimally and generally only for 'course correction.' A pleasant disposition and a sense of humor are far more effective than the exercise of any formal power." [44]

Gordon Alexander replaced the Captain after his sudden retirement, due to a heart condition. The new Captain reviewed the situation with his commanders, sergeants, and informal leaders. After careful consideration of the former shift commander's actions, Captain Alexander proceeded to change the social climate. His first act of leadership was to cancel the requirement of wearing a hat in the police cruiser. He calculated that wearing a hat on the midnight shift was unnecessary and uncomfortable. The new Captain's first act as shift commander won the hearts and minds of those he served. Captain Alexander was concerned about the welfare and comfort of his officers. His sergeants and officers returned the consideration and respect; commanders acknowledged his leadership skills.

LESSONS LEARNED: Resentment is often the result of over supervision in management. The Captain was confident and willing to take a risk. He gained his officers' respect because he was more concerned about "doing the right thing."

A recent NIJ study found that leader influence varies according to supervision style. An "active" supervisory style, involving "leading by example," appears most influential, regardless of potential drawbacks. Active leaders/supervisors appear to be crucial to the implementation of organizational goals and objectives. [45]

This Captain realized that the human priorities were more important than outdated arbitrary regulations. Sometimes rules and regulations do not make sense; officers are quick to notice when regulations are not purposeful. Not wearing a hat on midnight shift does not require disciplinary action and a letter of reprimand. Justice is an important leadership function, as well as concern for the welfare of officers.

The role of the manager is often relegated to organizing, planning, controlling and logistics. The role of the leader is to get things done and care for the morale of the department. Ideally, leadership and management are essential to successful accomplishment of the mission. For additional information concerning management versus leadership, review Table 4-1.

Table 4-1
MANAGEMENT VS.
LEADERSHIP

LEADERSHIP	MANAGEMENT
Gets things done with very little motion	Generates excessive paperwork
Instruction through deeds not words	Leads by memorandum and regulations
Keeps informed, highly visible	Lost in the details
Catalyst for change	Fears change
Accessible	Preoccupied with details
Does the right thing	Does things right
Coaches	Manages
Concerned with vision	Concerned with present
Understands the mission	Budgetary constraint issues
Leads from the front	Leads from the office
Defines goals	Concern for immediate tasks

SOURCE: Chinese philosopher Lao-Tzu (Left-Hand Column)

THE ROLE OF MIDDLE MANAGERS

Middle managers are the real power in any police organization. They have the influence to assist or resist even the smallest strategic reform in the organization. Middle managers derive their power from their positions and act as organizational "gate-keepers."

Captains and lieutenants have horizontal power that reaches across all functional areas of the police department. In addition, middle managers may serve as watch commanders, special unit commanders, or short-term project officers. Their managerial functions include setting goals, establishing procedures, controlling, and efficiently organizing.

"The role of mid-management has been primarily to extend the reach of management into the day-to-day operations of police departments by standardizing and controlling both organizational procedures and officer performance. As such, captains and lieutenants have been the leading edge of the control functions of police departments." [46]

Middle managers understand how departments work and the cultural issues involved. They know department secrets and sensitive issues. The traditional police manager commits to traditions and not "making waves." This commitment has served them well because they have advanced through the ranks by following the rules. Middle management is threatened by strategic change, how it impacts them and if they have the power to stop it.

Middle managers are there for the duration. They understand that they are young enough to survive the chief and senior leaders. They control first-line supervisors and their officers, and their combined power is often greater than the chief executive. Because the tenure of a police chief is usually short-term, time is on the side of middle managers. Moreover, strategic change depends on the cooperation of police middle managers.

ORGANIZATIONAL CLIMATE

Zero tolerance for failure is detrimental to creativity. "Officers will not be creative and will not take initiatives if a high value continues to be placed on conformity. They will not be thoughtful if they are required to adhere to regulations that are thoughtless. The wilful disrespect by officers for department policies, rules and regulations, may very well call for intolerance and recriminations by supervisors." [47]

"There are two kinds of mistakes—mistakes of the mind and mistakes of the heart. If you're doing something out of malice, then there is a problem. But if you're trying to do your job and you make an innocent mistake that may violate a rule, the entire circumstances should be taken into account. If we want people to take risks, we have to tolerate mistakes." [48]

Middle managers exercise leadership by changing the organizational climate from one of absolute control to empowerment of subordinates. Leadership may fear relinquishing some of its power; however, delegating power to subordinates actually reaps power and should be embraced, not feared. Middle management traditionally is not occupied by creative and innovative risk takers who encourage the same. Captains and lieutenants must learn creativity and apply participatory management techniques.

DOUGLAS MCGREGOR - THEORY X AND THEORY Y

Theory X and Theory Y describe two common styles of management. Theory X is an authoritarian leadership style based on two assumptions: one that employees do not enjoy working and two that employees need coercion to adequately perform.

Theory Y management emphasizes the positive aspects of the human spirit: that employees enjoy working, can be trusted, and are willing workers when given reasonable goals.

Some police middle managers subscribe to the Theory X style of management, the foundation for directive leadership, and the best management style in emergency situations. However, Theory X tends to stifle initiative in the everyday police environment and is inconsistent with both community-oriented and problem-oriented policing.

Theory Y is a humanistic approach to the encouragement of motivation and is superior to Theory X when applied to educated, highly motivated police officers. Theory Y reduces hostility and is consistent with community-policing and problem-oriented policing.

FROM CONTROLLING TO COACHING

Middle managers have functioned as "controllers" for years. Police officers often develop into this kind of manager because they identify with their leaders and ultimately become the kind of manager they resented. The transition from enforcer to facilitator and coach is not an easy transition.

In recent years, transformational leadership has emphasized that employees who participate are more productive. The most important aspect of transformational leadership is that the emphasis is on the employee. "Transformational leadership acknowledges people as the organization's most important resource, and empowers personnel to contribute to the organization's objectives. It empowers employees to take responsibility by allowing them to define the parameters of their work. It seeks out and solicits participation and input. It replaces organizational control with self-control. It advocates interdependence and autonomy rather than dependence and anonymity." [49]

"Transformational leadership is employee oriented management that share four key guidelines: creating an enabling culture and organization; practicing participative hiring; ensuring equitable recognition and reward; and demonstrating fairness during hard times." [50]

THE LOCUS OF CONTROL: EXTERNAL OR INTERNAL

Theory X promotes resentment, alienation, and ethical conflicts. This orientation is based on external controls, not internal controls. However, Transformational and Theory Y styles of management place responsibility for ethical behavior with the police officer.

Theory Y, participatory management, and transformational leadership empower police officers to perform well, even in the absence of the leader. This approach reduces resentment because it helps managers facilitate, not punish. It requires officers to think and reason, rather than blindly follow.

SHIFTING STRATEGIES

Police managers must realize that the hard-line approach will not work with better educated, youthful populations. Successful police leaders use positive management and avoid the punishing style of the past. This does not suggest the complete abandonment of punitive measures. Some officers require correction concerning violations of rules of conduct and professional ethics. There is a place for directive leadership and harsh discipline. However, it should be avoided when possible and applied only when necessary.

An advantage of progressive management is that it serves as a foundation for the transition from traditional policing to community-oriented policing. The new forms of leadership are consistent with community-oriented and problem-oriented policing and affect police personnel in many ways.

"First, it means a shift from telling and controlling employees, to helping them develop their skills and abilities...Second, it means listening to the customers, the citizens, in new and more open ways. Third, it means solving problems, not reacting to incidents. Fourth, it means trying new things, experimenting. Risk-taking and honest mistakes must be tolerated in order to encourage creativity and active innovation. Ideas must be permitted to "bubble up" within the organization. Finally, it means avoiding, whenever possible, the use of coercive power to bring about change." [51]

Additional research is needed about autocratic and coercive leadership styles. One hypothesis is that intelligent and capable officers resign under this type of leadership in search of more creative professional environments. Because individuals with lessor abilities remain, disorganization increases as well as police corruption and deteriorating police ethics.

MIDDLE LEADERSHIP TECHNIQUES

Middle managers normally spend much time in their offices overseeing internal departmental operations away from their officers. In a sense, middle managers are insulated from the daily police operations of sergeants and patrol officers. However, middle leaders should interact with their subordinates. The paper trail is merely functionary; it is not the function.

MENTORING AND COACHING

Captains and lieutenants are in an ideal position to serve as mentors because of their potential for influencing peers and subordinates. However, mentoring requires compassion and counseling skills. "Sharing the subtleties of the job with your subordinates, putting them in critical positions and allowing them to succeed is what mentoring is all about." [52] Further, mentors help people develop by educating subordinates, showing support, and expressing confidence. They encourage those who perform well.

All good mentoring incorporates the following: (1) it explains the purpose and importance of what is being taught; (2) it explains the process to be used; (3) it shows how it's done; (4) it observes the mentor firsthand and provides immediate feedback; (5) it expresses confidence when confidence is warranted; and (6) it follows-up. [53]

BUILDING TEAMS

Middle managers help integrate teams by encouraging collective thinking and actions that solve problems. Middle management builds support and demonstrates appreciation for contributions to the team effort. The fact is, teams help officers excel and confident leaders are never intimidated by outstanding team members or their performance. On the contrary, team members can accomplish what middle managers could not possibly complete alone. "Holistic management" does not emphasize functional areas, staff and line. It defines law enforcement officers and support personnel as a team. The simultaneous team actions of separate entities together have greater total effect than the sum of their individual effects.

Police officers depend on peer identification, for no call has higher priority than a fellow officer in danger. Police officers are also given an ego boost by the fact that they are readily identified by their uniforms and have certain powers above and beyond those of the average citizen.

"It is the police manager's responsibility to see that the officer does not lose this feeling of ego satisfaction (e.g., after a citizen has flashed him {or her} an obscene gesture) and continues to develop this sense of belonging to a unique profession geared toward helping one's fellow human beings." [54]

"All high performing teams have eight attributes:

* **Participative Leadership** - the creation of interdependency through empowerment, and service to others.

* **Shared Responsibility** - the creation of an environment in which all team members feel as responsible as the manager for the performance of the work unit.

* **Alignment of Purpose** - the possession of a sense of common purpose about why the team exists and the function it serves.

* **High Communication** - the creation of a climate of trust and open communication.

* **Focus on the Future** - the perception of change as an opportunity for growth.

* **Focus on the Task** - meetings that focus on results.

* **The Creative Use of Talents** - the application of individual talents and creativity.

* **Rapidity of Response** - identifying and acting on opportunities." [55]

EMPOWERING OFFICERS

Some officers are attracted to leadership for the wrong reasons. They are attracted to the power and control that come with the position. Unfortunately, inexperienced managers often fail to understand the responsibilities of command. Leadership is service to others that requires a tremendous amount of commitment, energy, patience and selfless service. The price-tag is high for those who seek leadership and command roles, and the satisfaction comes from serving members of the department, not being served.

"When you think about leaders you respect, they got to be leaders for exactly the opposite reasons that most officers start out seeking to be leaders. In most instances, leaders ultimately get power and control and are served by doing just the opposite. Effective leaders tend to empower their people, to free them up and to serve them." [56]

"Leadership is not so much the exercise of power itself as the empowerment of others. Leaders are able to translate intentions into reality by aligning the energies of the organization behind an attractive goal.... These leaders lead by pulling rather than pushing, by inspiring rather than ordering; by creating achievable, though challenging expectations, and rewarding progress toward them rather than by manipulating; by enabling people to use their own initiative and experiences rather than by denying or constraining their experiences and actions." [57]

Empowering officers does not mean delegating your power and walking away. Middle managers do not abdicate responsibility but they are responsible for their subordinates' behaviors. Middle managers are reluctant to empower subordinates because they are ultimately responsible to senior leaders and the chief.

Many are aware of "Murphy's Law" concerning the probability of something going wrong. A captain might be concerned that an officer's behavior could end his career. The worst scenario describes an officer who commits an illegal act and later testifies in court, "My captain told me to do it. He knew what I was doing. I thought it was the way we did things around here."

A set of non-negotiable behaviors that address lawful, constitutional, ethical and moral principles must be followed. Policing is not a license to use deadly force tactics. Leaders do not condone citizen abuse and total disregard for appropriate police procedures.

"Empowerment means coaching and supporting, not setting officers adrift and abandoning them. Giving pieces of power away at every rank allows a department to get more mileage out of the power. Don't just give power away—bargain over what you will get in return from the person who gets a piece of your power. You share power not because it's a nice thing to do but because you have other things to accomplish and you need others to exercise your power to get the job done." [58]

THEORY Z: ITS RELATIONSHIP TO BUILDING QUALITY TEAMS

In the first part of this chapter, Theory X and Theory Y leadership styles were discussed. In recent years, a new theory has been identified as Theory Z. This theory has gained prominence in the United States. It recognizes that the police cannot exist in social isolation and that social interaction is essential to the survival of policing.

Officers function in a larger community than the police organization. They work and interact amidst diverse cultures. Government, labor, and political institutions are not separate but interdependent entities. Cooperation is needed in all facets of society.

Theory Z considers the needs of employees. It recommends social change and the reform of Theories X and Y. The major goal of Theory Z is to view the organization in the total context of society.

According to Ouchi, Theory Z is based on three beliefs:

1. Management is concerned with production, as expressed in Theory X.

2. Management is concerned with the well-being of workers as productive employees, a basic assumption of Theory Y.

3. This belief distinguishes Theory Z from Theories X and Y. Organizations cannot be viewed independently of the larger social, economic, and political conditions in society. More importantly, the work setting must be understood along with other institutions in society, such as family and school.[59]

TOTAL QUALITY LEADERSHIP

Theory Z compliments problem-oriented policing by creatively approaching managing and encourages a positive relationship with officers and the community. Total Quality Leadership, developed in Japan and became popular in the United States during the 1970's and 1980's is directly linked to Theory Z. Public and law enforcement organizations began to notice the TQL process by the mid 1980's. The Federal Quality Institute provides a basic description of the concepts of TQL on the implementation level.

Organizations in both the private and public sectors that have adopted the TQL approach consistently increase value to customers, improve productivity, reduce total costs, improve products and services, achieve better planning and forecasting, reduce administrative overhead, reduce rework and waste, and improve employee performance and morale. Total Quality Leadership is therefore the means to achieving high-performing organizations. The TQL approach emphasizes: (1) Customer focus, (2) Alignment (internal and external) (3) Total involvement (4) Continuous improvement, and (5) Leadership commitment.[60]

While this approach helps to analyze social systems, it has problems in implementation. However, it can help focus policing at the community level, with all of policing's cultural implications. TQL is a useful theory for understanding the police and its relationship to the surrounding community.

USING QUALITY-CIRCLE PROGRAMS
TO BUILD TEAMS

Developed out of Theory Z, Quality-Circle Programs are useful concerning the motivation of police personnel. This approach is based on the assumption that officers working together to solve problems is superior to independent efforts. Cooperation and interaction provide the opportunity for growth and development.

Quality-Circle Programs are based on two assumptions: "First, interactions among employees should provide for the maximum growth of the individual. Quality circles are meant to enhance the ability of workers to improve themselves, both personally and professionally. Second, by providing conditions for the growth of employees, the organization will become increasingly effective. In short, it is in the best interest of the organization to promote the well-being of workers. Operating on these two assumptions, quality-circle programs are defined as small groups of employees, typically non-management personnel from the same work unit, who meet regularly to identify, analyze, and recommend solutions to problems relating to the work unit." [61]

Managers allocate time and resources that support police officers in their problem-solving and brainstorming efforts. "The research suggests that the use of Quality-Circle Programs greatly enhances the potential for producing small-scale improvements and improving work-unit morale among officers." [62] Importantly, managers must improve the social climate and morale of their officers. Quality-Circle Programs encourage participation in the problem-solving process.

FOCUS POINTS: CHANGE AND INNOVATION

Middle managers are in an excellent position to monitor and adjust the pace of change. They assure that the system is not overwhelmed and officers have the opportunity and time to adapt. Change and innovation are not always welcomed additions to police organizations.

"Middle managers should be aware of key factors concerning the adoption of innovations. These organizational
tasks apply to middle managers who attempt to implement
problem-oriented policing. Four central organizational tasks
lie before middle managers during the 'action phase' of a
team's innovation efforts: (1) Address interference; (2) maintain momentum; (3) address structural changes; and (4)
communicate externally." [63]

Some scholars and practitioners have portrayed middle
management as the main obstacle to the community-oriented policing movement. Middle managers have been threatened with early retirement, downsizing and organizational
flattening of the police hierarchy. However, others feel that
middle managers are important to basic police operations
and value their contributions.

Middle managers are caught in a cross-fire between top
management and line personnel. Senior leaders, who impose
community policing from the top, are under pressure from
political leaders to change. Sergeants and officers experience resistance when implementing the new reform strategies because of conflicts associated with the emergency
response system and traditional policing responsibilities.

CONCLUSION

What are the future changes in management theory? There is a movement away from Theory X (autocratic) management to Theory Y (participatory) management, that is, from controlling to participatory management. In recent years, Theory X (autocratic) and Y (democratic) have merged with Theory Z, the integrated approach toward Total Quality Leadership, which reaches beyond the organization to the total context of society. The synthesis of both approaches integrates well with community and problem-oriented policing because of its culturally oriented-approach.

Middle managers, captains, and lieutenants emphasize three basic situational theory leadership styles: coaching, supporting and delegating. They avoid micro-management whenever possible. Middle management develops the organizational climate and encourages senior leadership vision.

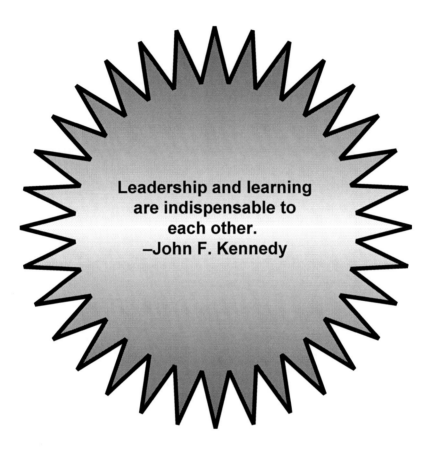

Leadership and learning
are indispensable to
each other.
–John F. Kennedy

Chapter 5
SERGEANTS AND POLICE OFFICERS

Sergeants and patrol officers serve as catalysts for joint police and community problem-solving endeavors.
- BUREAU OF JUSTICE ASSISTANCE

Problem-solving policing cannot be imposed but results from cooperation by sergeants and police officers. Situational Leadership encourages enthusiasm for change. Situational Leadership can be applied at every level of the organization, but most crucially by first-line supervisors. Sergeants are in a strategic position to identify problems and apply Situational Leadership Techniques which offer the flexibility necessary to respond appropriately.

THE SERGEANT
Sergeant is the first commissioned grade in the field of law enforcement and thus pivotally positioned to encourage problem-solving policing. The sheer number of sergeants and their direct contact with officers in the field provide many opportunities for them to encounter problem-solving opportunities.

The importance of sergeants in police organizations is best stated by "the old adage: 'Generals win battles but sergeants win wars'—true of the military and of police departments. A department's meaning to officers on the street and citizens in the community directly results from what sergeants are and do." [64]

79

Sergeants enable police forces to achieve accountability and performance objectives. However, sergeants also need time to be with their officers. "Sergeants spent only 11 percent of their time in face-to-face contact with the officers they supervise." [65] Most of a sergeant's time with officers is during roll-call. Poor supervision and limited officer contact leads to inadequate performance.

Sergeants sometimes emphasize paperwork rather than leadership. "Many of these sergeants never having experienced constructive guidance as patrol officers, did not know how to give it when they got promoted to sergeant." [66] Sergeants are often promoted on orders and the next day report for work without any training on "how to be a sergeant." The selection of well-motivated sergeants is the starting point for improving supervision. However, training is essential if they are to achieve their leadership potential.

The sergeant should be a proactive leader concerned with direct leadership, her primary role to teach and direct. Her three essential areas of competence include: (1) experience, (2) expertise, and (3) training/education. Situational Leadership provides an understanding of training and progressive leadership fundamentals. [67]

Police sergeants and their officers are daily decision makers, more so than CEO's of many large firms. Sometimes, decisions are made in a split-second without the benefit of prior consultation or research. Sergeants also advise subordinates on their decisions.

Successful decision making at the sergeant level requires identifying all parts of a problem and the appropriate solution. The evaluation of an officer's performance in a particular situation should be based on the technical knowledge and observations of the sergeant. First-line supervisors lead primarily through their human relations skills and their knowledge of their officers' role requirements.

PROACTIVE SUPERVISION

The quality of service to the community is directly linked to the quality of supervision. Police sergeants develop proactive methods of motivating, monitoring, coordinating and training their officers. If this proactive approach is absent, efficiency will depend on the efforts of a few motivated officers.

Sergeants and corporals should occasionally respond to calls with officers to evaluate police services and review officer-citizen contact. An after-action briefing also may be appropriate.

Praise can be an excellent means of building rapport. Helpful recommendations can also improve service. Field encounters with officers provide supervisors excellent opportunities to display positive leadership techniques.

TRANSFORMING LEADERSHIP

Sergeants who demonstrate transforming leadership set the example and provide training and guidance. They are reasonable, avoid excessive criticism, and praise generously. These leaders carry out their responsibilities lawfully and equitably.

Transactional leadership "occurs when one person takes the initiative in making contact with others for the purpose of an exchange of valued things.... Their purposes stand within the bargaining process and can be advanced by maintaining that process. But beyond this, the relationship does not go.... A leadership act took place, but it was not one that binds leader and follower together in a mutual pursuit of a higher purpose."

Transforming leadership, on the other hand, "occurs when one or more persons engage with others in such a way that leaders and followers raise one another to higher levels of motivation and morality. Their purposes, which might have started out as separate but related—as in the case of transactional leadership—become fused. The transforming sergeant sets the example and provides training and guidance. She is reasonable and careful about criticism. In addition, not stingy with public praise. [Ultimately,] transforming leadership...raises the level of human conduct and ethical

aspiration of both leader and led, and thus has a transforming effect on both." [68]

SERGEANT LEADERSHIP RESPONSIBILITIES

To be a successful supervisor, sergeants must manage
social change and be a productive force within the agency.
Supervisors: (1) attain organizational goals through line and
staff police personnel, (2) meet individual needs through
appropriate supervision, and (3) cope with the changing
goals and needs.

Motivating personnel begins with proactive leadership:
"The relationship of two or more people, in which one attempts to influence the other(s) toward the attainment of a
goal, or many goals. The key to understanding the concept
of leadership is to look at it as an influence process." [69]

A sergeant's operational plan ensures that subordinates
are properly equipped, trained, and motivated to perform
their missions. The skilled supervisor re-evaluates the planning process and pays particular attention to Murphy's Law:
"Anything that can go wrong will go wrong." Excellent
supervisors pay attention to detail, delegate tasks, and follow-up on goals and objectives. When details are tended to,
the larger tasks seem almost to accomplish themselves.

LEADERSHIP FRAMEWORK

The four factors that police supervisors are concerned
with are: (1) the leader, (2) the follower, (3) communication,
and (4) the situation. Each group of police officers requires
a specific style of leadership. A general understanding of
human nature and a clear understanding of one's
subordinates are necessary for successful leadership.

Sergeants must have an honest understanding of their
own abilities, informational requirements and performance
needs. Effective two-way communication is essential for accomplishing the tasks that support the mission. Since tactical situations are often different, appropriate leadership
requires clear analysis and judgment.

SITUATIONAL LEADERSHIP

This chapter attempts to develop appropriate supervisory responses based on four hypothetical case studies. With each officer the sergeant will be able to select the appropriate leadership style to accomplish the mission. The chapter aims to describe, in a proactive manner, how to develop subordinates.

KEY TERMS AND CONCEPTS [70]

The diagnostic ability of a leader is important. Equally important is an ability to vary leadership style to meet the demands of the environment. Moreover, there are so many environmental variables that managers cannot hope to evaluate every possibility before making a decision. Situational Leadership provides a valuable approach by focusing on the key situational variables of the leader and the follower(s.) This approach has proven to be a framework of practical value to leaders for almost three decades.

The concept is based on an interplay of the following: (1) the amount of guidance and direction (task behavior) a leader gives; (2) the amount of socio-emotional support (relationship behavior) a leader provides; and (3) the readiness level that followers exhibit in performing a specific task, function, or objective. It provides leaders with some understanding of the relationship between follower readiness and effective leadership. Followers in any situation are vital because they can individually accept or reject the leader, and also because they determine as a group how much personal power a leader has.

For the purpose of Situational Leadership, the terms "leader" and "follower" should be understood as relative terms. In any given situation, the leader is the individual trying to influence the behavior of others and may not necessarily be the highest ranking person.

Situational Leadership contends there is no one best way to influence people; the most effective leadership style depends upon the readiness of the followers. Leadership style, it should be remembered, is the behavior of a leader in influencing others. There are two major behavior types: task and relationship.

Task Behavior describes the extent to which leaders clarify the duties and responsibilities of groups or individuals. Telling people what to do, how to do it, when to do it, where to do it, and who is to do it.

Relationship Behavior describes the extent to which leaders effectively communicate, that is, how leaders listen, facilitate, and support certain behaviors. Task and relationship behaviors are independent activities; excellence in one does not necessarily suggest excellence in the other.

The four basic leadership styles are:

Style 1: Above average amounts of task behavior, below average amounts of relationship behavior.

Style 2: Above average amounts of task and relationship behavior.

Style 3: Above average amounts of relationship behavior, below average amounts of task behavior.

Style 4: Below average amounts of both relationship and task behavior.

Readiness of the Followers or Group

There are a number of factors in any given environment. The leader, follower(s), superior, associates, organization, job demands, and available time all impact on a situation. The crucial variable is the interaction between leader and follower(s). There is no leadership without someone following.

To maximize the relationship between leader and follower(s), the leader must first clarify the task or mission. If the leader is not clear about outcomes, objectives, and subtasks, there is no basis for determining follower readiness or the appropriate leadership style.

Readiness Defined

Readiness is the extent to which a follower can or will accomplish a specific task. Readiness is not a personality quality; people tend to be more or less ready depending on the task. A leader may have to assess the readiness of an entire work group as well as the readiness of each individual. In many instances, the leader may find that the behavior of a group differs from the behavior of an individual within the group.

There are two components of readiness: ability and willingness.

Ability describes the knowledge, experience, and skill an individual or group brings to a particular task or activity.

Willingness defines the extent to which an individual or group has the confidence, commitment, and motivation to accomplish a specific task.

Willingness also suggests self-confidence. While subordinates may find insecurity in unfamiliar situations, their unwillingness suggests regressive performance.

Change in either willingness or ability affects the other component. The more willing a person is, the greater the improvement in ability; and the more ability a person develops, the greater the likelihood of increased willingness.

The specific combination of ability and willingness defines the readiness level. The Center for Leadership Studies has expanded the continuum of follower readiness to include behavioral indicators of the four readiness levels.

Readiness Level 1 (R1)—Unable and unwilling. The follower is unable and lacks commitment or motivation; or, is unable and insecure. The follower may lack confidence.

Readiness Level 2 (R2)—Unable but willing. The follower lacks ability but is motivated and makes an effort; or, is unable but confident. The follower lacks ability but is confident as long as the leader provides guidance.

Readiness Level 3 (R3)—Able but unwilling. The follower has ability to perform the task, but is not willing to use that ability; or, is able but insecure. The follower has the ability to perform the task, but is insecure or apprehensive about doing it alone.

Readiness Level 4 (R4)—Able and willing. The follower has the ability to perform and is committed—or, able and confident. The follower has the ability to perform and is confident about doing it.

Going From R1 to R2 to R3

At R2, followers have become confident, but at R3 they revert to insecurity again. This is not regression, but an indication of the shift in emphasis from leader-directed to self-directed behavior. This shift may result in apprehension or insecurity. Note that the right side of Figure 5-1 involves leader-directed behavior, while the left side of the figure involves follower-directed behavior.

Selecting Appropriate Leadership Styles

In Situational Leadership it is the follower who determines the appropriate leader behavior.

R1:S1—For followers at Readiness Level 1, the appropriate leadership style is known as Telling. This style consists of above average amounts of tasks behavior and below average amounts of relationship behavior. See Figure 5-1 and 5-2.

R2:S2—Readiness Level 2 defines a style known as Selling, in which the leader uses above average amounts of both task and relationship behavior; the task behavior provides direction for the lack of skill while relationship behavior reinforces the individual for trying.

R3:S3—The appropriate style is called Participating, which incorporates above average amounts of relationship behavior, with below average amounts of task behavior. People at R3 know what, when, how, and where to perform but lack confidence or willingness. Relationship behavior encourages them to develop that willingness or confidence.

R4:S4—The appropriate style is called Delegating, which is below average amounts of both relationship and task behavior. These individuals know how, where, when to do their jobs, and have the willingness and confidence to get on with it. Leaders must simply allow them to perform their job.

Situational Leadership is not a prescription with hard-and-fast rules, but an attempt to improve managerial effectiveness and leadership success. Figure 5-1 and 5-2 comprehensively summarizes appropriate leadership behavior for four follower-readiness levels.

DETERMINING APPROPRIATE STYLE

The answers to several questions determine leadership style:

1. What objective(s) do we want to accomplish? The manager must decide what aspects of an individual's or group's activities to influence.

2. What is the individual's or group's readiness? The manager must evaluate the current readiness level of the group or individual in regard to each of these aspects. Readiness level is not a general reflection of overall ability or willingness. A person may be highly ready in one or several aspects of the job, of average readiness in other aspects, and have low readiness in yet others.

3. What leadership action should be taken? The manager employs Figure 5-1 to determine the appropriate style to use with that individual or group for each aspect of the job.

4. What was the result of the leadership intervention? The manager assesses the results to see if they match expectations and determine follow-up action if necessary.

5. What follow-up, if any, is required? If a gap appears between the performance and the desired performance of the individual or group, then follow-up is required and the cycle begins again.

Figure 5-1
FOLLOWER READINESS

When a leader behavior is used appropriately with its corresponding level of readiness, it is termed a high probability match. The following are descriptors that can be useful when using Situational Leadership for specific applications:

S1	S2
Telling	Selling
Guiding	Explaining
Directing	Clarifying
Establishing	Persuading

S3	S4
Participating	Delegating
Encouraging	Observing
Collaborating	Monitoring
Committing	Fulfilling

Source: Adopted from Paul Hersey, Situational Selling (Escondido, California: Center for Leadership Studies), p. 35.

Figure 5-2
HOW TO USE THE
SITUATIONAL
LEADERSHIP MODEL

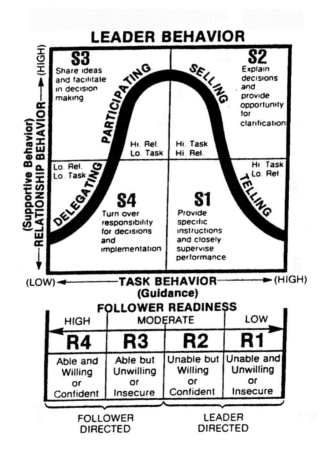

LEADER BEHAVIOR

S3 Share ideas and facilitate in decision making

S2 Explain decisions and provide opportunity for clarification

PARTICIPATING

SELLING

Hi. Rel. Lo. Task

Hi. Task Hi. Rel.

(HIGH) RELATIONSHIP BEHAVIOR (Supportive Behavior)

Lo. Rel. Lo. Task

Hi. Task Lo. Rel

DELEGATING

TELLING

S4 Turn over responsibility for decisions and implementation

S1 Provide specific instructions and closely supervise performance

(LOW) ◀——— **TASK BEHAVIOR** ———▶ (HIGH)
(Guidance)

FOLLOWER READINESS

HIGH	MODERATE		LOW
R4	**R3**	**R2**	**R1**
Able and Willing or Confident	Able but Unwilling or Insecure	Unable but Willing or Confident	Unable and Unwilling or Insecure

FOLLOWER DIRECTED   LEADER DIRECTED

Source: Adopted from Paul Hersey, Situational Selling (Escondido, California: Center for Leadership Studies, 1996), p. 19.

Figure 5-3
FOLLOWER READINESS

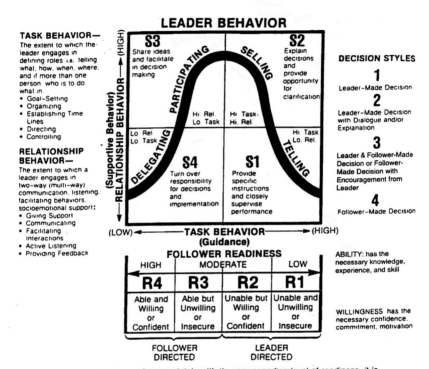

When a Leader Behavior is used appropriately with its corresponding level of readiness, it is termed a High Probability Match. The following are descriptors that can be useful when using Situational Leadership for specific applications:

S1	S2	S3	S4
Telling	Selling	Participating	Delegating
Guiding	Explaining	Encouraging	Observing
Directing	Clarifying	Collaborating	Monitoring
Establishing	Persuading	Committing	Fulfilling

Source:
Adopted from Paul Hersey, Situational Selling (Escondido, California: Center for Leadership Studies), p. 35.

Effective Task Statements

A well-formulated task statement must be developed to assess individual readiness. The task statement must present clearly defined and measurable performance standards for the task. [71]

Situational Leadership is based on the premise that there is no one best way to lead. Effective leaders adapt their style to the situation. To develop the people working for you into peak performers, you must think about leadership style. The pattern of behavior must fit the abilities of the officer, as well as the situation.

Research indicates that leadership styles vary from situation to situation. While some sergeants direct their officers' activities (task behavior), others concentrate on building personal relationships with their followers (relationship behavior). Sometimes various combinations of task and supportive behaviors are required. Thus, specific task and socio-emotional leader behaviors are not "either/or" leadership styles. Each of the four leadership styles represents a different combination of specific task and socio-emotional leadership behaviors. These combinations differ depending on (1) the amount of direction the leader provides, (2) the amount of support and encouragement the leader provides, and (3) the amount of subordinate involvement in the decision making. [72]

IN SUMMARY

A sergeant using *Task Behavior* uses one-way communication to spell out the officer's role, and telling him/her what to do, where, when, and how to do it; he or she then closely supervises performance. Six words can be used to define *Task-oriented Behavior*: *goal setting, organizing, directing, controlling, and supervision.* [73]

A sergeant using *Relationship Behavior* uses two-way communication, listens, provides support and encouragement, facilitates interaction, and involves subordinates in decision making. Four words can be used to define *Socio-*

emotional Behavior: *active listening, communication, and feedback.*[74]

The key is to know when to use the appropriate style. Many variables influence which leadership style is appropriate in which situation, but the main factor is the *readiness level* of the subordinate to perform the specific task. Always remember that *optimism* is a positive force generator when dealing with officers learning a new task.

APPLICATION OF SITUATIONAL LEADERSHIP

As the readiness level of the officer increases from (R1) to (R4), confidence and willingness fluctuate. Most officers are enthusiastic and ready to learn (R1) when they begin a new task in which they have little prior knowledge or experience. Once they begin the task, officers may find the task more difficult or less interesting than they had expected. "This transition from leader-directed to self-directed may result in apprehension or insecurity."[75]

If officers advance from this level of readiness, and learn to perform the task with help from their leader, most individuals go through a self-doubt stage where they question whether they can perform the task well on their own. Their leader says they are competent, but they are not sure. These alternating feelings of competence and self-doubt cause their commitment to fluctuate from excitement to insecurity. With proper supportive behaviors, most officers eventually can become peak performers (R4) who demonstrate a high level of competence, motivation, ability, and willingness.[76]

CASE STUDY

Sergeant Roberta Jones has been fortunate enough to attend a basic supervisor course established by the training academy. During the course, this new sergeant had the opportunity to study Situational Leadership, the functions of the first line supervisor, and a new crime reporting system. Roberta is faced with this problem: How can she get four officers to understand and employ the new reporting system? The program is on-line and involves a new computer. The goal is to achieve exceptional performance from four officers with varying expertise and experience.

After considering the following information about each subordinate, Sergeant Jones has to identify the correct leadership techniques using the Situational Leadership model. The sergeant must implement the new reporting system and seek feedback on its efficiency. Sergeant Jones must apply Situational Leadership and assess each officer at the tasks.

CASE STUDY #1 – Officer Able

Officer Able is probably the best officer on the shift. He is experienced with the computer and has helped the department in its planning with suggestions for the new reporting system. He is constantly one step ahead of the other officers, and has served in the patrol division for the past ten years. His enthusiasm and motivation are contagious and demonstrate positive spirit and morale. The Chief is so pleased with Able's performance that he is being considered for promotion to sergeant. At times, Officer Able seems frustrated when given a routine task and told how to do it.

CASE STUDY #2 – Officer Baker

Officer Baker has been with the department for about four years. He is skilled, competent and a good patrol officer. He probably performs better than he credits himself. At times he seems insecure about his abilities, and he is reluctant to make suggestions when he has good ideas. He keeps the ideas to himself because he fears they may sound obvious or impractical. If he could overcome some of his uncertainty, he would become an outstanding officer.

CASE STUDY #3 – Officer Crumb

Officer Crumb has been with the department for about a year. Initially, he showed enthusiasm. He demonstrated innovative ideas, organized social functions, and developed a new self-defense program for the training academy. In recent months, however, his attitude has changed. His enthusiasm is no longer present. He has stated, "I'm discouraged, and report writing on the new system has taken longer and is more difficult than expected." He feels some degree of discouragement because he was just beginning to master the old system.

CASE STUDY #4 – Officer Daily

Officer Daily is the newest officer on the shift, and graduated from the academy eight months ago. She does show promise, moreover, she is excited about serving in the department, and really didn't expect to be turned loose on her own so soon. She is intelligent and should learn the new system quickly. What she lacks in ability, she makes up for in enthusiasm. Officer Daily will certainly look for opportunities to prove herself in the field of law enforcement.

SOLUTIONS TO HYPOTHETICAL CASES

CASE STUDY #1
DELEGATING LEADERSHIP STYLE
Officer Able

Officer Able is at readiness level (4), willing and confident. The appropriate leadership style (S4), must include delegating with low relationship and low task support. Because he is competent, he does not need support from the leader. As a peak performer, he will be frustrated when given a routine assignment and told how to do it, a normal reaction to micro-management. The delegating style (S4) has the highest probability of being effective.

CASE STUDY #2
PARTICIPATING LEADERSHIP STYLE
Officer Baker

Officer Baker is at readiness level (3), high relationship and low task. Uncertain about his abilities, he has low confidence and is insecure. Leadership style (S3), relationship behaviors with low direction and high support is appropriate. Because he is competent, he does not need close supervision by the sergeant. Because his commitment is variable and he is an apprehensive or reluctant contributor, however, he needs Sergeant Jones' praise, encouragement, and support to help overcome this insecurity.

CASE STUDY #3
SELLING LEADERSHIP STYLE
Officer Crumb

Officer Crumb is at readiness level R1, unable and insecure, or unwilling. A disillusioned learner, he initially shows much enthusiasm (was committed and enthusiastic in the past). He seems to learn, but still feels discouraged. The appropriate leadership style is (S2), selling with high task and high relationship support. Sergeant Jones needs to give him some direction and guidance, while supervising him closely. He needs explanation and clarification to help him overcome his disillusionment.

CASE STUDY #4
TELLING LEADERSHIP STYLE
Officer Daily

Officer Daily is at readiness level 2 (R-2), unable but willing or confident. Key phrases from the case study substantiate that she is an enthusiastic beginner. She is the newest officer, which could indicate low ability since she works on a new task. However, she is excited, which reflects high willingness and enthusiasm. Although she lacks ability, she should learn the task quickly. The appropriate leadership style is (S1), supervising with telling and directing. Sergeant Jones must provide close guidance.

FOCUS POINTS: LEADERSHIP APPLICATIONS

As a result of the new technology, it may be appropriate for Sergeant Jones to provide specific leadership behaviors. However, great tact is required when using style (R1:S1), telling style (R2:S2), selling, because it is difficult for officers to face their lack of knowledge within this new area of expertise. With excellent rapport and training, the officers should make a rapid transition to style (R3:S3) participating, and style (R4:S4) delegating.

Sergeants must be able to organize, plan, and evaluate their officers to reach department objectives. Frustrated police personnel can lead to negative productivity. To accomplish their missions, sergeants must take a "hands-on" approach and know each of their officers' weaknesses and strengths. The basic skills to be effective are diagnostic abilities, adaptability, flexibility, and the ability to apply the correct leadership style according to each emerging situation.

"Supervising others may be compared to keeping corks under water—no sooner is one problem resolved than another one pops to the surface. A good supervisor must want to perform the job and work the hours necessary to keep subordinates moving toward the goal of making the community a safer place in which to live and work." [77]

In summary, Situational Leadership is essential to problem-solving policing. The sergeant who applies the principles of Situational Leadership helps officers plan their time and develop work plans. The first-line supervisor is in the best position to coach police officers and apply Situational Leadership. The problem-solving process gives officers the freedom to experiment with new approaches.

CONCLUSION

A sergeant should demonstrate flexibility and patience. No other rank holds as many responsibilities in first-line supervision, leadership, and training. A situational leader must demonstrate flexibility, diagnostic ability, and contracting leadership styles. The junior leader must concentrate on the Situational Leadership model and the needs of officers. The sergeant must be concerned with the welfare of officers, sustain an ethical climate, and accomplish the mission.

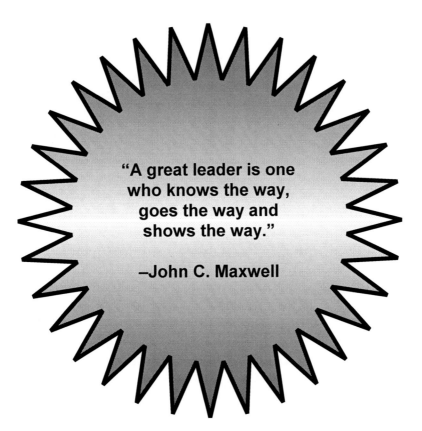

"A great leader is one who knows the way, goes the way and shows the way."

–John C. Maxwell

Part III
DIRECTION AND EXCELLENCE

MOTIVATING POLICE OFFICERS

* DEFINE EXCELLENCE

* DEFINE THE GOALS AND OBJECTIVES

* EVALUATE PERFORMANCE

* REWARD PERFORMANCE

TRAIN TO WIN

* DEFINE THE STRATEGIC TRAINING PROGRAM

* TRAINING BUILDS PERFORMANCE

* TRAINING BUILDS MORALE

* TRAINING BUILDS CONFIDENCE

MANAGING CONFLICT

* ASSESS CONFLICT

* DEVELOP CONFLICT MANAGEMENT PLANS

* DEAL WITH INTERNAL CONFLICT FIRST

* MANAGE COMMUNITY CONFLICT

PART III

LEADERSHIP FOUNDATIONS	GUIDEPOST BEHAVIORS
Assess organizational climate	Promote individual responsibility
Demonstrate leadership by example, model behaviors	Earn respect and achieve accountability
Identify training needs and train officers to achieve success	Coordinate and evaluate realistic training
Mentor officers and assess human resources requirements	Establish policy and standards, hire the best officers
Identify sources of conflict	Encourage positive listening skills
Encourage communication and open discussion	Develop feedback and build trust
Develop a win/win philosophy and solutions	Plan positive interventions

Chapter 6
MOTIVATION AND POLICE PERSONNEL

Interest and attention are just as important to people as grease and oil are to a machine. Without it they don't run smoothly, never reach top speed and break down more frequently.

- ANONYMOUS

Employees are challenging to motivate and supervise, for they are not, like inanimate objects, easily manipulated. Motivating officers to accomplish missions requires imagination and leadership. Personnel motivation must be a primary management goal.

Law enforcement administrators and supervisors ask themselves: "How can I build a positive and proactive work climate?" The chief and senior leaders are responsible for the assessment of the organizational climate.

Commanders assess the environment to cultivate a positive organizational climate and promote an individual sense of responsibility. They demonstrate their leadership by example, and serve as an inspiration for motivation. Excellent leadership provides direction and enhances officer motivation.

DEFINING MOTIVATION

Motivation is a process of obtaining compliance and the accomplishment of a specific goal or objective. Motivation may relate to an inner drive to accomplish a task, or it may evolve externally. Motivation is possible when organizational and individual needs coincide.

"Leadership is the ability get things done under the right circumstances." [78] The challenge is encouraging motivation and accomplishments of others. "The term motivation describes the effort and persistence committed to an activity or task. Like preferences and personality traits, motivation is not directly observable; it must be inferred from behavior." [79]

The motivation of officers to accomplish strategic goals and objectives is essential to the success of any department. The chief, senior leaders, middle managers and first-line supervisors address the question: Where are we going? This question is essential to the task of encouraging motivation. The U.S. Army Infantry motto, "Follow Me!" may be useful; however, the question, "Where?" must be answered.

MOTIVATION: THE ROLE OF SENIOR LEADERSHIP

The chief and senior leaders are responsible for strategic management that establishes a climate that motivates officers to pursue organizational goals and objectives. They have the primary responsibility for building a professional climate that encourages a "winning" attitude. Top management establishes a professional environment that allows subordinates to feel connected and supported, and that develops personal motivation and esprit de corps.

MOTIVATION: MIDDLE MANAGERS

Middle managers are responsible for implementing the chief's strategic goals and objectives. They are coaches and motivators for accomplishing the mission and empowering subordinates. Middle leadership emphasizes empowerment and accountability through the tasking process.

Power is entrusted to first-line supervisors who complete the mission by defining tactical objectives for sergeants and officers. Sergeants establish objectives for key tactical results that are considered important to mission success.

GOAL COORDINATION

Unless the department's mission and direction are translated into measurable objectives, outcomes cannot be measured. Operational objectives should be set by middle managers and first-line supervisors, with the participation of police officers. Empowering officers heightens their motivation and creates a sense of accomplishment.

Table 6-1
STEPS FOR MOTIVATING OFFICERS AND STAFF

❖ Try to see things from the line officers' point of view.	❖ Include officers in decision-making activities and listen to them.
❖ Give officers responsibility and hold them accountable.	❖ Reward officers for contributions, and give credit where it is due.
❖ Publicly commend officer accomplishments.	❖ Mentor and support officers.
❖ Challenge officers to explore new ideas.	❖ Treat officers, as they want to be treated.
❖ Be firm when necessary.	❖ Be honest with officers.
❖ Participate in officer activities.	❖ Care about officers.

Source: Table created by the author from Steven J. Sarver, "Twelve Steps to Getting the Most Out of Your Employees," The Chief of Police 10 (October 2003): 46-52.

Chief Steven J. Sarver comments: "Chiefs must be willing to tell an employee that they value the person as much as they value them as an employee. Openly praising them and discussing their accomplishments demonstrates this commitment.

Chiefs should take all the things they have admired in their supervisors over the years and put them to use. Then they should take all the things they have hated about their supervisors over the years and avoid doing what they did. If they follow this simple plan, chiefs cannot help but be more effective." The Chief recommends the twelve effective steps cited in Table 6-1 to improve officer motivation. [80]

POLICE COMMUNITY GOALS

The word "motivation" implies movement toward the accomplishment of goals, which must be identified before we can motivate individuals to accomplish them. Two traditional goals of policing are (1) maintaining order and (2) protecting life and property. Many sub-goals and objectives emanate from these two goals.

Other goals emerge under the community-oriented policing philosophy. The active support of the community becomes the main priority. This goal suggests that the police need the assistance of their community to achieve successful policing goals:

COMMUNITY-ORIENTED POLICING

*   Reducing the fear of crime

*   Developing community rapport

*   Providing services

*   Preventing crime

*   Neighborhood policing

*   Problem-solving policing

TRADITIONAL POLICING GOALS

* * Suppressing criminal activity

* * Enforcing laws

* * Preserving the peace

* * Protecting civil rights

The previously mentioned goals can be mentioned in the department's mission statement, which describes desired outcomes. Goals should be written in a broad manner that describe desired results. Objectives derived from goals have measurable outcomes that officers can identify and reach within the allowable time. It may take the accomplishment of numerous objectives to achieve a general goal.

MOTIVATION: DEFINING OBJECTIVES

Develop mission orders that tell officers what the mission requirements are. This kind of order explains what should be done, but not how to do it. The "how to" is left to the officers involved. Objectives must have a specific task, condition, and standard. Conditions are forces that officers operate under in the field. The standard allows for the proper evaluation of the task. The objective must be specific and measurable.

EXAMPLE 1

TASK: Alpha Team will conduct a monthly community-oriented neighborhood meeting.

CONDITION: This monthly meeting will be conducted with members of the Neighborhood Community Organization.
Location: Kennedy High School

PURPOSE: To discuss increased burglary and drug offender activity in the neighborhood.

STANDARD: Obtain a positive attendance rate from members of the organization.

EXAMPLE 2

TASK: Alpha Team will improve the arrest and closure rate for burglary in the Hill Section of the city.

CONDITION: When not responding to "calls for service," patrols will conduct an intensive patrol of residential area - Sector A.

PURPOSE: To reduce residential burglaries in Sector A.

STANDARD: An improvement in the arrest and closure rate of burglary.

WRITING OBJECTIVES

Objectives identify who will implement the desired tasks, which must be reasonable and attainable. If objectives are not attainable, officers become disenchanted and morale plummets. Objectives should motivate and inspire each officer toward a higher degree of proficiency.

*   Does the objective make sense? Is it important to all levels of the organization?
*   Does it fit with other organizational goals?
*   Does it have operational, financial or political risks?
*   Do personnel have the knowledge, skill and resources to accomplish it?
*   Can achievement be verified in some measurable way? [81]

WORK PLANS

Work plans, specific but flexible, identify the teams, steps, and procedures necessary to accomplish objectives. Once the sergeant develops work plans, they are assigned to individual teams or officers. Work plans help define who, what, where, when, how, and why. At this point, leadership and motivational factors begin to influence productivity.

WORK PLAN EXAMPLE

* Adopt the community-oriented policing approach to cultivate police-community involvement.
* Develop a neighborhood crime prevention program for the Hill Section that addresses the level and fear of crime in that community. Implement the following techniques: **(1) Neighborhood Watch (2) Neighborhood Advocacy (3) Citizen Patrols and (4) Crime Prevention Surveys.**
* Gather crime statistics and conduct a crime analysis for the neighborhood residents.
* Distribute pertinent information and other relevant data to each Neighborhood Watch Program. Organize the community and instruct in crime prevention techniques, i.e., target hardening etc.

MOVEMENT TOWARDS THE GOALS AND OBJECTIVES

Setting goals and objectives comprises the most practical system of motivation, an ideal method to motivate police officers that involves presenting officers with goals and objectives and convincing them that they can achieve positive outcomes. A winning attitude is cultivated and officers realize that they can achieve their objectives if they expend the effort. The sergeant evaluates task completion, then praises the effort. Goals and objectives establish the "path to success" and a sense of accomplishment. If the task is worth doing, it is worth doing well, especially when it is evaluated by leaders.

Goals are the most powerful determinants of task behaviors. Goals serve to direct attention, mobilize effort, help officers develop strategies for goal achievement and continue their efforts until the goal is reached. That leads, in turn, to even higher goals. Commitment to goals is often proportional to the height of the goals set. However, the leaders must be perceived to have legitimate authority, confidence in followers, and clear standards for performance. [82]

Officers become motivated to take action when the following three-step process takes place:

1. A motivating factor—a need or goal—exists which is important to the officer.

2. The officer believes that by exerting the required or requested effort, the job can be performed.

3. The officer believes that by successfully performing the job as requested, the need will be satisfied or the goal achieved. [83]

In summary, the officer will perform the task if three conditions are met: (1) The officer can do the task; (2) The officer will be rewarded if they follow through on the task; and (3) The officer values or sees the reward as important.

MOTIVATION: REWARDS

Rewards can influence officer behavior; these may include pay raises, preferred assignments, and promotions. However, rewards can provoke problems, for officers may view rewards as signs of favoritism while some may resent the manipulation, others may work only for the reward, reducing their performance after the pay-off.

Positive motivation develops responsibility in subordinates, and from responsibility comes initiative. Set high not minimum standards for officers and hold them accountable for the results. However, leaders must clarify performance expectations. Encourage officer initiative and enthusiasm; praise rather than punish for the former is the best motivator and do not forget to reward.

THE AWARDS SYSTEM

One of the most impressive rewards is a ribbon or medal which athletes compete for and police officers die for. Ribbons and medals can motivate officers to high performance levels for they provide visible proof of dedication and professionalism. Every police department should provide merit and valor awards.

The National Association of Chiefs of Police recognizes this need with a National Awards System. The Medal of Honor Award, the Silver Star for Bravery, the Legion of Honor, General Commendation and police service medals recognize individual accomplishments.

"Happy employees can't be bought with dollars. One survey indicated the biggest long-term motivator was working for a leader with vision and values (32.6 percent). This was followed by pay raises and bonuses (27.5 percent), being given greater responsibility (20.7 percent), developing the respect of subordinates and peers (16.6 percent), recognition from supervisors (12.5 percent) and other (8.7 percent)." [84]

Financial rewards are important, but money is not the only option for officer motivation. External rewards (money, status, etc.) help promote compliance to organizational rules and regulations. However, achieving internal motivation (winning the hearts and minds of the officers, etc.) requires excellent leadership, values, and vision.

PUNISHMENT

Historically, punishment has been the primary motivating factor in police organizations. While supervised punishment may occasionally work, its long-term consequences may be adverse. To maintain discipline, sanctions must be selectively applied, for most police officers are in patrol cars, distanced from supervisors. They need internal motivation, not external punishment. Most officers respond to negative reinforcement in two ways: (1) **fight** or (2) **flight**. Punishment should be the last resort. Positive motivation, not negative, is the preferred approach.

Undesirable effects of punishment emerge when punishment is perceived as arbitrary or unnecessarily severe. However, punishment under certain circumstances may be necessary. When leadership fails to act on undesirable or unethical behavior, it inadvertently encourages those behaviors. Moreover, properly administered punishment does not have undesirable, emotional side-effects. [85]

ASSESSMENT OF THE INDIVIDUAL OFFICER

As the sergeant glances around the squad room, gazing at a sea of blue uniforms, he/she may not sort out, much less acknowledge, all the unique personalities. When each officer is recognized as an individual, and made to feel important, morale, efficiency, and performance improve. When the sergeant knows each officer's idiosyncracies, what motivates and discourages him/her then the sergeant can match individual talents to individual assignments.

Police officers are not a "thin blue line of automatons." Despite the same police uniform, each officer is unique. Police leaders must understand what is significant to their officers to motivate them to accomplish the mission. Police officers differ in their educations, experiences, intellects, personality traits, attitudes, values, and preferences. The personal characteristics of the individual officer must be appraised to motivate them.

MOTIVATION: THE ROOKIES

Generally, "rookies" are easily managed and can be directed to tasks and objectives with explanations. However, an exception may be the "rookie" with a great deal of relevant education, experience, and motivation. The sergeant must be sensitive in the assessment of new officers who have prior military or civilian police experience. If these officers are treated "as rookies," the consequence may be resentment. Respect should be demonstrated for their individual expertise and education.

"Rookies" tend to be enthusiastic, but inclined to make mistakes. They respond to excellent leadership that is organized and directive and are anxious to please their sergeants to whom they look for leadership and support. Sergeants on the other hand are role models who assign tasks and objectives, and follow-up to ensure the latter have been completed properly. Sergeants provide constant coaching and feedback to the "rookies" to maintain motivation and performance. They should perform frequent field checks and supervise the assignments.

MOTIVATION: EXPERIENCED PATROL OFFICERS

Experienced officers generally have five to ten years experience in high profile assignments; thus, "rookies" identify with these officers, who have street experience and know how to handle calls. Experienced officers can influence new officers because of their peer status and seniority.

Police "rookies" can be profoundly influenced by experienced officers, while less experienced officers may seek advice from senior officers. This happens informally in the field and in car-to-car conversations. Often, the advice concerns performance improvements; however, this advice can be double-edged, leading to the circumventing of goals and objectives.

Experienced officer influence is often positive as well as negative, for example, in proper task performance; or negatively in avoiding tasks. In addition, the experienced officer influence may operate against formal objectives.

Every precaution must be taken against rookies fraternizing with negative officers. The "rookies" should train under positive role models to encourage enthusiasm and motivation. Sergeants should assign new officers to highly motivated field training officers, not to negative officers who may have adverse influences for years to come.

The sergeant makes an assessment of experienced officers to determine the source of their motivation. What is their direction or motivation? How can that direction and motivation be channeled toward organizational goals and objectives?

Styles and substance patterns emerge at the experienced officer level. Some officers remain proactive, while others passively retreat. Proactive officers seek challenging assignments and are committed to the profession of law enforcement.

Passive officers become demoralized, avoiding work and not committing to missions. Others experience burnout. Some have experienced embarrassment in the courtroom and avoid testifying. They have become disillusioned with the legal system.

MOTIVATION: SENIOR PATROL OFFICERS

Senior officers with ten to twenty years of service can perform effectively. Generally, an informal leader will emerge from this group, officers whose key opinions have great informal power. The sergeant must work with the informal leader or leaders to accomplish the mission.

Their power may be formative and even coercive, but the leader/follower relationship is a two-way street. For senior patrol officers can make a leader appear incompetent by following orders to the letter. Senior officers have learned to say, "Yes Sir!" at the same time applying the order until dysfunction. They will not use judgment and the proper use of discretion, which may result in junior leaders looking ridiculous in front of managers.

MOTIVATION: "PAID RETIREES"

There are passive officers serving in a full-time capacity who are "retired" from the department. They may be Rookies, Experienced Officers, or Senior Patrol Officers. These officers occupy space, but do not contribute to the mission or their department. They have a full-time job with little work. Many have outside employment that leaves them exhausted during their tours of duty.

The officer in a full-time "retired status" is not productive and has a profound morale problem. This officer may be depressed and unable to concentrate on required tasks and objectives. Recognizing the problem begins with the observation of an officer's deteriorating physical appearance and sloppy uniform. The sergeant should be able to recognize poor performance, including sleeping or loafing on duty.

These officers cause others to suffer as they continuously shift responsibility to those who are already overburdened.

They do not carry their "fair share" of the work load, thereby creating morale problems in the organization. For example, a full-time, "paid retiree" might encounter an accident and break radio contact to use the telephone in a fire station. This strategy causes the officer's absence from his/her beat, forcing the dispatcher to assign someone else to the accident.

This pattern can result in officers in adjoining beats working 50 accident calls outside their area of responsibility. In addition, "paid retirees" often avoid the "hot calls," deflecting stress and responsibility to others. This pattern is obvious to other officers working the shift, but in most cases, they will not report the incompetence to their supervisor.

When leadership fails to respond to inappropriate behaviors, others become disenchanted and alienated, resulting in reduced motivation for the entire shift. "Paid retirees" then pass their morale and motivation problems on to others, at which time problems escalate, such as lateness or unexcused absences. There may also be violations of department rules, regulations and procedures; damaged equipment; and inattentive behavior resulting in minor and major cruiser accidents. More extreme behaviors may include verbal attacks on the department and its officers; unethical practices; criminal violations such as burglary, rape, and graft; and even occasional dealings with organized crime.

Full-time, "paid retirees" must be identified early before problems escalate, for early intervention by first-line supervisors deters the escalation of serious violations and their negative impact on other officers. Address the early stages through non-punitive, supervisory counseling sessions, which should be recorded to maintain a record of the meeting. If the problem cannot be resolved, formal disciplinary action should be taken. To ensure due process, formal letters of reprimand will then become necessary. The most difficult officers who engage in the "paid retired" status, are those who remain slightly above the "paid retiree" syndrome. They perform minimally, yet do not engage in obviously detrimental behaviors. These individuals are in a "survival mode," not the proactive mode.

They fail to contribute, take little risks, and simply maintain the status quo. They work day-to-day to collect a pay check and have little impact on the department's daily performance requirements. They expend all their energies on "survival behaviors," which includes the manipulation of the power structure. If they directed their energies at work instead of themselves, they would accomplish much.

CASE STUDY : SERGEANT PAUL TREVINO

Sergeant Paul Trevino is an eight-year veteran of a police department in New Mexico and recently graduated from the Southern Police Institute's first-line supervisor's course. The Sergeant rotated from the first platoon to the second platoon and was assigned to supervise unfamiliar officers.

Sergeant Trevino's department has 100 officers, 10% of whom perform duties outside the area of field operations. The department's sworn personnel consists of a 20% minority population. Sergeant Trevino is responsible for six officers in the city's highest crime sector.

Before the sergeant assumes command, he studies personnel files of officers to familiarize himself with each individual. He also interviews the former sergeant before meeting officers. The sergeant attempts to identify sensitive issues so he may address them positively.

The deliberate gathering of information may prove helpful before formally addressing his squad in the briefing room with a welcoming demeanor. At first, Sergeant Trevino does not change the methods of the former supervisor but allows time for him to gain acceptance of his leadership. After assessing the police officers, the Sergeant formulates where he is going and how he will get there.

Sergeant Trevino meets with each officer to establish rapport. He is a team player and recognizes that the members must cooperate to establish a winning climate. His leadership style is situational and the Sergeant "pulls" rather than "pushes" the officers in the proper direction.

Sergeant Trevino understands that the "rookies" will be easy to influence if he has the support of both experienced and senior patrol officers. The most important person to influence is the informal leader, Officer Tom Frazier, a twenty-year member of the department and a successful police officer. He has refused the rank of sergeant three times to stay in the patrol division.

Tom has been informally controlling the shift for about a decade, although in the past, he conflicted with the former sergeant. This dissension led to the presence of cliques and low officer morale. The former sergeant practiced a passive, laissez-faire leadership where people ran themselves without direction. Officer Frazier filled the gap in leadership and direction.

Sergeant Trevino realizes that the challenges would be difficult because they are assigned to a sector with a high crime level. He acknowledges that teamwork will be essential to establishing community support, and expresses concern about squad conflict and tension. He wonders how the squad can respond to the community when it is divided in leadership.

The Sergeant appeals to Tom Frazier's concern about the mission and the welfare of the men and women on the shift and expresses his commitment to the department's philosophy, mission and values. He explains to Tom that they must work together for the good of the community and officer safety. Both would work on reducing group conflict and improving morale in the future.

Both men agree to communicate frequently and cooperate to establish the best climate for effective policing. The Sergeant understands that without Tom's support, he is doomed to repeat the former sergeant's mistakes, that Officer Frazier's informal power is a significant force. Sergeant

Trevino's understanding of group dynamics is essential to his success.

Sergeant Trevino responds dynamically to problems and his officers. He interacts with each officer based on the tactical situation. The Sergeant cannot apply the same leadership technique to every officer. Instead, he must assess the individual needs of each officer.

In a single tactical situation, Sergeant Trevino may need to respond to each officer differently. He has two "rookies," three experienced and one senior officer to communicate with. He also reasons how officers may respond to each other differently with a change in leadership.

LESSONS LEARNED: Sergeant Trevino understands that Officer Frazier has a great deal of rapport with the experienced officers and through them has indirect and direct influence over the "rookies." Without Officer Frazier's support, he will have a difficult time leading and influencing squad members. The sergeant's primary goal is to influence the informal leader to obtain support for department goals and objectives.

Sergeant Trevino understands that successful leadership requires influence and certain desirable behaviors from officers. The Sergeant must know how to change officer attitudes and behaviors. Indifference and uninvolvement reduces the Sergeant's ability to lead. He must recognize that followers have power and influence. Sergeant Trevino is fully aware that gender, culture, and diverse backgrounds influence perceptions and thus remains sensitive to the individual needs and diversity of his officers.

PRAISE AND CONSTRUCTIVE DISCIPLINE

Discipline is a form of training designed to produce appropriate officer behaviors. Positive discipline emphasizes leadership by example. The sergeant or police leader who conforms to rules and regulations and exemplifies appropriate behaviors will witness a lowered need for negative discipline. Further praise can effectively encourage higher levels of performance, efficiency and morale.

Blanchard and Johnson suggest that one minute praising works well when managers:

1. Praise people immediately.

2. Tell people what they did right - be specific.

3. Tell people how good you feel about what they did right. [86]

Constructive discipline is the last option for controlling inappropriate behavior. While leaders should praise officers for performing well, they should criticize officers for performing improperly. But do not accuse an officer before you know who is at fault. Leaders should research the facts before assigning blame. Always distinguish hearsay or rumors from the facts which include who, what, when, where and why.

Self-control is important when criticizing an officer, and never act in haste. Confront officers behind closed doors and in private. Never criticize in front of others, and begin and end interviews with praise. Allow officers their dignity; avoid demeaning or sarcastic statements.

Disciplinary records must be kept in the officer's personnel file and provide evidence if further disciplinary action is required, especially in cases of dismissal. The first step is verbal and the next written, followed by further documentation. Improper documentation may help reinstate unsatisfactory officers; accurate evidence and records prevent reversals.

The one minute reprimand works well when leaders:

1. Tell people beforehand that you are going to let them know how they are doing and in no uncertain terms.

THE FIRST HALF OF THE REPRIMAND:

2. "Reprimand people immediately.

3. Tell people what they did wrong specifically.

4. Clearly tell people how you feel about what they did wrong.

5. Stop for a few seconds of uncomfortable silence to let them feel how you feel.

THE SECOND HALF OF THE REPRIMAND:

6. Remind them how much you value them.

7. Reaffirm that you think well of them, but not of their performance in this situation.

8. Realize that when the reprimand is over, it's over." [87]

There are several other common mistakes supervisors should be aware of:

* Don't condescend. [Treat subordinates like adults.]

* Don't berate. [This will lead to denial.]

* Don't bellow.

* Don't attack.

* Don't belittle.

* Don't be ambiguous.

* Have a solution in hand.

* Don't show prejudices. [88]

Discipline must be appropriately applied and penalties should be directly related and appropriate to the offense. Generally, enlightened supervision will follow several steps depending upon the severity of the offense. The formal process would start with an oral reprimand and then escalate to written reprimand. If necessary, suspension, demotion and finally discharge from the service could result from the administrative decision.

Probably, the single most important factor in determining how a leader is viewed by subordinates is the disciplinary process. A leader who is perceived as arbitrary and inconsistent is regarded as threatening. Erratic behavior alarms, creates confusion, and destroys morale.

From a patrol officer's point of view, leadership that demonstrates fairness and justice is respected. Leadership that demonstrates bias and the favorable treatment of "fair-haired boys and girls" is resented. Paternalistic leadership is offensive, especially to those who are educated and trained. This style of leadership may be interpreted as benevolent by those who are favored, and results in a great deal of hostility by those who are not.

THE SERIOUS INCIDENT INVESTIGATION

Unfavorable reports from citizens, as well as others, may be founded or unfounded. If police leaders do not conduct objective investigations, both groups are done an injustice. Police leaders need to have all of the facts before confronting an officer.

The first step in a discipline investigation, is to be as thorough as any criminal investigation. The second step is to interview all of the relevant parties before interviewing the officer. The third step is to gather all of the evidence necessary to refute or affirm the charges.

If the evidence and the investigation requires an interview with the officer, every attempt must be made to secure the officer's side of the story. After listening carefully to the officer's explanation, the police leader should schedule a second interview. The third interview should exonerate or confront the officer with the evidence. The evidence should point out the inconsistencies in the officer's explanation of events or affirm the officer's position. After careful consideration by a disciplinary board, and with the concurrence of the sergeant or other high ranking officer, punishment may be administered and in accordance with due process and departmental regulations.

However, if the officer has been exonerated of the charges, an apology should be made as soon as possible. The apology should be specific with an explanation for the errors made during the investigation. The sergeant, at the conclusion of an investigation, should attempt to empathize and establish rapport with the officer.

FOCUS POINTS: MORALE AND LEADERSHIP

Police leaders extract minimum employee performance with salary and benefits only. Officers may be physically present and punctual, but for officers to be productive, leadership must instill enthusiasm and win their hearts and minds.

Morale climbs high when officers identify with the organization and its goals but department leadership must clarify these goals and objectives. When officers do not understand these, they cannot be expected to achieve them.

Successful police leaders are able to identify the symptoms of poor morale, which include sloppy appearance, absenteeism, excessive grievances, complaints and high turnover. The leader also needs to identify less obvious symptoms of poor morale. Some subtle indicators may be found in excessive sick leave, coming in late, and disrespect for leaders. The causes of these issues must be identified and remedied in the early stages.

Addressing morale means assessing the situation, communicating effectively, and accepting others. Sometimes it is the very simple things that count. For example, remembering a birthday, awarding a medal or a "pat on the back" for a job well done.

Leadership must seize the moment and demonstrate its concern. Managers must treat each person as an individual and remember that job satisfaction and morale are linked to meeting important individual needs. An opportunity to win or fail may generally revolve around the larger issues that touch the lives of individual officers.

For example, important morale issues may stem from the death of an officer in the line of duty or suicide. How police leaders handle these incidents builds respect and the sense of compassion for their officers. The failure to handle these issues sensitively will bring the morale of the department down on the leadership and morale will be destroyed. In fact, it will be extremely important to reestablish morale after a devastating event.

The mishandling of death notifications is an indication to every officer of how their own families will be treated if they were in a similar situation. Police executives make sure that they have established the proper policies concerning sensitive issues that may develop.

When an officer is injured in the line of duty, leaders must personally appear at the hospital. If that officer is not hospitalized, a personal contact should come forth. Excellent leaders take every opportunity to express concern, empathy, and gratitude at critical moments in their officers' lives.

CONCLUSION

Goals and objectives are at the heart of highly motivated officers. They know when they are winning and also understand that the lack of clear direction leads to apathy and low morale. Inspirational leadership demonstrates a proactive program that initiates positive action and outcomes.

When the philosophy, mission statement, goals, objectives and work plans are clearly defined, the motivation of police officers may be accomplished. Without decisive direction, police leaders do not have the right to complain about poor motivation and low morale. When a leader says, "Follow Me!," it is necessary to clearly define the goals and objectives. Only then will officers be able to follow and achieve desired outcomes.

Chapter 7
POLICE TRAINING

Tell me and I will forget; show me and I may remember; involve me and I will understand.

- CHINESE PROVERB

Why is training important? While mission statements, goals, and objectives answer the question "Where are you going?" training is essential to answering the question "How will you get there?" Strategic training focuses on officer competencies to accomplish the mission. Strategic training should revolve around four major themes: (1) community-oriented policing; (2) police ethics; (3) use-of-force training and (4) civil liabilities. If these interrelated issues are properly addressed by police leaders, community support and crime control will improve in the twenty-first century.

TRAINING: COMMUNITY-ORIENTED POLICING

Poorly trained officers are deficient in the skills needed to follow-through on basic tasks that secure general goals and specific objectives. Inadequate training fosters the development of officers who lack confidence and are not mission-oriented. Street level officers must be trained in police problem-solving techniques for the community-oriented philosophy to succeed.

Training programs, at every level of the organization, are necessary to fulfill the basic tenets of the community-oriented policing philosophy. The implementation of this philosophy is at risk if appropriately trained officers are not available to conduct the problem-solving component.

The mission and value statements assure that every member of the department "sings the same song." Training programs prepare officers to "read the music." Otherwise everyone sings "off key" without the ability to "harmonize." This state of affairs leads to disharmony, a lack of direction and poor morale.

Without strategic training that incorporates the philosophy of community-oriented policing, resistance comes forth. Implementing strategic objectives, like community-oriented policing, directly connects to strategic training. "The shift to community policing has significant implications for training. If all aspects of training are driven by the philosophy and mission of community policing, training becomes the key to promoting and institutionalizing this fundamental change in policy." [89]

Learning may be defined as a change in behavior. The absence of training and acquisition of new skills leads to the department's inability to implement new directions and focus on the improvement of services. Even if police officers are instructed on where they are going, without appropriate community-oriented training, they will not have the skills to get there.

POLICE PROFESSIONAL ETHICS TRAINING

Quite often, the topic of police ethics is considered the least important component in the policing training curriculum, ironic when considering how vital police professional ethics are to decisions officers make. Ethical decision-making is at the heart of the police discretionary process, including every arrest and administration of the criminal law. Every police training program should require a comprehensive coverage of value choices and ethical case studies.

Ethics should be integrated throughout the curriculum, not taught in isolation. Ethical case studies should be a significant component of each session on the laws of arrest, search and seizure, the administration of the criminal law, and the investigative process. Ethics should be the first consideration of every police academy class as well as in-service training programs.

Ethics training should not be delegated to outside training agencies or programs of higher education. This topic is important because many police officers obtain law enforcement employment without the benefit of a college ethics course. However, even if an officer has completed an ethics course, it remains essential that the officer be exposed to the Police Code of Ethics.

"Ethics in policing now is more important then ever. As policing becomes more decentralized and community-based in structure, accountability to the public becomes a highly relevant issue that affects police services. Perhaps management through values will provide the method by which police provide quality service and protection to the public while remaining faithful to the rule of law and exemplifying the highest ethics of public service." [90]

Few employment choices require the kind of critical thinking, problem solving and moral complexity than that of a police officer. Law enforcement officers have a peace keeping role that requires involvement in numerous ethical dilemmas. Police officers have the power to make life and death decisions.

USE-OF-FORCE TRAINING

The vast majority of officer activity involves community service. A small percentage involves the use-of-force. However, it is the most sensitive area and when handled poorly, results in a broad societal response. That response can quickly erode community support and build contempt and disrespect for the police. Poorly trained officers may overreact because of insufficient training and a lack of self-confidence. When police academies emphasize firearms training without the proper ethical training, improper use-of-force results. With proper community support, the use-of-force is infrequent because of mutual respect and cooperation. Citizens of the community should feel that it is "their police department."

TRAINING: CIVIL LIABILITIES

Police training is a legal mandate, an investment in the police department as well as individual officers. Cutting training programs is not prudent. The numerous law suits that have followed inadequate training over the last twenty years provide ample insight into the possible consequences. Case study examples should be made available to those who have the power to make decisions regarding funding for police training programs.

Police executives play a proactive role in the area of legal liability. Police misconduct litigation is fast becoming a cottage industry for the legal profession. Suits are being won and small municipalities have the most potential for exploitation and financial devastation.

Insufficient training is often at the core of a law suit. The most common grounds for suits and complaints being filed are under negligence or failure to train. The theory that underlines these suits is negligence. The plaintiff will argue that the injury was not that the conduct was malicious in nature, but that the injury and damages resulted from a police officer's failure to perform a duty with care. The officer's behavior is assessed concerning the legal culpability or liability that may have resulted because of negligence or failure to give proper attention or care to duty.

The foundation for legal liability can be located under Title 42, Section, 1983, of the Civil Rights Act:

"Every person who, under color of any statute, ordinance, regulation, custom, or usage, of any State or Territory or the District of Columbia, subjects, or causes to be subjected, any citizen of the United States or other person within the jurisdiction thereof the deprivation of any rights, privileges, or immunities secured by the Constitution and laws, shall be liable to the party injured in an action at law, suit in equity, or other proper proceeding for redress..."

Generally, the plaintiff will file actions up the chain of command, to include supervisors, managers, training academy staff members, and even the Chief of Police. Frequently, the charge will be made that the alleged officer acted intentionally to cause harm and injury. In addition, higher ranking personnel failed to take proper action.

Strategic police leaders acknowledge their role in the establishment of excellent training to avoid civil liability. The best way to escape civil litigation is to provide quality training programs and maintain accurate records. To accomplish this goal, training standards must be identified and accountability for implementation established.

POLICE TRAINING: MOTIVATION

Police training is one of the most significant management functions. Training supports the mission, at the same time cultivating motivation and morale. Effective training enhances police performance as well as personal related competencies (e.g., coping with stress, thinking when exhausted, maintaining self-control).

The positive accomplishment of the mission is dependent on executive support. This emphasis is demonstrated through the adequate training of officers. Appropriate training is essential for excellent performance. "Police training should help officers feel a sense of growth and development in their jobs because it contributes to a sense of well-being." [91]

Training builds human resources and the motivation to perform the mission. It also assists in defeating obstacles that prevent team building. For example, problems such as personnel turnover, potential racial tension, and drug/alcohol abuse make it difficult to build teams.

Inexperienced police executives and managers may regard such problems as isolated from the training mandate, a serious miscalculation, for they fail to include topics that address stress management, post-shooting trauma, and suicide prevention. These topics are equally important as target shooting, laws of arrest and the criminal law.

Social survival skills often provide the "glue" that holds the organization together. The establishment of prevention training programs can help improve respect for race, gender and individual differences. This kind of training can help to encourage and maintain discipline and social cohesion.

Men and women training together, working toward common goals, are far less susceptible to tension from within and outside the police organization. Well-trained officers are more likely to cooperate under stress and perform the mission more successfully. They develop a winning attitude and are more confident when performing tasks and objectives.

SENIOR LEADERSHIP RESPONSIBILITIES: STRATEGIC TRAINING

The chief and senior leaders are responsible for identifying strategic training needs and objectives. Strategic training at the highest level supports the mission statement, goals and objectives. The chief is also responsible for financial forecasting and the training budget, which supports training and is coordinated with government officials. The chief's job is to "sell" an adequate training budget to produce positive training outcomes.

Senior leaders help identify training needs in their respective functional areas, and conduct a financial analysis to determine how to effectively use monetary resources. Their role is to assess training and to forecast.

MIDDLE MANAGER RESPONSIBILITIES: TRAINING MANAGERS

Middle managers supervise police training programs and establish the training climate. Like senior leaders, they assess training needs and evaluate programs. They also coordinate the master training schedule that has department wide implications. They are responsible for organizational training as well as individual training.

"Training is universally recognized as a major management function. It is a fundamental responsibility of management in any organization to train the people in that organization. The efficiency and effectiveness of an organization is directly related to the amount and quality of training conducted within that agency.

* Training is a means of management communication.

* Training improves productivity.

* Training reduces liability.

* Training increases self-discipline." [92]

Middle managers develop a core strategic plan for training. The preparation of a carefully designed training plan is essential for implementing a successful training program whose plans are based on comprehensive assessment and progress toward established objectives.

Occasionally, minor adjustments will be needed to meet unexpected requirements. The training schedule is middle management's plan to facilitate the training program. The training schedule has two important management functions: (1) planning and (2) controlling.

FIRST LINE SUPERVISOR RESPONSIBILITIES: PRIMARY TRAINERS

Sergeants serve as the primary trainers of police officers, and possess most of the technical skills that police officers need to succeed. More than any other leader in the chain of command, sergeants are best suited to accomplish on-the-job training. Their training can be conducted in the field, based on the individual needs of their officers. Because they have ample opportunity to know their subordinates, sergeants occupy an ideal position to conduct training assessments.

Sergeants who coordinate with corporals or senior officers determine individual training needs because they are the closest to field operations. In addition, they are strategically positioned to help train newly assigned police officers through Field Training Officers (FTOs). First line supervisors are coaches and teachers. The best sergeants are selected as instructors for the police academy and in-service training programs.

TRAINING MANAGEMENT ISSUES

The most pressing problem in police training remains the failure to train managers and supervisors, which results in inadequate training programs because managerial supervisors constitute the primary teaching staff. This remains the critical starting point to achieve excellence in training. In far too many jurisdictions, first-line supervisors, middle managers, and senior leaders operate without necessary training.

American policing does not need additional officers on the street. However, money would be better spent on upgrading training for present and future law enforcement leaders. The funds should be spent on regional training centers, established possibly at major universities. The use of existing classroom space and instructors would save construction costs and full-time training staff salaries.

These centers would establish national, regional, state and local certifying standards. For promotion a candidate would need to successfully graduate from a designated course, which would certify area specialization and/or command rank. The First-Line Supervisor's Course would prepare officers for the rank of sergeant and would concentrate on the basic principles of leadership and supervision, emphasizing junior leadership skills. The Lieutenant's Course would certify entry level, middle managers, and shift commanders, emphasizing basic middle management skills teaching shift commanders how to relate to first line supervisors.

The Captain's Advanced Course would certify captains as advanced middle management staff officers and training management specialists. It would develop training managers, emphasizing the development of staff officers.

The Senior Leader's Course would develop executive skills including command and staff procedures. This course would develop conceptual and indirect leadership skills. The emphasis would be on vision and planning requirements for the future.

The completion of a national, state or local certification program, prior to selection for promotion, would enhance individual supervisor, middle manager, and senior leadership abilities. These basic competencies would be established before assuming command, thereby preventing the "learn-on-the-job" or "hit-or-miss" system that presently exists. In addition, this accreditation process and merit-based system would help remove some political factors in police promotional systems.

TRAINING MANAGEMENT AND CURRICULUM

Managers determine both individual and organizational training goals; formulate training goals; and specify learning objectives, tasks, conditions and standards. The objectives are specifically defined by measurable criteria and the time is identified in which they will be achieved.

"The planning function is assisted when the curriculum defines the units of instruction, places them into a logical sequence, prescribes officer learning outcomes, and delineates in instructor guides the strategies for reaching the intended outcomes. A well-written curriculum will also identify instructional aids, establish practice sessions, and specify achievement tests and other events that are planned to occur at predetermined intervals during the course.

When a curriculum calls for certain critical instruction which was proved not to have been given or to have been given imperfectly, an accusation of negligence can be supported, and perhaps even directed at the particular training officials who failed in their responsibilities." [93]

TRAINING: THE LEARNING CURVE

Police trainers should understand the "learning curve." A knowledgeable police trainer actively seeks to train up to the required level of proficiency in the minimum amount of time. Skills are minimally enhanced by additional training.

The trainer must also understand that without on-going in-service training proficiency will decrease. If the training is not updated and sustained, the "forgetting curve" will follow peak proficiency.

Every "learning curve" contains a "forgetting curve," a quantitative curve that leads to a decline in the learning process. Intensive once-a-year training is simply not enough to provide proficiency and readiness, as in self-defense and firearms training. In addition, training that is sensitive and complex needs to be recycled during the training year. This retraining process will help reaffirm skills that were formally taught.

TRAINING PLANS

The police planning phase is important and serves as the foundation for excellent training. Trainers would be wise to use the "backward planning" sequence. This process begins by determining the desired outcomes of training, then works backward, to determine what needs to be accomplished. The planning process is necessary to provide an overview of training plans such as long-range, short-range, and near-term plans. The following case study will illustrate police planning and training requirements.

CASE STUDY: CAPTAIN SHANNON BROOKS (TRAINING SPECIALIST)

Captain Shannon Brooks was the first female officer hired by the Charles City Police Department. She has served as an outstanding police officer for the past ten years. Shannon earned her bachelor's degree at a small liberal arts college of some distinction where she majored in criminal justice and minored in education. Captain Brooks consistently maintained a high grade point average and graduated with honors. Prior to her present assignment, Shannon served in the police department Operations Bureau.

The Captain was approached by many members of the department requesting that she develop a use-of-force and self-defense program. Many officers felt uncertain about appropriate use-of-force procedures. They hoped that an in-service training program would prepare them for field confrontations.

Captain Brooks previously received use-of-force training from Prof. McGrath, her former criminal justice professor. The professor held the rank of black belt in judo and occasionally taught at the local judo club. The Captain was active in the judo program during her four years at the University and earned her brown belt by competing in competitions and passing rigorous martial arts testing.

Captain Brooks approached her former professor for advice concerning the establishment of a use-of-force and self-defense program. While she would implement this in-service program, the professor would coordinate its research and design.

Captain Brooks realized that she must clearly define and state the problem before reviewing numerous professional journals and related literature. Her goal was to develop an interdisciplinary program based on the martial arts, judo, and karate. She planned to develop the program through principles of curriculum development.

The literature review was enlightening and helpful in the development of strategies, procedures, and techniques. Captain Brooks concluded from her research that psychological factors were more important than psychomotor self-defense tactics. This information would impact on the content of her program.

WRITING PRECISE LEARNING OBJECTIVES

Specific learning objectives are normally developed after the formulation of a philosophical statement and general goals. The final development may occur when the curriculum and learning design nears completion. Learning objectives are derived from the general goals and constitute those specific tasks, conditions, and standards that are applied to the learner. They: (1) focus on the individual; (2) relate to a dimensional need; and (3) result in precise learning. As an example, Shannon based many of her specific learning objectives on the performance-oriented tasks.

SELECTING MEANINGFUL LEARNING EXPERIENCES

Captain Brooks knew that learning occurs most efficiently and effectively when an officer has the opportunity to engage in active learning whose best format is a simulation or practical scenario. The ultimate test for judging a learning experience demands evidence that this opportunity, activity, or instructional invention is actually creating the desired responses. Learning experiences should evoke desired changes in the learner. Shannon knew that if the Use-of-Force Program did not produce the expected or desired outcomes, it would be considered "invalid." Any trainer who is involved in shaping or influencing learning should be able to identify the presence or absence of the principles associated with meaningful training experiences.

These principles are:

* **Appropriate practice**

* **Satisfaction**

* **Learner capability**

* **Variety**

* **Multiple outcomes**

Captain Brooks knew that for her to apply these principles to a meaningful police training program, she must devise learning experiences that:

(1) focus on the individual;

(2) relate to dimensional needs; and

(3) result in explicit learning.

In short, the Captain realized that most officers learn best by doing, not listening to long lectures that do not meet dimensional learning needs.

DEVELOPING POLICE TRAINING EVALUATION PROCEDURES

Captain Shannon Brooks understands that most in-service police training programs neglect the evaluation process. She also acknowledges that evaluation is essential in answering the final and most important question: How will you know when you have arrived?

Informal evaluation tends to vary in quality; thus, an inclusive process of evaluation is necessary to validate police training and determine the effectiveness of instruction and the overall program design. Police training evaluation procedures are required to determine whether learning experiences function properly in producing desired outcomes.

Without evaluation procedures there can be no rational basis for training. While the behavioral and content aspects of learning objectives guide the development of police training and evaluation procedures, the learning objectives indicate the kinds of behavior to be appraised and evaluated.

LESSONS LEARNED

Captain Shannon Brooks learned some valuable lessons while conducting the use-of-force, self-defense program, information which should prove valuable during the next training cycle. The information gained from teaching the first class, should prove invaluable when conducting future classes.

What did Captain Brooks learn? The more difficult techniques were too time consuming and costly with regard to training time. Teaching basic positioning and a few simple techniques seemed of value to officers, and received the best response from the group. The officers found that complex judo, jujitsu, and karate techniques were difficult to retain. Teaching simple techniques proved a superior defensive system. Psychology, communication, verbal judo, planning, and correct defensive positioning strategies were more likely to be remembered.

TRAINING EXCELLENCE

Excellent police training requires officers to participate in the critical-thinking and problem-solving process, skills required in the field, and which are the essence of every police training program. Police officers should be confronted with real-world situations they may encounter in their communities. The emphasis should be on active learning based on field scenarios, role playing, and learning simulations.

What does excellent training accomplish? Excellent training produces officers who successfully perform mission requirements and enables officers to understand where they are going. The training process provides the skills for accomplishing essential field tasks. Police officers must learn to meet challenges similar to those in their community.

PERFORMANCE-ORIENTED TRAINING

Law enforcement training must be performance oriented, not classroom oriented. The lecture method should be a small part of the training unit. When the lecture method is used, the trainer should follow-up with a field demonstration. The demonstration should include trainee participation and interaction. For police training to be meaningful, it must facilitate active learning, not passive learning.

"Training that reflects actual work conditions assists in identifying problems that require special officer attention. This kind of training under real-life conditions saves lives. Night training should address procedures related to traffic and pedestrian stops, searches of persons and vehicles, use of artificial light sources, use of handcuffs and other prisoner restraints, weapons and self-defense training, and first aid."[94]

FOCUS POINTS: TRAINING

The lecture system has been overused for years because it makes instructors feel safe. Because the lecture is a passive style of learning, instructors rarely encourage or respond to questions. Some lecturers may feel uncomfortable answering an officer's question. The lecture describes "a process by which facts are transmitted from the notebook of the instructor to the notebook of the student without passing through the minds of either." [95]

"Involving students in training is more difficult, more time consuming and requires more teaching skill, creativity, and greater depth of instructor knowledge. However, it is widely accepted that application is an integral and essential part of the training process. The first failure should occur in the classroom." [96]

Active learning is more than instructor/lecture oriented, it requires interaction between instructors and officers as well as interaction with other learners in the classroom. Encouraging peer interaction allows officers to learn from each another.

Active learning encourages an exchange of ideas and feedback, the latter essential to learning. Critical thinking and problem solving encourages officer involvement in the feedback and learning process. Role playing and learning simulations maximize instructor and student feedback.

The basic training strategy should be lecture/theory first. Theoretical information may then be applied to "hands on" role play scenarios followed by a critique and discussion. The performance-oriented training should approximate field conditions.

"Today, realism seems to be the watchword, with training exercises designed to resemble closely street scenarios. Although academies still emphasize classroom lectures, at least half of a cadet's time is spent in the field. In addition, technology has also given birth to simulators, particularly in the area of firearms training... Driving simulators are another popular training tool." [97]

Even the ancients understood the value of active learning. Aristotle once taught centuries ago, "What we have to learn to do, we learn by doing." This principle is still valid today. Unfortunately, police training continues to rely on the lecture/classroom method. However, in recent years, some police departments have attempted to move toward more innovative instructional methods.

A few talented instructors who mix humor with anecdotal case studies are indeed entertaining, effective instructors. However, most instructors do not possess these attributes. In most cases, diversity of instructional methods will be the best approach.

"Should instructors simply cover the material—or empower our participants to perform better on the job?

"We retain: 10% of what we read
              30% of what we see
              50% of what we hear and see
              70% of what we say
              90% of what we say and do" [98]

Police training is a dynamic process that is essential to mission success; however, poorly trained officers will be unable to perform essential tasks. They will be deficient in the skills necessary to obtain the department's goals and objectives. The relationship between leadership, training and motivation cannot be ignored. Leadership defines a department's directions and training provides opportunities for officers to learn the skills to get there.

CONCLUSION

The first step to the successful management of training is to train the trainers. The second step is to prioritize readiness training. The third step identifies training needs based on needs identification, goal setting, curriculum development and evaluation. The training cycle requires constant evaluation, flexibility, and innovation. Strategic training addresses the larger conceptual issues. The four strategic issues central to police excellence are: (1) community-oriented policing; (2) police ethics; (3) the use-of-force and (4) preventing civil liabilities. All four of these strategic issues interconnect and are essential in winning community support.

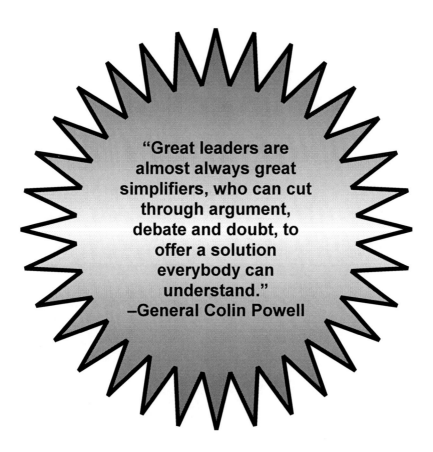

"Great leaders are almost always great simplifiers, who can cut through argument, debate and doubt, to offer a solution everybody can understand."
–General Colin Powell

Chapter 8
HUMAN RESOURCES
MANAGEMENT

Treat people as if they were what they
ought to be and you help them to
become what they are capable of being.
- JOHANN WOLFGANG VONGOETHE

Human resources management is a core leadership responsibility. Police leaders must develop the vision for meeting future staffing requirements. Thus, strategic recruitment planning policy is an essential step to selecting the best officers.

The most important influence on the quality of a police department is the competency of its officers. The recruitment of qualified officers helps ensure excellent police service to the community. Police leaders play an active role in the recruitment and selection process and a successful recruitment plan may provide the key for selecting the most qualified candidates. "Sound personnel practices, therefore, may well be the single most vital consideration in the quest for effective law enforcement." [99]

Police strategic objectives, achieved in three areas, serve as the foundation for policing: (1) community-oriented policing; (2) a tradition of police ethics, and moral behavior; and (3) recruitment of candidates who can assist in problem-solving policing strategies.

THE KEYS TO SUCCESSFUL RECRUITING

Excellent recruiting is the active pursuit of qualified applicants for positions in the police department, the keys to which include: (1) leadership and vision, (2) the implementation of policy in harmony with community-oriented policing philosophy and the mission of the department, (3) analysis of the candidates who possess problem-solving abilities, (4) an adequate job description, (5) the development of written support documents, (6) the training of recruiters, (7) an aggressive recruiting program that is continuous, and (8) financial support that maintains the recruiting program.

To off-set future recruiting limitations, basic standards need to be refined: (1) clearly define recruit qualifications, (2) improve testing procedures, (3) select officers with emotional intelligence, (4) improve psychological testing, and (5) develop improved methods of recruiting quality officers.

ASSESSING POLICE NEEDS

Leaders with vision determine the foundation for the recruiting assessment process. Strategic leaders understand where they want to go and provide a map that defines how to get there. This knowledge will be essential for police recruiters who chart the course. The effort to recruit and select police personnel should start with an assessment of the department's needs, a complex process involving the analysis of police organizational goals and objectives.

JOB ANALYSIS AND DESCRIPTION

The level at which an officer must perform can be predetermined through the job analysis process. Once the mission and values statements, goals, and objectives are formulated, then the position can be described in specific terms. This information will assist recruiters as well as the officers who perform the job.

Job analysis helps to formulate critical information concerning tasks and job performance. It also provides a tool for gathering purposeful and systematic work-related information. The job description identifies who, what, why, where, when and how. "A job description describes the job as it is being performed. In a sense, a job description is a snapshot of the job as of the time it was analyzed. Ideally, [it is] written so that any reader, whether familiar or not with the job, can 'see' what the worker does, how and why." [100]

Thoughtful job analysis considers more than the physical requirements. Character and emotional intelligence are two essential requirements for a police officer. The job description must address the emotional requirements for successful policing.

CHARACTER FOUNDATIONS

The selection process is a primary leadership staffing function that supports the mission. Character is significant in the police selection process. Police recruits who lack character and integrity are incapable of producing excellent service that supports the immediate mission.

Police leadership must emphasize staff functions to employ men and women of high moral and ethical character. "Can do" leadership develops suitable entry level standards, necessary to select officers who have the potential for leadership.

Most human resources management difficulties can be traced to the administration of personnel services and the quality of police recruitment/hiring practices. "The staffing of an organization is the pivotal process that puts in place the individuals who will carry out the organization's mission and plan." [101] Without the proper selection process, efforts directed at motivating and training police officers will be less effective.

ESTABLISHING NEW STANDARDS

Various standards have been established to provide criteria for police recruitment and selection. Many police departments have been challenged by applicants concerning entry level standards. Hopefully, the police selection process will continue to evolve while in the past, the recruitment emphasis has been on physical standards. Police leaders in the future will likely acknowledge the importance of emotional and social intelligence.

Generally, police departments have attempted to measure the basic intelligence of police applicants, probably, too narrow a measurement. New instruments are needed to assess the emotional intelligence of police applicants.

The job description should imply the human qualities that make-up the ideal police personality. Qualities such as impulse control, self-motivation, empathy and social intelligence are essential traits for community-oriented and problem-solving policing.

"These are the qualities that mark people who excel in real life, whose intimate relationships flourish, who are stars in the workplace. These are also the hallmarks of character and self-discipline, of altruism and compassion—basic capacities needed if our society is to thrive." [102]

Interestingly, "Here the argument for the importance of emotional intelligence hinges on the link between sentiment, character, and moral instincts. There is growing evidence that fundamental ethical stances in life stem from underlying emotional capacities. For one, impulse is the medium of emotion; the seed of all impulse is a feeling bursting to express itself in action. Those who are at the mercy of impulse, who lack self-control, suffer a moral deficiency: The ability to control impulse is the base of will and character. By the same token, the root of altruism lies in empathy, the ability to read emotions in others; lacking a sense of another's need or despair, there is no caring. And if there are any two moral stances that our times call for, they are precisely these, self-restraint and compassion." [103]

Recruitment remains the most important strategic objective. Without an adequate recruiting and selection program, other police strategic objectives cannot be accomplished. The recruitment of excellent police officers enhances the potential of the entire department; therefore, recruitment programs must select the most capable officers. Character and emotional intelligence remain essential personality characteristics for police applicants.

EQUAL OPPORTUNITY LEADERSHIP

Being an equal opportunity leader means respecting individual differences. The police mission and welfare of personnel are mutually interwoven and cannot be separated. Excellent leaders support their officers' efforts to accomplish the mission. Taking care of police officers and department civilians builds trust and respect that increases morale, performance, and efficiency.

Trust in leadership involves the way police officers perceive leaders who demonstrate an interest in their welfare. Equal opportunity leaders are cautious about treating the people they like too well, avoiding the appearance of preferential treatment. Everyone will be watching for double standards.

Once the best applicants are hired, they must be given fair and equal treatment. "Can do" leaders have attitudes and skills that effectively understand the needs of people of different races, gender, ages, and lifestyles. Excellent leaders have the cultural sensitivity and willingness to investigate the reasons why people display diverse different cultural behaviors. Excellent leaders talk to officers from different cultural backgrounds and communicate to them their importance to the department.

Fair employment practices require that police job specifications be job related and realistic. If not, a discrimination complaint may be filed with the Equal Employment Opportunity Commission (EEOC). The test of job related "content validity" will determine whether individual rights in employment procedures have been violated. Police agencies should be able to demonstrate that selection procedures actually represent requirements for performance on the job. The evidence of job relatedness is determined by carefully reviewing the job analysis, job specifications and police job description.

146   Chapter 8

RECRUITING POLICE PERSONNEL

The recruitment of police personnel should be based on carefully specified criteria. In recent years, recruiting practices have received considerable scrutiny from the courts. Unless the criteria can be validated and proven to be job related, the agency is at risk for legal actions and remedies.

Many standards are related to physical requirements like eyesight, hearing, and physical agility. Some strength and agility tests may be discriminatory. In most cases, it is illegal to eliminate candidates based on a handicap without examining the whole person and their ability to perform the job. Handicapped individuals may also necessitate reasonable accommodation.

LEGAL REQUIREMENTS

Numerous federal and state laws can impact on the hiring and civil rights of an applicant. Some laws that have been proven to be significant are:

*   Civil Rights Acts of 1964 and 1970 prohibit race discrimination in hiring and placement.

*   Title IX of 1972 Education amendments prohibits discrimination in education benefits based on gender, race, color, religion, or national origin.

*   The Rehabilitation Act of 1973, amended in 1980, prohibits discrimination against handicapped individuals for federal contractors and the federal government.

*   The Age Discrimination of Employment Act (ADEA) of 1967, amended in 1978, prohibits discrimination based on age for people between the ages of 40-70.

*   The Americans with Disabilities Act of 1990 (ADA) prohibits discrimination based on physical or intellectual handicap for employers with 15 or more employees.

The increased recruitment of minorities and women will continue to enhance the present police culture. Police personnel changes will eventually mirror America's diversity. The number of women and minorities in police departments should grow significantly, enabling them to serve with distinction as they uniquely contribute to law enforcement.

Equal opportunity leaders appreciate the meaning of diversity and treat people fairly so that everyone is made to feel part of the team. "Can do" leaders build integrated teams. They evaluate performance fairly and equitably.

KEYS TO POLICE PRODUCTIVITY

Leaders are constantly making evaluations about performance. In most organizations, both formal and informal evaluations are conducted. Police organizations must stress the role of formal evaluation which ensures accountability and responsibility for the actions of each officer.

A formal evaluation is the most efficient method of evaluation, but may include informal elements. For example, informal comments provide an excellent opportunity to reinforce good performance or discourage poor performance. The formal evaluation document becomes a permanent record based on specified performance objectives.

The best evaluation system has a double leadership approach comprised of one primary rater and one senior rater. The primary rater writes comments on performance, while the senior rater affirms or discounts the primary rater's comments. The senior rater outranks the primary rater and generally restricts comments to leadership potential.

Police performance evaluations attempt to measure how well the officer performs, generally measured in three areas: (1) effort, (2) ability and (3) direction. For the officer to obtain an acceptable level of performance, these three factors must indicate positive achievement.

Leaders enhance excellent performance by encouraging officers to develop their potentials and abilities. The leader is also responsible for clearly communicating what an officer must do to accomplish organizational objectives, where the officer is going professionally and what the officer is expected to accomplish.

The job description remains the foundation for personnel evaluations and is developed through the position analysis process. Its purpose is to communicate to officers what is expected concerning performance. However, sergeants play a key role in developing specific objectives related to the job description.

Developing and clearly communicating an accurate job description, including specific behavioral objectives, is the first step in the performance/appraisal process. The second step is personal observation by the leader, usually made in the field, but occasionally at other places. The third step is documentation based on personal observations.

CONDUCTING PERFORMANCE INTERVIEWS

The rater should appraise progress on objectives defined in the job description and should not appraise personality. The leader should strive for objectivity in an evaluation that mirrors performance. Personnel evaluations should incorporate the entire rating period, not just the last week.

The purpose of communicating the performance evaluation is: (1) to provide the officer with a clear understanding of the rater's thoughts about performance; (2) to clear-up any misunderstanding or miscommunication; (3) to establish new objectives and review how to improve performance on past objectives; and (4) to improve rapport between the rater and ratee.

Evaluated officers should understand rules and procedures concerning appeals and grievance complaints, and should fully understand the evaluation process. Officers should approach the evaluation process positively, for performance evaluation is a tool, not an end. The evaluation provides feedback on the successful execution of specific tasks and objectives; its purpose to keep officers motivationally focused on behaviors needing improvement. Excellent leaders use strategies to bring the best out of their officers, their mentoring a valuable tool for encouraging positive professional behaviors.

EXCELLENT MENTORSHIP

"Can do" leaders who evaluate officers recognize talent and potential. They are usually older and more experienced but may come from the same departmental level. However, one does not need rank to mentor, an act of leadership that requires time, energy and coaching abilities. Mentors also serve as helpers and confidants.

Excellent mentors provide emotional support and career development opportunities. Most police officers who have risen through the ranks had excellent mentors. Mentors assist officers with career advancement by sponsoring and nominating officers for favorable positions and promotions. Powerful and successful leaders often look for subordinates to replace them. Without this kind of sponsorship, police officers will find it difficult to get promoted. The more powerful the mentor, the more likely the officer will advance professionally.

Mentors point out obstacles, while encouraging problem-solving and personal development. Therefore, mentors are essential to learning how to avoid obstacles. They often give advice to officers on how to improve their skills, avoid mistakes, and provide assistance in technical problem-solving. For example, they may make simple comments like, "Have you considered this as a possibility?" "Can do" leaders allow their officers to problem solve rather than offer pat solutions. Trust and emotional support may be more important than information.

How can one be an effective leader and mentor? Police leaders who "take care of their officers" shape a positive social climate. Leaders who successfully show concern for the development of their officers or civilians mentor well. "Can do" leaders encourage career development and provide advice on how to succeed. Positive mentoring encourages officers to train for success. Generally, "can do" leaders are in a position to provide on-the-job skill development and excellent training assignments. Most importantly, mentors encourage positive achievement and promote the success and reputation of their officers. The following case study is an example of mentoring techniques.

CASE STUDY: THE MENTOR

Tom Jenkins, a college professor and former police officer, now a retired reserve military police colonel, received an important telephone call from a local public safety director. The Director was working on a Department of Justice grant and needed the advice of a police consultant. He knew that Tom Jenkins was a forty-year veteran and a police specialist with the University.

The professor taught community policing and problem-solving policing strategies and could serve as a technical consultant. Both men agreed that this would be an excellent opportunity for the community; therefore, Tom accepted the position. However, in spite of this excellent start, problems were already on the horizon.

Jenkins soon learned that the political problems the department was experiencing would impact on the implementation of the grant. While town council had appointed a new Director of Police Services, the former Chief of Police was still in place. The council was attempting to modernize the department with grants that would financially assist the community. However, the former Chief was against change and modernization, placing the new Director at a serious disadvantage.

The Director hired Jim Watson, a civilian crime analyst and part-time police officer with exceptional intelligence, education, and people skills. This officer made a mid-life career change after serving as a manager in the civilian sector. Jim was now caught in a conflict between the Chief and the new Director of Public Safety. The new crime analyst was confronted with the classic unity of command conflict: serving two leaders at the same time, at the same level.

The professor was a trustworthy advisor, assisting the crime analyst in his successful transition to leadership. The advice was straight and simple: stay out of the leadership conflict and demonstrate your loyalty to the Department. The second part of this advice suggested that Jim should remain trustworthy and available to both leaders, and work in areas that had success potential and would gain community support.

Jim was advised that the Neighborhood Watch program would be the starting point for gaining community support. Jim hesitated and explained that the former Chief had not been successful at this endeavor. Jenkins acknowledged that this would be a difficult assignment; however ,the professor would provide support.

The trust began to build and as a result, Jim engaged in some risk taking and community activities that recruited eighty new members in the Neighborhood Watch program. Once Jim learned that an effective leader takes responsibility, he accomplished the mission. Jim had the desire to be a winner. He read books that the professor made available and applied the problem-solving approach, while implementing several successful crime prevention countermeasures.

The professor continued to show concern for Jim, the new crime analyst. He allowed Jim to struggle a little, but was available for advice or support. The consultant continued to promote Jim's career and reputation, and Jim would eventually gain confidence and take charge of the Neighborhood Watch program and related crime prevention activities. Jim received several national awards for police service and published the results of the program in police professional journals.

Jim continued to make progress in areas that were unopposed by the Police Chief. The conflict between the Police Chief and the new Public Safety Director continued to escalate, resulting in the resignation of the Director and the retirement of the Chief. Jim Watson, the part-time officer, was promoted to a full-time position and continued to coordinate the grants. His efforts and professionalism led to recognition by the town council and community. Jim's selfless service eventually led to his appointment as Chief of Police. Much of this success is credited to his learning abilities and the sponsorship and support he received from his mentor.

LESSONS LEARNED:

The term "mentor" means trustworthy advisor. The advice Jim Watson received was essential due to his short tenure in the field of law enforcement. His mentor promoted his efforts and recommended him for national awards and ultimately for Chief of Police. Most successful police officers have mentors and sponsors, who provide excellent career advice and coaching information on avoiding social obstacles. In this case study, Jim Watson was confronted with many social and political obstacles, but he managed to achieve all of his objectives and successfully execute the grant. Finally, and most importantly, mentors provide emotional support, friendship and role modeling, which helps overcome adversity.

COACHING POLICE OFFICERS

Coaching police officers is an art directly related to mentoring; however, the coach must be discreet, a master of diplomacy. A low profile approach enhances communication, breaks down barriers, and increases openness. The approach may be directive at times but usually, non-directive. The coached officer must trust the leader's judgment and experience, whose advice must be competent and concrete.

Ultimately, the goal of coaching is performance, which necessitates officer cooperation and therefore the breaking down of barriers. Coaching requires a soft interviewing style, not a police interrogation. One way to tear down these barriers is to avoid acting like an interrogator.

The most effective coaching method is to use positive rather than negative motivators. Constructive advice can break down barriers and improve coaching effectiveness, as in the following: "Your job performance in most areas is above average. However, if you made a few changes, you could be one of the top officers in the department. As a police officer, you have tremendous potential and, if you apply your many talents, opportunities are available. The department needs you; we must pull together as a team."

Good coaching requires a relationship and excellent rapport. Officers may have difficulty expressing concerns about their performance, so an open-ended question rather than a specific "yes" or "no" response is often the best format. For example, you might ask, "How do you feel about your new assignment?" This is an excellent opportunity for the coach and the officer to reflect on content and meaning. Coaches rephrase the question and just listen.

The coach is a facilitator who possesses values, ethics, and expertise. The leader respects and understands that helping others is a noble task. Being interested in the growth and development of others is a prerequisite. While recognizing organizational controls, the leader often allows a wide range of behaviors when the officer is learning. The first step is listening to others; the second, observing behavior and giving feedback.

Identification with the coach is an important part of the learning process. Furthermore, the officer must be willing to follow the coach's recommendations. Achieving insight is the ultimate goal.

Coaching involves explaining the standards, how to get there and how to evaluate outcomes. It may mean raising the standards or at least teaching basic standards. Occasionally, productivity and the ability to complete essential tasks requires in-depth instruction. Police officers learn best when confronted with a crisis, where there is motivation to learn. Critical to this explanation is how to avoid tripwires and social land mines.

Important points to consider when coaching include discrepancies between desired and actual performance. Establish realistic goals for the officer, which help expand capabilities instead of failures. The ability to achieve a commitment to change may be the most difficult part. Pay close attention to what is being said and the feelings behind the words. Most importantly, the coach should look for impediments that are beyond the officer's control. In most cases, gaining commitment simply requires asking officers what they would do differently.

SUPPORTING POLICE OFFICERS

Everyone needs support sooner or later. Police leaders may be reluctant to assume a supportive role for fear of losing objectivity. This would be a mistake because the support process is an excellent opportunity to demonstrate concern for the welfare of police officers.

The leader is in the best position to use organizational and personal power to resolve conflicts or problems. The effective leader coaches, suggesting useful ideas for improvement. This is followed by encouraging the officer about possible solutions.

In some cases, an independent police officer can actively resist leader support. Leaders must respect the officer's right to privacy and independence. An effective role model, available for assistance, may be the wisest course of action. However, "can do" leaders make every officer feel valued and supported.

FOCUS POINTS: HUMAN RESOURCES

Without an adequate selection program, police strategic objectives cannot be accomplished. The recruitment of excellent police officers enhances the department's potential. The recruitment program must select the most capable officers. Character and emotional intelligence are essential to successful police performance.

Emotional intelligence remains the key ingredient of a successful police officer. What matters is not what is on the outside, but on the inside, unique qualities that must be included in the job description and actively recruited in the labor market.

Job specifications are qualifications needed to perform police missions. When a camera lens is focused on the police job description, the image becomes discernable concerning the skills required. The snapshot reveals that emotional intelligence is the essence and blueprint of excellent police performance.

CONCLUSION

Hire the best police officers and treat them as if they are world class potential. Make everyone feel that they are a valued member of the team. This means avoiding exclusiveness and encouraging inclusiveness; no officer is left out. Equal opportunity leaders encourage diversity while recognizing individual needs. Coaching and mentoring are essential leadership skills to retaining and motivating new talent and acknowledging lengthy service. Once recruited, new officers represent a legacy to be nurtured for the future of the department and community.

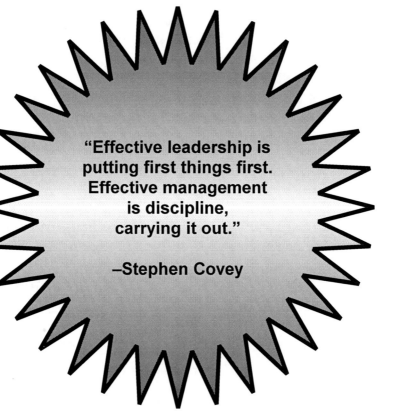

"Effective leadership is putting first things first. Effective management is discipline, carrying it out."

–Stephen Covey

Chapter 9
CONFLICT MANAGEMENT

> *What happens is not as important as*
> *how you react to what happens.*
> - THADDEUS GOLAS

Police leaders are constantly confronted with conflict; how they manage it is their litmus test. Failure to control conflict places the police organization at considerable risk. Two major strategic objectives in conflict management are (1) internal and (2) external conflict. To build a bridge to the community, leaders must acknowledge and manage internal conflict. Once negative internal conflict in a department has been minimized, leadership can manage external community conflict. This places them in a position to implement a community-oriented policing philosophy and problem-solving approach.

Effective leadership skills require an awareness of how to maintain positive conflict and avoid negative conflict. Conflict resolution skills work for the benefit of the department. Learning how to deal with conflict is one of the most challenging aspects of a police officer's profession, regardless of rank.

TYPES OF CONFLICT

While conflict can facilitate creativity, productivity and growth, it can also create turmoil and dissension. Conflict is a significant part of the police profession, presenting itself to officers on a daily basis. Conflict originates from many sources: (1) intrapersonal; (2) interpersonal; (3) structural; (4) strategic and (5) community. Social change in itself presents conflict, which "occurs when change is imposed or introduced without adequate preparation and involvement of those affected by the change." [104]

157

DEFINING CONFLICT

We all experience conflict in our daily lives. Leaders can create conflict among subordinates when they lack leadership skills, for conflict is about power, control and frustration. Conflict is not the problem; how we handle conflict is important!

"Conflict is a condition that results when one party feels that some concern of that party has been frustrated or is about to be frustrated by a second party. The term party in the previous sentence may refer to individuals, groups, or even organizations." [105] "Conflict can be defined as people's striving for their own preferred outcome, which, if attained, prevents others from achieving their preferred outcome, resulting in hostility and a breakdown in human relations." [106]

POSITIVE AND NEGATIVE CONFLICT

When we hear the word "conflict," our thoughts may turn to confrontation or rivalry. In its deadliest form, conflict is combat or warfare. Positive conflict can be competitive and productive of excellence, but extreme competition can lead to negative conflict. The following definitions demonstrate the difference between negative and positive conflict.

"Negative conflict. Individuals view others as adversaries. They are more concerned about protecting themselves and less, or not at all, concerned about the basic human rights of others. They try to win at all costs and often see people as expenses rather than as investments. They often take negative statements personally and do not try to elicit the true thoughts and feelings of others. They play mind games.

Positive conflict. Individuals, with differing points of view and personalities, show mutual respect for each others' thoughts and feelings; they consequently develop effective partnerships. In short, they are supportive of each other. They are secure enough to communicate openly. They avoid playing mind games. Rather than taking negative statements personally, they assert themselves to achieve positive results." [107]

Positive conflict can be healthy, leading to growth and change, and police leaders should encourage it. Negative conflict, however, is a source of social disorganization and dysfunctional behavior, and this should be avoided.

STAGES OF CONFLICT

Leaders are occasionally surprised when interpersonal conflict erupts and stand dismayed in its midst despite the many signs of it that were apparent. "Conflict is a dynamic process that does not usually appear suddenly. In fact, conflict generally passes through several stages, or cycles.

* **Latent conflict.** At this stage, the conditions for conflict exist but unrecognized by the parties.

* **Perceived conflict.** The conditions for conflict are recognized by one or both of the parties.

* **Felt conflict.** Internal tensions begin to build in the involved parties but are still unapparent.

* **Manifest conflict.** Conflict is out in the open, its existence obvious to uninvolved parties.

* **Conflict aftermath.** Conflict has somehow stopped, establishing new conditions that lead either to new conflict or to more effective cooperation." [108]

Not all interpersonal conflicts pass through each of these stages. Officers involved in conflict may not be at the same stage of development. One officer may demonstrate the beginning stage, where the other may be at the perceived stage of conflict. Leaders must take positive steps in the early stages of the conflict.

Conflict may represent "danger" or "opportunity," depending on how it is managed. Negative conflict often results from poor communication and listening skills.

ACTIVE LISTENING

Police leaders must be "active listeners" to intervene and manage conflict in a professional manner. What does the term "active" or "focused" listening mean? It means careful listening by leaders for the underlying message as well as the obvious message. Active listening includes postponing judgment until a "speaker" had ample opportunity to express feelings and concerns.

While this technique has some risks, both parties are often rewarded with increased rapport and communication. Simply stated, you cannot listen if you are talking! "Listening well requires concentration and, at times, risks. But the payoffs are worth it.

ADVANTAGES TO FOCUSED LISTENING

* "Fewer mistakes. Quality often increases when associates listen to, understand, and respectfully question procedures, policies, and expectations.

* Increased objectivity. Instead of overreacting or hastily acting, focused listening increased intelligent response.

* Increased efficiency. While more time initially may be spent listening, time spent solving problems and mending relationships will ultimately decrease." [109]

Barriers to effective communication arise between officers, middle managers, and senior leaders. Rank hierarchy intrinsically contains status barriers that need adjustment. "There is a need at all levels to recognize barriers to communication to improve listening and speaking skills.

THE MOST COMMON BARRIERS

* Time. Since there is so much emphasis on 'urgency,' people often rush their communication.

* Perceptions. Due to the nature of work, there are many
  ways to view issues. Are others' views taken into consideration?

* Prejudices. Preconceived thinking causes some managers
  and associates to listen selectively.

* Distractions. No matter what the work environment
  quality, a lack of focus can literally be the difference between life and death." [110]

FEEDBACK AND FOCUSED LISTENING

Feedback helps officers understand how their behavior
impacts on others. Feedback is vital to listening because it
ensures clear communication. One way of implementing
feedback is for the receiver to rephrase the speaker's comments to see if the revision corresponds to what the officer
had in mind. This technique may take time but will clarify
communication and enhance rapport.

Feedback describes but does not evaluate an officer's
statements. By avoiding language that evaluates, defensive
responses are reduced. Frustration results when an officer
is reminded of some personal shortcoming—especially, when
the officer does not receive guidance and direction from the
leader.

Feedback must be timely and is most effective after specific behaviors. However, timing often depends on the other
party's willingness and readiness to receive the feedback.
Feedback must be specific, not general, directed at behaviors the officer can adjust. Finally, feedback is counter-
productive when it serves only the leader's needs and not
the officer's.

POLICE INTRAPERSONAL CONFLICT

Conflict can be internal or external, the former defining
intrapersonal conflict, which is internal to the officer and
difficult to assess. Intrapersonal conflict connects to the officer's needs and goals. The officer's needs are not being met

because of external and varied conditions. These internal conditions may be physical or mental.

Intrapersonal conflict develops when obstacles exist between the officer's drives, motives, and his goals. For example, an officer not promoted because of race or ethnic discrimination may experience internal conflict leading to aggression. Severe frustration may sabotage management objectives.

One type of intrapersonal conflict can develop because of goal conflict, which occurs when an officer's goals have positive and negative components, or when competing or conflicting personal goals are present. There are three basic forms of goal conflict:

* Conflicting positive goals develop when an officer must choose between two or more positive goals. For example, if an officer is offered promotion to detective or sergeant and views both opportunities as equally positive, goal conflict may result. This is the classic approach-approach conflict and produces the least frustration and aggression.

* Goals with positive and negative conflict occurs, for example, when an officer is offered a promotion to sergeant and identifies positive as well as negative aspects. The positive features may include an increase in pay and status, while the negative features may include separation from friends and dealing with other officers' problems. This is the classic approach–avoidance conflict, selecting one positive decision that may include negative consequences.

* Goals that have two negative consequences occur when an officer is confronted with two or more negative goals. For example, a sergeant facing disciplinary action that includes reduction in rank or dismissal. This is an avoidance-avoidance conflict, a "lose-lose" choice between two negatives.

CAUSES OF INTRAPERSONAL CONFLICT

Intrapersonal conflict often results from poor training and insufficient professional knowledge, which create inconsistent policies, goals, and objectives. This kind of intrapersonal conflict influences motivation and productivity, creating further conflict.

Intrapersonal conflicts, such as domestic and financial problems, can lead to ethical dilemmas, including corruption and may result in heavy drinking, insubordination, excessive use of force, and off-duty conflict. In many cases, intrapersonal conflict leads to interpersonal conflict with other officers.

The first step in deciding whether to handle intrapersonal conflict is to listen actively and assess the officer's performance and productivity. If intervention is indicated, the second step is to identify the problem. Third, determine if the intervention risk is worth a positive outcome, and finally, assess if rapport can be established and the conflict resolved.

FIRST-LINE SUPERVISOR RESPONSIBILITIES

The sergeant is in an ideal position to recognize conflict situations providing he/she has a positive relationship with the officer. Generally, intrapersonal conflict is resolved through intervention with first-line supervisors assisting by identifying problems and causes.

When an officer requests assistance with a problem, the sergeant identifies signs of intrapersonal conflict; however, the sergeant should be cautious in giving personal advice. In most cases, professional treatment is most appropriate.

If intrapersonal conflict affects officer performance, the sergeant must follow up with positive steps toward effective intervention. The following case study is an example of the process involved:

CASE STUDY: INTRAPERSONAL CONFLICT
OFFICER JEB STONE

Officer Jeb Stone is a 14-year veteran of the police department. His work record has been above average, but in recent years his performance has dropped. Jeb was an officer who took pride in his personal appearance and always wore his uniform in the finest tradition. In recent months, however, he came to roll call looking as if he had slept in the uniform.

At age 43, Officer Stone appears much older than his years. Jeb has always been a heavy drinker, but now it is impacting on his health and appearance, and more importantly on his performance. In addition, Jeb is chronically late or absent and appears depressed and withdrawn.

THE INTERVENTION: Sergeant Mathews sensed problems but was reluctant to intervene. He hoped that Jeb's demeanor and behavior would improve. After several observations, however, Sergeant Mathews decided to act on the problem instead of ignoring it, a flawed response. Other members of the department had voiced their opinions about Jeb's drinking and behavior.

Officer Stone's reliability in an emergency was doubtful. Sergeant Mathews wanted to approach Stone in a manner that would ensure the officer's dignity, emphasizing his past service and performance.

The Sergeant would display self-control, patience and encouragement. Most of all, Sergeant Mathews would show Officer Stone fairness, balanced with honesty. Sergeant Mathews realized that balancing the rights of Officer Stone with the rights of fellow officers and the community would be a difficult task.

Sergeant Mathews arranges an interview with a clear understanding of where he is going. The sergeant recognized that alcohol, divorce, and financial problems may be blinding Officer Stone to what mattered most to him—his love of law enforcement and his work. His position on the police department was the key to resolving Officer Stone's problems.

The sergeant is concerned about doing the right thing in this case. His primary goal is a positive counselor referral that will increase the officer's self-awareness and understanding of the important issues in his life. Sergeant Mathews acts with caution and restraint, realizing the risks involved.

To manage intrapersonal conflict, leaders must take risks. Ignoring a problem is easy but in most cases fails. Sergeant Mathews approaches the situation as an opportunity to positively intervene and professionally contribute.

The Sergeant's first step is to establish rapport with Officer Stone. Sergeant Mathews wants to put Jeb at ease, demonstrating that he wants to listen. The Sergeant avoids criticism and demeaning remarks. Such communication will only put the officer on the defense; it will not enhance the intervention process or lead to positive outcomes. Even if Sergeant Matthews wins the argument, he will lose. So he begins by asking Jeb a few probing questions encouraging discussion and demonstrating his willingness to listen.

Initially the interview focuses on Officer Stone's strengths and accomplishments. He encourages Officer Stone to consider what he has control over and to focus on the future. The sergeant relies on his interpersonal skills and sensitivity to gain rapport with Jeb. Now he can obtain feedback, answer questions, and clarify misunderstandings.

Sergeant Mathews attempts to prevent further conflict by developing a common understanding of the problem. The Sergeant encourages Jeb to continue to communicate and concentrate on those things he hopes to have control over, for example, not arriving late. Sergeant Mathews sustained the flow of information by remaining quiet for a few seconds after Jeb responded to his questions. He waited for Jeb to fill in more information, while pausing occasionally.

The Sergeant understands that periodic pauses in the dialogue are important. He knows that if he talks too much he cannot be an effective listener. The Sergeant focuses on active listening techniques, summarizing Officer Stone's feelings while asking for periodic clarification. He paraphrases Officer Stone's statements to delineate, gain feedback, and reach a better understanding of his problem.

Jeb responds to the silence and open environment by providing additional information. The Sergeant is grateful for the additional information he receives during the conversation. The information gives the Sergeant a better understanding of Officer Stone's problems.

PROBLEM SOLVING: Officer Stone admits that he was shaken by the third divorce, saying, "I'm not sure of anything in my life any longer." Sergeant Mathews responds, "Jeb, perhaps you should have someone to help you cope with these issues. I think I can help you. Would you be willing to meet with a counselor who can help you deal with your feelings? You don't have to handle this alone. I can set everything up and make it as easy as possible. Your privacy will be respected."

Both men agreed that Jeb's problems were hurting Officer's Stone's professional and personal life. The Sergeant allows Officer Stone to take ownership for the problem and the solution. At the end of the interview, both men agree that Officer Stone seek help through the Employee Assistance Program (EAP), which provides assistance for psychological and counseling services. The intervention would include stress, marital and chemical dependency counseling.

LESSONS LEARNED: Sergeant Mathews's active listening and conflict resolution techniques proved to be essential leadership skills that improved the social climate. The Sergeant realized that even excellent conflict management techniques do not necessarily succeed. However, a proactive approach creates an opportunity for resolution. More often than not, the passive approach fails to resolve conflict situations and may even compound the problem.

INTERPERSONAL CONFLICT

Competitive personalities may lead to interpersonal conflict, the main cause of which is opposing personalities and value systems. This conflict may occur with managers or supervisors, including the chief. Interpersonal conflict may evolve from peer competition.

A sergeant experiences strong peer relationships before being promoted. Jealously and envy can become increasingly evident if a fellow officer feels that he or she should have been the one promoted. New supervisors may encounter this kind of conflict. A transfer to another shift can reduce this kind of conflict for new supervisors.

INTERPERSONAL CONFLICT MANAGEMENT SKILLS

More often than not, the sergeant confronts interpersonal conflict situations evolving from direct supervision and must decide whether to arbitrate the conflict that develops from the interacting officers. "Under what circumstances should the manager intervene? Leaders should ask themselves the following questions before getting involved in personality clashes:

*   Do I have the ability, the experience, and the willingness to help resolve the situation?

*   Do they want your help?

*   What are the consequences of the conflict?

*   Recognize your power, role and vulnerability. (Third, parties are in as power position, but also make very convenient scapegoats.)" [111]

The following case study illustrates the stages of interpersonal conflict:

INTERPERSONAL CONFLICT
CASE STUDY: SUSAN LIGHTFOOT

Sergeant Louis Clark has recently been promoted in a small police department for which he was given a promotion party. All of his "old buddies" from the shift were present, including a new officer, Susan Lightfoot, a Native American. It was a gala event, and everyone agreed that Louis Clark was the best person for the job.

As the months passed, Susan Lightfoot was becoming disenchanted with her new Sergeant. He was inclined to rely on his old "comrades in arms" for significant assignments, while Susan was treated as an inadequate rookie. This made her unhappy because she was the only college graduate in the department and felt that she was treated unfairly.

The "good old boy" network made jokes about her college degree every time she made a small error or mistake. She harbored the feeling that Sergeant Clark did not respect her because she was a woman. She believed that discrimination was a factor and that one particular individual was harassing her. Susan's perceptions about Officer Tom Jones were accurate. She was actually well-liked by most members of the department. Tom's remarks, however, were periodically demeaning and insensitive.

Susan began to withdraw from the other officers and became silent about her feelings. As her frustration increased, the conflict accelerated. On one occasion, Susan had an emotional exchange with Officer Jones over the way a domestic case had been resolved. The verbal exchange was loud enough so that other officers could overhear.

Sergeant Clark should have sensed her anger through her silence, but did not perceive her hurt feelings important enough to take action. Anger, however, is a form of communication that indicates conflict. The recent incident with

Tom focused Clark's attention on the conflict between the two officers.

Unfortunately, the department's leadership failed to recognize Officer Lightfoot's change in behavior. Sergeant Clark did not understand how it felt to be the department's only woman and Native American. His lack of empathy made it difficult to eliminate interpersonal conflict for this new officer.

The members of the department did not view Susan's silence as indicating a problem. They rationalized their behavior as appropriate for a rookie. It had always been a tradition to tease new members of the department. Generally, assignments that seasoned officers did not want were given to new officers as training for future responsibility.

Susan was in a different stage of the conflict cycle than her peers. She was at the perceived conflict level, while her peers were at the latent level, unaware that conflict existed. Officer Lightfoot decided to bring the conflict into the open. She felt excluded and considered leaving the department.

Susan's personal conflict grew daily with members of her shift. With the frustration mounting, she decided to quit. She loved her job but did not feel that her treatment was fair. This is the classic approach-avoidance conflict, positive and negative goals. Officer Lightfoot walked into the Sergeant's office and stated, "I quit, effective immediately." This startled the Sergeant and he replied, "Susan, I do not want to lose you. It would be a real loss to the Department."

Susan replied, " I thought you wanted me to quit because you were prejudiced toward women." The sergeant replied, "I feel that you are making a considerable contribution to the department and have an excellent future as a police officer. Let's sit down for a moment and discuss your decision. What information can you give me concerning your reasons for leaving?"

CONFLICT MANAGEMENT RESPONSE

Conflict resolution techniques vary. Approaches can range from ignoring the conflict to attacking the conflict directly. The Sergeant's strategy was to confront the problem in a manner that would enable Susan and other members of the department to achieve their goals.

Sergeant Clark continued to probe for more information. Now focused on the conflict, he communicated his position to Susan. This misunderstanding was creating conflict and a sense of rejection for Susan. Sergeant Clark has identified steps that are needed to resolve the conflict. He has "broken the ice" and focused his attention through the active listening process. The Sergeant provides feedback to Officer Lightfoot designated to establish common understanding.

Susan's interpersonal conflict had been acknowledged during the interview. She decided to give another opportunity to members of her department, in particular, Tom Jones. The sergeant realized that he and the other department members have not handled interpersonal conflict well.

On the positive side, Officer Lightfoot has established boundaries of what she considered acceptable peer behavior. Furthermore, she has established her presence as an equal partner in the field of law enforcement, which other officers are beginning to appreciate and respect. Her self-respect has been maintained.

LESSONS LEARNED: In the future, Sergeant Clark will be watchful to prevent this kind of misunderstanding. He will strive to communicate to the others how Susan felt. The Sergeant is an equal opportunity leader who encourages cultural sensitivity in the future. He will contact Officer Jones immediately to understand his position in this interpersonal conflict.

Open communication should be encouraged, and perhaps Officer Lightfoot's morale and job satisfaction will improve. Sergeant Clark will follow up to ensure that Officer Lightfoot's adjustment is complete. Every member of the department should learn from this interpersonal conflict, and especially Tom Jones and Susan Lightfoot.

STRUCTURAL CONFLICT
Structural conflict results from how a department is organized and is independent of the personalities involved. For example, while the detective division may come into conflict with the patrol division, patrol officers may come into conflict with standing undercover operations.

An officer may discover minor street drug activity directly related to a large-scale operation. The patrol activity may interfere with an important drug trafficking buy that has been scheduled for a particular day. Competition to eliminate drug dealers may lead to poor communication and conflict among operating divisions.

GOAL CONFLICT: Each police department has a subordinate structure, like bureaus, divisions, sections and units. Ideally, they contribute to the department's overall goals. Unfortunately, at times, these subordinate units may come into conflict and become counterproductive to the mission. Police leaders have the responsibility to discourage structural conflicts as they coordinate the goals of the department.

MUTUAL DEPENDENCE: When two divisions depend on each other for support, the potential for structural conflict arises. For example, although the Investigative Division may need additional support from the Patrol Division, prior commitments may reduce resources for the operation. If the Patrol Division is not supportive, mass arrests of drug traffickers and the execution of search warrants may not take place on schedule.

UNEQUAL DEPENDENCE: Potential for conflict also exists when a unit or section depends on a larger bureau or division for support. For example, Headquarters Staff may need the assistance of line officers. Patrol officers may resent higher headquarters and not accept a particular set of staff recommendations. Police officers may resist the implementation of staff officers' recommendations and fail to cooperate which may lead to further conflict when support from headquarters staff is needed.

COMMUNICATION BARRIERS: Conflict that develops from communication barriers is often encountered in situations where departments have decentralized operations. The physical separation of the precincts from the Headquarters has the potential to create structural conflict for personnel coordination, and logistical support is strained in decentralized police departments.

MANAGING STRUCTURAL CONFLICT

Management can create communication barriers by building territorial imperatives in police organizations, thus encouraging a "them versus us attitude." Unfortunately, the department's structure may reflect this attitude. A self-serving organizational structure reflects only the needs of personalities rather than the mission of the department. Most often, the solution can be found in reorganization and reassignment of officers.

RESTRAINING FORCES: STRUCTURAL CONFLICT

Community and problem-oriented policing is often viewed as a threat to police organizational structure. Empire building also may hinder the development of strategic reform, thus the department's structure must be analyzed to eliminate restraining forces and opposing personalities.

Change is another obstacle that impedes a department's desire for security. Many officers feel comfortable with familiar situations, even if it would be prudent to modify some practices. The problem with change is that dealing with the unknown may produce further conflict. Change may be encouraged in three phases: (1) the unfreezing of an old pattern of relationships, (2) the switch to a new pattern through change induced by an agent, and (3) the refreezing of a new pattern of relationships. [112]

When addressing structural conflict, additional social change may produce a more chaotic degree of conflict. For long-term results, it may initially require "biting the bullet," in the short run. Unfortunately, the situation may need to worsen before it improves.

STRATEGIC CONFLICT

Intrapersonal and interpersonal conflicts may spontaneously arise from a variety of situations, while strategic conflicts are usually planned and intentional. Often strategic conflicts promote the self-interest of individual officers, or a group of officers seeking to obtain an advantage. For example, control over strategic changes like community-oriented or problem-oriented policing is viewed as an important source of power.

Presently, differences in philosophy and values is creating strategic conflict in many police organizations. Two distinct groups are setting the stage for strategic conflict. First, the progressive younger group, college-educated, who support the philosophy of community-oriented and problem-oriented policing and who tend to emphasize the civil and constitutional rights of citizens, emphasizing crime prevention.

The second group is composed of traditionalists who emphasize crime control and pragmatic solutions. This conservative element seeks to resist change by maintaining traditional methods and the "old ways of doing things." They fear change and resent the "attack" on their methods of policing.

Differences in culture, status, power and interdependence must be addressed, for strategic conflict may create organizational ambiguity and competition for scarce resources. The drive for autonomy and independence will often create competition, frustration, conflict and even aggression.

STRATEGIC CONFLICT: WIN/WIN SOLUTIONS

The conflict between traditional policing, the "status quo," and the reform community-oriented and problem-oriented policing is on-going. The proponents of traditional policing view community and problem-oriented policing as social work, not law enforcement. They perceive the field of policing as law enforcement and response to emergencies.

The reformers regard problem-solving and crime prevention as the main concern. Fortunately, a large percentage of officers are open to mediation and compromise. In actuality, both approaches can reduce crime and enforce the law.

Traditionalists and reformers have much in common, for their individual goals are not mutually exclusive and unattainable. Strategic reform is possible and the retention of traditional policing and enforcement still plays a vital role in achieving community goals and objectives.

The best hope for strategic change involves a win/win philosophy. The balance between traditional policing and community-oriented policing is delicate. The win/lose position will lead only to resentment and lose/lose consequences.

Win/win is a frame of mind and heart that constantly seeks mutual benefit in all human interactions. Win/win means that agreements or solutions are mutually beneficial, mutually satisfying. With a win/win solution, all parties feel good about the decision and feel committed to the action plan. Win/win sees life as a cooperative, not a competitive arena.

"Most people tend to think in terms of dichotomies: strong or weak, hardball or softball, win or lose. But that kind of thinking is fundamentally flawed, based on power and position rather than on principle. Win/win is based on the paradigm that there is plenty for everybody, that one person's success is not achieved at the expense or exclusion of the success of others. Win/win is a belief in the third alternative. It's not your way or my way; it's a better way, a higher way." [113]

The differences between successful and unsuccessful leaders is often determined by how officers are influenced. The best leaders encourage others to follow them. Superior leaders have the conflict resolution skills necessary for excellent leadership.

CONFLICT RESOLUTION SKILLS: The community-oriented and problem-oriented policing controversy is not going to vanish. "Conflict is here to stay and we should learn to deal with it effectively and manage it proactively.[114] There are four specific strategies for win/win mediations:

* Separate the people from the problem....The partici-pants...should come to view themselves as working together to solve a particular problem.

* Focus on interest(s), not positions.

* Look at the options.

* Establish that a single opinion without dialogue is unsatisfactory."[115]

The revolutionary approach to community-oriented poli-cing is win/lose oriented, resulting in a lose/lose situation for strategic reforms. The win/win approach to the traditional and community-oriented policing will result in a better way, a higher way.

STRATEGIC AND INTERPERSONAL CONFLICT
Occasionally, leaders will demonstrate their power through a win/lose conflict resolution approach. It would be more productive if they would "pull their horns in" and meet their officers half-way. The win/lose conflict is all too common in policing today.

"Win-lose produces frustrated and often irritating re-sults; organizationally, interpersonally and situationally. It has limited application in today's complex organizational world, and, and, like salt, should be used sparingly." In win/win solutions, focus on the basic merits of each side, rather than "interpersonal haggling." [116]

All too often, the win/lose approach results in a lose/lose situation for both parties. In lose/lose conflict situations, the conflict is negotiated through an ineffective compromise, both sides feeling they have not accomplished their purposes. This kind of compromise is usually considered a "quick-fix" solution, with officers sometimes engaging in future aggravated conflict. The temporary suppression of feelings and unresolved conflict may flare up with a new triggering event.

DEALING WITH SOCIAL AND STRATEGIC CHANGE

Some of the basic barriers to change are (1) fear of the unknown; (2) economics; (3) inconveniences; and (4) threats to interpersonal relationships and social interaction. To implement a community or problem-oriented police approach, all of these issues must be addressed.

"Resistance to change can be strong and the reaction from officers negative. Some of these negative consequences range from visible frustration to outright mutiny. This backlash is frequently encountered when chiefs attempt to impose community policing on a department. To reduce or eliminate such backlash:

* Train the entire department in the community policing philosophy from the beginning.

* Develop a management style and organizational structure that gathers input from all members of the department.

* Constantly stress to both the department and community that the agency will always perform traditional police duties.

* Go slowly...In most cases, it will take 10-20 years to change our current incident-driven response to a community-oriented partnership.

* Don't take it personally when members of the department demonstrate backlash." [117]

COUNTERING RESISTANCE TO CHANGE

The sergeant is responsible for implementing change and holding officers accountable for goals and objectives. First-line supervisors can affect an officer's acceptance of change. Because fear of the unknown is one of the obstacles to implementing change, building trust with officers is the foundation for achieving it.

Obstacles can be overcome by discussing with the officers any changes that take place. Officers must be allowed to ask questions with straight-forward answers forthcoming. Police officers must be actively involved in the change process, for effective implementation. Officer involvement is the key to the successful execution of new goals and objectives.

NEIGHBORHOOD-ORIENTED CONFLICT

Community-oriented conflict is resolved through a block-by-block approach. The term "neighborhood policing" has become incorporated in the community-oriented and problem-oriented police vocabulary. This approach has had varying degrees of success and failure. This police partnership with the community is based on communication in dealing with the various sources of conflict in the community.

"The fight against crime is going to be won at the neighborhood level, community by community, and police departments must work closely with these communities if we are to be successful. This can be accomplished by:

* Organizing community-based crime prevention activities neighborhood by neighborhood.

*   Focusing city resources, within neighborhoods, to ad-
     dress the identified causes of specific types of crimes.

*   Keeping the community updated on the results of
     police operations in their neighborhoods." [118]

The goal of neighborhood policing is the cohesion of the
members of the community and individual block watch
programs. Cohesion exists through strong bonds of mutual
respect, trust, confidence, and understanding of community
block watch members. Cohesion results from the officers'
respect, confidence, caring and communication.

Officers should assess community opinions about the
delivery of the department services in the community and
specific block watch programs. All too often, officers assume
that they are doing an excellent job without surveying their
customers. The old adage, "The customer is always right,"
is seldom applied to citizens. However, progressive departments are attempting to measure and evaluate the quality
of their services.

Community perceptions may be more important than
officers' perceptions:

> "It is not how good you are, it's how good those
> people out there think you are that is important.
> Officers may think they are the best at what they do;
> however, if the people, the citizens, the community,
> and the civic groups do not think they are the best or
> do not think they are doing the job they should be
> doing, the officers have not accomplished anything
> positive....
>
> "Neighborhood-oriented policing is an interactive
> process between police officers assigned to specific
> beats and the citizens that either work or reside in
> these beats to mutually develop ways to identify pro-
> blems and concerns and then to assess viable solu-
> tions by providing available resources from both the

police department and the community to address the problems and/or concerns." [119]

The most difficult part of implementing a successful neighborhood-oriented policing philosophy involves dealing with diverse community groups, whose expectations may vary. Officers who participate in these responsibilities must understand basic leadership principles and group dynamics.

FOCUS POINTS: CONFLICT MANAGEMENT
The first step in managing conflict is to train police leaders in conflict management skills and how to recognize early signs of conflict. Conflict management programs should begin with the training and development of conflict management instructors.

The second step involves an assessment of conflict in the department. A plan for gathering and analyzing the data must be ongoing. The analysis and interpretation of the data should lead to problem-solving techniques, which will prove most valuable in recommending appropriate remedial action.

The third step involves an evaluation system, which helps clarify the effectiveness of the conflict management efforts. It would be pointless to continue interventions that do not lead to successful mediation and solutions.

CONCLUSION

Police organizations consumed with conflict are not likely to reach their goals and objectives. They will become lost in the web that conflict weaves, causing distractions, loss of focus, time and energy. The path to where they want to go will become more burdensome than necessary, causing low morale and a lack of motivation. Conflict obscures an organization's goals and objectives.

The "distractions" that result from conflict distract police officers from answering two basic questions: (1) Where are we going? and (2) How will we get there? Ultimately, this could mean they cannot determine whether they have achieved organizational goals and objectives.

Part IV
CHARTING THE COURSE

EFFECTIVE STRATEGIC PLANNING

* IDENTIFY THE MANDATES

* IDENTIFY THE PRESENT STATE

* IDENTIFY THE DESIRED FUTURE STATE

* IMPLEMENT THE STRATEGIC AND TACTICAL PLANS

ESTABLISH THE EVALUATION PROCESS

* EVALUATE GOALS AND OBJECTIVES

* SELECT THE EVALUATION SYSTEM

* DETERMINE RESULTS

* DETERMINE NEW DESTINATIONS

INTELLIGENCE-LED POLICING

* PULLING IT ALL TOGETHER

* INTELLIGENCE SHARING

* JOHARI WINDOW FEEDBACK

* STRATEGIC PICTURE FRAMING

PART IV

LEADERSHIP FOUNDATIONS	GUIDEPOST BEHAVIORS
Develop the vision, include staff and officers	Assess strengths and weaknesses
Forecast potential crime trends and related problems	Define the department's problem(s)
Develop strategic plans and assessment procedures	Plot the course, direction and destination
Identify strategic goals and objectives	Promote the vision, goals and stay the course
Develop tactical plans and decision requirements	Apply COP, POP and SARA
Define the mission(s) and logistical support requirements	Define what needs to be accomplished and related operational procedures
Evaluate strategic goals, objectives, and procedures	Design the assessment and determine the quality of outcomes

Chapter 10
CRITICAL THINKING, PLANNING AND PROBLEM-SOLVING

When you've exhausted all
possibilities, remember this:
you haven't!

- ROBERT H. SCHULLER

"Can do" leadership requires strategic planning, problem-solving and decision-making and have three major purposes. They: (1) encourage and support the development of vision, (2) focus on the department's goals, and (3) encourage the application of the department's resources and logistical support of those goals.

Senior leaders and middle managers have the primary responsibility for looking to the future. **Chapter 3, SENIOR LEADERSHIP**, discusses the need to develop vision. In this chapter, we will focus on the critical thinking skills and strategic planning strategies that help make vision and future forecasting possible.

"Can do" leadership skills make it possible to answer our three basic questions: (1) Where are we going? (2) How will we get there? and (3) How will we know when we have arrived? These questions continue to serve as the vehicle for leadership, providing a map to the department's destination.

STRATEGIC PLANNING

Intelligence-Led Policing (ILP) is the umbrella management philosophy that encourages strategic planning strategies and criminal information coordination. Planning is a means to an end; it engages the mind. Strategic planning is the centerpiece of the planning process, and is directly related to problem oriented policing (POP) and long-term planning. In addition, there are two other contingency feedback-planning models: (1) intelligence analysis, and (2) crime analysis.

Critical thinking and logic represent foundations for the ILP management philosophy. Excellent logic and strategic planning leads to calculated goals, objectives, and tactical action plans. Proactive ILP intelligence gathering procedures provide support for intelligence and crime analysis strategies.

There are many intelligence analysis definitions and facets of meaning. The fundamentals include *collection* of raw data, *analysis,* and meaningful *dissemination.* The essential quality is *analysis* of the information; otherwise, it is merely a collation of facts or raw data.

The six steps of the Intelligence Cycle offer the systematic collection of pertinent data and criminal information. The process of collection, analysis, and dissemination provides the means for law enforcement leaders to make excellent and timely decisions. Refer to Figure 10-1 for an analysis of the Intelligence Cycle.

Efficient planning for collection focuses on the target. Collection planning requires that at different phases of the investigation, methods of collection are coordinated according to the specific target. The proper coordination of collection avoids the use of numerous logistical resources by avoiding duplication of effort. In addition, it provides the correct distribution of personnel resources.

Generally, threat assessment concerns criminal activity, followed by recommendations and remedial solutions. Analysts inspect data and historical facts, predicting future crime patterns. Threat assessment represents one of many intelligence products available for analyzing criminal behavior. The final intelligence product may include an assessment based on human expertise that includes conclusions and recommendations.

Figure 10-1

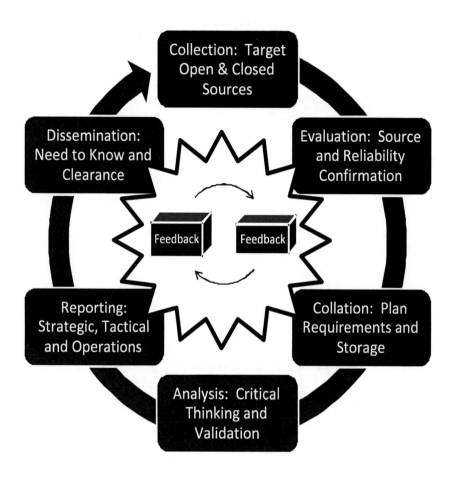

Intelligence Cycle Figure

ILP philosophy eventually improves leadership effective-ness and criminal information applications. This manage-ment approach is a powerful and pragmatic apparatus of law enforcement that offers leaders opportunities to make informed decisions. Moreover, ILP strategic intelligence strategies form the ideal foundation for successful policy and strategy development.

Sound policies that enhance positive crime prevention, intervention, and crime control outcomes evolve when lead-ers incorporate sound social science and statistical informa-tion in the decision-making process. These considerations suggest the possible synchronization of ILP management, strategic and tactical planning.

The consolidation and synthesis of Community-Oriented Policing **(COP) + Problem-Oriented Policing (POP) + SARA planning model = COPPS.** The most recent component of the equation would include CompStat, a form of focused policing, plus the leadership and technology components.

Therefore, the new intelligence-led policing approach would include **ILP + COPPS + CompStat + Quality Leadership = Police Excellence.** The updated formula serves as a pathway and necessary progression to the evolu-tion and development of an intelligence-led policing grand strategy. ILP should have a strong affinity for the COPPS philosophy strategy in the United States. For additional information concerning ILP refer to **CHAPTER 13.**

DEVELOPING ACCURATE CRIMINAL INFORMATION

The chief and senior leaders comprise the strategic plan-ning team. Their decisions must be based on accurate intel-ligence, usually solicited criminal information. To achieve a flow of accurate information, channels of communication must remain open. Community-oriented and problem-orien-ted policing provide this essential stream of information from citizens.

THE CRIMINAL INTELLIGENCE CYCLE

Crime analysts are responsible for coordinating and managing criminal intelligence. Without crime analysis, missions cannot be accomplished. Criminal intelligence is a complex physical and intellectual endeavor involving criminal activities and patterns. While trends may be projected, predictions are not possible.

The criminal intelligence cycle includes the collection and storage of data, evaluation, analysis and dissemination of criminal information. The result most often is an informed judgment, or best educated guess. This thoughtful description of facts or near facts is called the criminal information/intelligence cycle. The process may be defined as the handling of individual items of information for their conversion into material useful for investigative purposes.

COLLECTION: Information processing is primarily conducted by the crime analyst or investigating officer. Information must be coordinated to ensure it is not duplicated. It must be constantly updated to reflect realistic objectives; gaps must be filled where they exist. Categorize the information collected according to its use. Strategic intelligence is broad, global, and long-term; while tactical obtains near-term objectives.

PLANNING AND COLLECTION FUNCTION: The collection must be focused against a target to be efficient. Moreover, several methods of collection must be coordinated with respect to the target. Collection planning should be reviewed several times at different phases during the investigation with the methods of collection coordinated according to the target. This saves resources by avoiding duplication of efforts.

TARGETING: A targeting system collects and stores information concerning a target. Targets may vary according to the community's concerns, for example, concerns about criminal activity or specific buildings or community businesses. The target collection folder is a management tool used to identify, track, record, analyze and manage information about specific targets. This information is frequently reviewed to ensure timely analysis and is available to police officers and field investigators.

TARGET SELECTION AND EVALUATION: The key to successful target selection and evaluation is to deal with a narrowly defined target area, a particular business, for instance, rather than a whole community. Debriefing and follow-up questioning of individuals in the target activity who have been arrested for other offenses are necessary for the development of essential information.

COLLECTION METHODS: Collection methods can be divided into two general areas: (1) overt collection and (2) covert collection. Overt collection identifies many open sources from which valuable information can be obtained. Available sources should be used to develop data on criminal activity. Covert collection may be quite expensive due to the use of paid personnel and physical surveillance or electronic methods.

SOURCES OF INFORMATION: Primary sources include the victim, neighbors, informants, and complainants. Other law enforcement agencies which provide meaningful exchanges of intelligence are also important sources. Essential criminal information should be exchanged on a regular basis with rules for dissemination established and followed.

EVALUATION OF CRIMINAL INTELLIGENCE: Evaluation can be divided into two basic parts: (1) a judgment of the validity of the information, and (2) an assessment of the truthfulness and reliability of the source. Information must be continuously evaluated to determine its pertinence, reliability, accuracy and corroboration.

COLLATION: Criminal intelligence must be organized in order to make deductions concerning collected data so that it may be used. Collation is the first step in the process of translating raw data into criminal/intelligence information and includes the removal of useless or incorrect information. It also involves the orderly arrangement of collected material, concepts, and data so that the proper connective relationship and elements can be identified. Basic to the collation process is a system for the filing and retrieval of gathered information.

ANALYSIS: The central issue to criminal intelligence is the analysis system, an important phase directly related to collation. Analysis requires the ability to think critically and develop stated and unstated assumptions. The analyst studies fragments of criminal information and attempts to assemble them into logical patterns.

Constructed fragments of information are then inserted in the hypothesis to test tentative conclusions. In addition, the analyst may develop several alternative hypotheses. The analyst must understand how to conduct applied research and evaluate criminal information. The formation of patterns or hypotheses forecasts potential criminal activities, which may lead to new strategic and tactical intelligence objectives.

DISSEMINATION: The ultimate value of criminal intelligence is to assist police officers in the field. The value of the information is often determined by the speed and accuracy of its dissemination to those who legitimately need it. However, dissemination must respect the privacy of individuals and must be implemented with safeguards for its ethical release on a need-to-know basis.

THE PLANNING PROCESS

Planning bridges the gap between where we are and where we want to go. It helps identify and select the best methods to achieve positive goals and objectives. Defining how we will get where we want to go describes the planning process.

Planning involves determining what is to be done, when it is to be accomplished, where it is to be completed, who will be tasked and held accountable, and how the task will be accomplished. The essence of planning is decision-making and goal setting. Planning has many forms and three major facets: (1) strategic planning, (2) traditional planning model, and (3) tactical planning. [120]

STRATEGIC PLANNING

To plan and develop vision, police leaders must remain actively involved in the critical thinking and planning process. While vision may include intuitive judgements, the planning process gathers information to help facilitate effective planning and decision making. This information permits police leaders to function in an ever changing social environment. Excellent strategic and tactical planning encourages the police management team to respond rapidly to fluctuating conditions.

The chief and senior leaders are involved in the strategic planning process, a comprehensive plan that may require as many as five years. Strategic planning concerns what might happen and involves uncertainty. There are seven basic steps for conducting strategic planning: [121]

1. Introduce strategic planning within the agency

In police organizations, the most difficult obstacle to overcome is establishing the need for strategic planning, particularly, in small or mid-size police departments.

Police leaders anticipate and shape events rather than being controlled by each crisis. The strategic planning process has three basic objectives: (1) Help clarify the mission, goals and objectives, (2) Improve the analysis of various problems confronting the agency, and (3) Help identify and anticipate solutions.

2. Clarify agency mandates

Police leaders analyze their organizational mandate, which clearly describes the department's present conditions and identifies the means for dealing with the problem. Analysis of the mandate will encourage understanding by members of various functional areas, ie., traffic, patrol and investigative. Some of these mandates include court decisions, county government charters and coordination with other jurisdictions.

3. Specify the agency mission and values

Mission and value statements are concise definitions and reasons why organizations exist (See **CHAPTER 3, POLICE SENIOR LEADERSHIP**). The ideas presented are representative of many police agencies. Bryson suggests answering six questions in formulating a mission statement:

* **What is the organization's identity?**

* **What social and political needs does the organization fulfill?**

* **What does the organization do to respond to these needs?**

* **How does the organization respond to the key stakeholder (anyone affected by or who can affect the operations of the institution)?**

* **What are the organization's philosophy and fundamental values?**

* **What makes the organization distinctive?** [122]

4. Examine external conditions – threats and opportunities

Threat analysis is an important part of strategic planning. The threats may be internal or external. For example, poor morale and motivation must be quickly addressed to form the foundation for dealing with external threats like budget cuts or force reductions. The planning process should identify weaknesses and vulnerabilities.

Tactical/action plans are then designed to counter various threats and vulnerabilities, which may then be turned into new opportunities. Threat analysis is generally based on criminal intelligence/information. This provides planners and personnel with detailed information on threats or adverse circumstances likely to be encountered. The threats are isolated and identified, which provides essential information to field officers.

Many of these threats can be turned into positive opportunities. For example, community groups that work to the detriment of the police department can now be realigned into support groups. As opportunities emerge, every effort must be made to turn adversity into opportunity.

5. Examine the internal situation – strengths and weaknesses

All too often, police leaders focus on external threats in the community, law enforcement's main weakness. Assessing this side of the human element should be an on-going essential task. The impact of leadership on morale should be constantly evaluated. The motivation of personnel is largely based on the behavior of leaders.

6. Evaluate strategic issues facing the agency

Only after successfully completing the earlier stages, can one proceed to the next stage: compiling a list of strategic planning issues. This appears an easy step but may in fact prove the most difficult. Obviously, individual personalities and philosophies will differ. Some will insist on the traditional approach to policing, while others will favor new techniques and innovations.

The current social and political trends of community-oriented policing and social diversity continues to influence police operations. These forces represent a large constituency and will have a dramatic impact in the future. To ignore the forces of social change will only lead to disorganization and the failure to respond appropriately.

7. Design strategies to respond to issues

The last step in the strategic planning process encourages innovative methods in response to strategic issues. Problem-oriented policing remains the vehicle for accomplishing those strategies that have the potential to deal with dramatic community issues. This approach is proactive rather than reactive, creating new challenges and opportunities [123].

THE TRADITIONAL PLANNING MODEL

Police departments have generally used the traditional planning method, which is based on rationality and assures optimal achievement of the desired goals of the situation. "Police administrators are more apt to appreciate a planning model centered around problem-oriented goals and priorities (such as the reduction of burglaries in a given residential area) than around more abstract notions (such as the reduction of crime and delinquency)." [124]

The traditional planning model describes an eleven step planning model:

(1) Preparing for Planning; (2) Describing Present Situation; (3) Developing Projections; (4) Considering Alternative Future States; (5) Identifying Problems; (6) Setting Goals; (7) Identifying Alternative Courses of Action; (8) Selecting Preferred Alternatives; (9) Planning for Implementation; (10) Implementing Plans; (11) Monitoring and Evaluating Progress. The cycle is then repeated. [125]

SETTING THE STAGE: STRATEGIC AND TACTICAL PLANNING

Once the strategic planning process is in place, middle managers can engage in administrative planning while first-line supervisors concentrate on developing operational planning and intelligence data. Sergeants, however, are concerned with tactical planning, which they develop from strategic planning and the intelligence cycle.

Strategic and tactical planning will dictate personnel and logistical support requirements. These cascading plans move from the top downward, involving everyone in the planning process. The planning process occurs at every level of the department.

TACTICAL AND ACTION PLANNING

Lieutenants and sergeants are essential contributors to the tactical planning process and leaders should involve them in the planning process. However, if possible, leaders should implement and comply with previously prescribed tactical procedures when developing action plans. The first step in tactical and action planning is to analyze any available broad strategic intelligence while developing tactical intelligence for the operation. The leader should use this information to prioritize objectives and determine how they will be achieved.

"Can do" leaders should carefully answer the following tactical questions to effectively develop tactical or action plans:

1.   What is the mission?

Leaders should precisely define the purpose of the mission. This process helps leaders determine what actions are necessary to reach their objectives.

2.   What are the possible alternatives?

All actions are designed to move toward the achievement of the mission. However, a leader's decision regarding what actions will be taken, greatly impacts on the outcome of the mission. Alternative actions should be formed into a solution and alternate solutions. These solutions may be ranked according to the best, second best and, third best solutions. Generally, one or two solutions are recommended to the chief or subordinate commander.

3.   Why must it be accomplished?

A rationale statement for the mission will help pin-point the purpose and need for the mission. Effective leadership will consider if an action and its related risks are truly necessary, especially force.

4.   When and where will the mission be accomplished?

Dates and time schedules are essential details that require careful consideration. The success of the mission may depend on the timing and location where the action takes place. This decision may have considerable impact on the safety of citizens and participating officers.

5.   How will other unrelated events and activities be coordinated?

Leaders must consider what events are taking place during the same time frame and how they may impact on the successful completion of the mission. Again, timing can "make or break" an operation.

6.   Who should carry out the mission?

Leaders will need to select personnel who will participate in the mission. The appropriate selection of officers will significantly impact on the mission outcome.

7.   What skills and abilities will be needed to perform the mission?

Once this is determined, officers who have demonstrated the appropriate skills and abilities should be identified and assigned to the related tasks.

8.   Where should the officers assemble?

This will be determined by the mission, location, and the mission's execution plan. Officer and citizen safety should always be considered.

9. How should the mission be planned and executed?

Strategic and tactical intelligence dictate certain requirements. The intelligence needs reviewing by the intelligence analyst for changes. This new information may impact on revisions in the planning process.

10.   What methods and procedures should be followed?

Each situation is unique. However, prior experience may give leaders insight into successful outcomes. Information from informed sources can also enhance the possibility of the mission's achievement.

11.   Will innovative techniques and procedures be necessary or will prior plans be implemented?

Innovation is risky, but the potential for rewards is great. Because a method has been previously successful does not guarantee future success. Each situation is unique and dictates its own requirements.

12.   What logistical support, weapons and tactical teams will be necessary?

The logistical support, weapons and teams must be uniquely matched to the situation and the mission. Failure to adhere to these requirements could lead to a tactical disaster, including loss of personnel and equipment.

13.   How will leaders evaluate the outcome of the mission?

The after-action report develops information on performance and recommends future tactical planning and operations. Debriefing officers assists in uncovering past mistakes and lessons learned from them.

DECISION-MAKING

Decision-making skills are essential for successful leadership. Most of the operational decisions should be made at the lowest level, near the officers most affected. Strategic decisions are made by the chief and senior leaders. Middle managers make administrative decisions, while first-line supervisors make operational decisions.

Command decisions refer to decisions made by leaders or commanders on their own, a kind of decision making that should be seldom exercised. Because command decisions are made alone, they may be unsupported. Command decisions should be reserved for emergency situations. If a decision does not have to be made immediately, one should consult others who are affected.

"The following recommendations and guidelines help improve positive decision-making:

Is the decision:

1.   **Consistent with the agency's mission, goals and objectives?**

2.   **A long-term solution?**

3.   **Cost-effective?**

4.   **Legal?**

5.   **Ethical?**

6. **Practical?**

7. **Acceptable to those responsible for implement-ing it?"** [126]

Failure to identify and apply the above listed questions will result in the rejection of the recommendation(s). More importantly, it can reflect adversely on the recommender's judgement and ability to make decisions. A poor decision that fails to answer these questions may run full-circle on the originator and generate ethical and legal liabilities.

COMMUNITY AND PROBLEM SOLVING POLICING (COPPS)

Chapter 1, PHILOSOPHY, introduced the principles of problem-oriented policing (POP). The SARA planning model need not be a separate entity, but should serve as the foundation for community-oriented policing (COP). Problem-solving policing requires accurate intelligence, strategic, and tactical planning. Problem-oriented policing is the vehicle for problem-solving and decision-making. The following case study illustrates the above mentioned strategies.

* PROBLEM-SOLVING: CASE STUDY

In a small town in Pennsylvania, a local park that was once a safe, quiet area that local residents and children used for recreation became the object of repeated calls for police service. Many of the complaints involved vandalism and substance abuse-related offenses. For example, drug dealers and juveniles terrorized elderly residents in an adjacent apartment complex and destroyed property owned by citizens living in the area surrounding the park. The vandalism appeared to result directly from drug and alcohol abuse. Also, the littered appearance of the park area and the over-grown shrubs that hid an adjacent railroad property encouraged these deviant behaviors. As a result, this area served as a crime "hot spot" for drug abuse and sexual activity that, in turn, helped generate a fear of crime among residents.

Using the SARA (scanning, analysis, response, and assessment) model of problem solving, law enforcement agencies can address crime in particular areas of a community. The SARA model helps police reduce the crime rate, as well as the fear of crime among citizens.

PROBLEM-SOLVING STRATEGIES

In recent years, the philosophy of community-oriented policing has gained a significant position in American law enforcement procedures. The strategic planning process for the philosophy remains the problem-solving policing model of SARA. [127] These problem-solving strategies focus on crime generators and hot spots that plague law enforcement agencies in the United States. Specific problem-solving activities to eliminate these hot spots include working with citizens through such programs as Neighborhood Watch and coordinating with potential "guardians" (e.g., local business owners and residents) to increase surveillance and territorial control. Law enforcement agencies base SARA solutions to hot spots on information obtained from citizen and crime prevention surveys.

Why focus on hot spots? Residential locations can generate as much as 85 percent of the repeat calls for service. Moreover, research indicates that in many communities, more than 50 percent of the calls for service come from only 10 percent of the locations. [128] Identifying these hot spots through crime analysis and crime-specific planning can lower the level and the fear of crime.

SCANNING: IDENTIFYING THE PROBLEM

Why are crime prevention surveys and crime-specific planning important? Community involvement remains the essential ingredient for reducing the fear of crime. Crime prevention surveys provide core information concerning criminal behavior for police patrol and Neighborhood Watch programs.

After developing criminal intelligence, police officers can use this information as the foundation for coordinating community programs. Without the development of accurate criminal information, little opportunity exists for planned citizen involvement or successful tactical strategies. Moreover, only when agencies conduct the assessment of the present condition (Where is the department now?), can they project its future status (Where is the department going?). Therefore, prevention represents an ongoing process that requires planning strategies, implementing responses, evaluating effectiveness, and modifying approaches.

Crime prevention surveys gather information that can help police officers eliminate the motives, opportunities, and means for individuals to commit crimes. This information provides officers with the exact times and kinds of offenses committed, the offenders' methods of operation, the targets of attack, and the crime generators and hot spot locations. Furthermore, crime prevention surveys can determine the underlying causes of crime, aid in eliminating opportunities for offenders to detect victims or criminal targets, and assess situations based on individual needs.

After gathering this information and carefully analyzing the problem and causative factors, officers can implement appropriate responses. For example, they can pinpoint hot spot locations through Geographic Information Systems (GIS) mapping. Then, they can outline the problem by numbering the offenses, plotting the times and places crimes occurred, and noting the techniques used to commit the crimes. Finally, by establishing goals and priorities to determine where they need police patrols, officers can attack these hot spots in an effective and efficient manner.

Although similar to problem-oriented policing, crime-specific planning approaches crime problems by considering the underlying factors that characterize each type of offense. Crime-specific planning aids problem-oriented policing by using proactive measures aimed at protecting citizens and property. [129] For example, law enforcement agencies task police personnel and allocate equipment based on crime analysis results and crime-specific programming. Also, crime analysis can improve community relations by graphically illustrating criminal patterns to citizens' Crime Watch programs. The SARA model expanded on these early strategies by examining the geographic, cultural, and economic aspects of the hot spot location, along with the relationship between the victim and the offender.

ANALYSIS: CHOOSING THE RESPONSE

Officers must understand the actions and interactions between offenders, victims, and the crime scene before developing appropriate responses. Criminal intelligence information gathered in crime prevention surveys serves as the foundation for this analysis. However, the intelligence process also includes analysis and dissemination of criminal information.

A crime cannot occur without the presence of three elements that form a crime triangle: the offender, the victim, and the crime scene or location. [130] Accordingly, crime analysts must discover as much as possible about all three sides, while examining the links between each. By asking who, what, when, where, how, why, and why not about each side of the triangle, as well as observing the way these elements interact, analysts can understand what prompts certain crime problems. [131]

Law enforcement agencies use crime potential forecasts to attempt to determine future crime events. Forecasting depends primarily on historical analysis of cyclic, periodic, or specific events. The historical data can explain the context of the present and anticipated crime, while focusing on problem locations. Officers benefit from using crime maps and computers when targeting crime sites and time frames from past experience and criminal information. Information from crime series and pattern analysis can provide assistance when estimating future target locations and times. For example, analysis of the neighborhood spatial, cultural, and psychological characteristics may produce valuable crime-specific data.

Spatial analysis generally focuses on a small geographical area and includes physical, demographic, and crime history characteristics. Geocoding neighborhood "hot spots" on a map that have a frequency of crime occurrences shows where most illegal acts occur, and subsequently, targets the locations and the levels of crime intensity. The crime analyst then applies the techniques of spatial analysis and crime templating.

Determining Spatial Relations

Criminals do not move randomly through neighborhoods—a predictable pattern usually exists. A criminal who is motivated to commit crimes uses cues to locate, identify, and target sites and hot spots. For example, familiarity with a neighborhood reinforces criminal patterns, a process often referred to as cognitive mapping or mental imaging. Consequently, offenders plan potential crimes and make decisions based on template information. [132] Designated hot spots provide criminals with mental images for safe havens— places where criminals feel they can commit crimes with less chance of detection.

Microanalysis of criminal behavior links this criminal conduct to geography. This type of analysis represents the processing and selection of mental cues and images selected by the offender. Therefore, police leaders use templates to understand offender patterns and predict likely courses of action.

Identifying Crime Templates

Crime prevention surveys also can assist in identifying the criminal mindset or template. Templates provide a means for continuous identification of offenders and their vulnerabilities. The templates can help reveal travel patterns and methods of operation and help officers predict how and where offenders may select activities and crime sites. The hot spots serve as focus points for analysis and crime prevention responses. In summary, templates have several advantages. They help: 1) estimate locations where critical events and activities might occur, 2) identify victims and crime scenes, 3) project time-related events within crime sites or hot spots, 4) present GIS mapping techniques, and 5) determine a guide for tactical decisions and proactive patrol allocations. While a template may be unable to predict exactly when and where a criminal will strike next, it provides information that can help police choose appropriate courses of action. For example, in many instances, police officers have determined that templates indicate crime often occurs only short distances from an offender's residence.

Travel Distance: Pathways to Crime

Offenders gain template knowledge from familiar environmental experiences (e.g. living in a certain geographical area). Most property crimes, such as vandalism, are committed within 2 miles' travel distance of the offender's residence. Moreover, offenders may avoid targets closer to home because of the risk of apprehension. Opportunity, reward, and fear of arrest determine the difference between "good" and "poor" crime hot spots. [133] An area that provides cover and concealment represents a favorable hot spot, whereas a well-lit, heavily patrolled area would prove a poor choice for criminal activity.

Analyzing Crime Data

In the park case study, police officers found that crime-specific analysis and crime templates revealed that the pattern of criminal behavior was restricted to a small geographical area. Crime statistics revealed a history of offenses surrounding the park. The data indicated that the offenders moved to and from an adjacent jurisdiction, often using a bridge joining the two areas.

The offenders and the victims remained close in time and space—only a walk of a distance of less than 400 yards. Mapping techniques traced the offenders to a particular residential area less than 2 miles from where they lived.

In this case, the juveniles obtained their drugs or alcohol and then hid in the overgrown brush along the railroad tracks. This secluded hot spot was adjacent to the bridge and park. The unkept vegetation obstructed the local residents' view, making natural surveillance impossible. Illegal activities remained undetectable by anyone passing through the area, thereby creating a hot spot. The guardians were unable to view and engage in surveillance. Poor park maintenance contributed to the destruction of the social environment. Crime template analysis revealed that when youths used drugs and alcohol, they committed more crimes. This social disinhibitor, alcohol, prompted them to target victims and engage in criminal behavior. An ideal crime site or safe haven reinforced these behaviors. A minimal risk of apprehension existed; therefore, the crime site continued to serve as a hot spot.

CRIME ANALYSIS AND GIS MAPPING

Crime-specific analysis and crime prevention surveys can systematically appraise the social and geographic features of a hot spot and safe haven. For example, in the case study, crime analysis revealed that sellers and buyers could monitor the approach of the police officers or individuals who might report illegal activities. The physical terrain and geography provided an awning for drug transactions. Moreover, offenders created several escape routes by opening holes in the surrounding park fence. After acquiring relevant accurate information, law enforcement officers developed numerous proactive responses.

Law Enforcement Responses

In the case study, law enforcement agencies developed and implemented several countermeasures based on crime prevention survey responses: (1) installing closed-circuit television surveillance cameras, (2) repairing damaged fences, (3) improving lighting, (4) locking the park fence during the evening hours, (5) limiting access, and (6) posting and enforcing such signs as "Park Rules and Regulations." In addition, pruning the shrubbery around the park and creating a defensible space improved natural surveillance. These corrective actions gave a visible warning that the police and local residents cared about the park and were determined to abolish criminal behaviors. For example, youthful offenders used a pay telephone to page drug dealers. However, with the cooperation of the telephone company, officers had the telephone booth removed. Coordination with railroad authorities helped eliminate overgrown vegetation that blocked public view. Officers also contacted the guardians with the best view and encouraged them to report suspicious activities in the park and surrounding railroad area.

The emphasis on crime analysis and proactive patrol reduced the need for redundant calls for services. Crime-specific planning improved tactical responses and freed patrol officers to respond to emergency situations more effectively. Spatial analysis and crime templates served as the foundation for identifying hot spots and patrol techniques in this community.

The concept of random patrol proved less productive than employing directed-deterrent patrol and target-oriented patrol. The department changed patrol coverage based on offender location and crime site. In the case study, directed-deterrent patrol and target-oriented patrol provided the best strategies.

Directed patrol differs from traditional patrol methods because patrol officers perform certain specific, predetermined preventive functions. Patrol movements are planned on the basis of crime-specific planning and systematic procedures. Officers perform preventive activities on the basis of spatial analysis, crime incidents, offender characteristics, methods of operating, and offender templates. For example, in some geographical areas, foot and bicycle patrols have several advantages because of terrain.

With target-oriented patrol, when officers are not responding to calls they may monitor particular routes to interrupt criminal patterns developed under analysis and crime-specific planning. Agencies target high-risk areas and selected types of crimes using location and offender-oriented patrol.

Victim Responses

The level and fear of crime lessen after communities successfully establish Neighborhood Watch and other community programs. Citizens feel safer when crime prevention initiatives give them an opportunity to become involved in their communities. Police departments can strategically employ bicycle and foot patrols, as well as coordinate with parents to determine their willingness to cooperate with nearby guardians. Police presence and high-profile tactics help to reduce fear of criminal behavior.

A crime newsletter and ongoing communication between the police and citizens proved beneficial to community residents in the case study. For example, in addition to the strategies discussed, monthly neighborhood meetings addressed accurate crime statistics and steps taken to improve the situation. Cooperation and communication between the police and local residents resulted in a reduction of crime, as well as the fear of crime.

Offender Responses

The police discovered that the same group of individuals committed a series of related crimes. Several unique, repeated incidents (e.g.,ringing doorbells of residents who lived in the immediate park facility) identified specific group activities. Crime-specific analysis revealed that drugs, alcohol, and party-oriented activities became the common denominators for these acts. Psychological disinhibitors such as drugs and alcohol often facilitate vandalism. These ingredients undermine social or moral inhibitions and impair judgment and restraint, making offenders less aware that they are breaking the law. Corrective actions (controlling drinking in public and semipublic areas) limit these factors.

In addition, during the summer, teenagers who do not participate in meaningful activities have too much leisure time and become bored. As a result, they loiter at many community locations and have more opportunities for criminal activities. The creation of summer recreation programs may assist in more productive leisure activities for these teenagers. Coordination with the partners, school district, and recreation department may provide some solutions.

ASSESSMENT: MEASURING RESULTS

When agencies design community crime prevention programs, they often neglect the assessment process, which measures the intervention results concerning the level and fear of crime. Statistical analysis of citizen surveys will help determine successful interventions. The evaluation phase consisted of a pre-assessment that provided information on hot spots and a post response assessment designed to evaluate the effectiveness of the policing tactics.

Moreover, prevention programs generally fail to address the effect of the program outside the target area. In the case study, areas external to the park should serve as control groups and receive comparison with the target area. The results of the intervention effort show that the level of crime tends to shift away from the park to areas there other law enforcement departments have not implemented crime prevention efforts.

A decreased level of crime that can be measured by such factors as lower levels of vandalism and drug abuse will provide the most dramatic indicator of the program's success. Another evaluation indicator of success is the level of the fear of crime. In the case study, a decrease in the fear of crime among individuals living near the park after the department implemented crime prevention measures indicated successful problem-solving.

Agencies should not displace the problem to another area. In the case study, the problems in the park could be displaced to a nearby jurisdiction across the bridge. Crime displacement–the movement from the crime hot spot to alternate crime sites–can occur in certain areas, by time, method of attack, victim of attack, and change of criminal offense. Departments must consider displacement when evaluating crime prevention programs.

FOCUS POINTS: PLANNING AND PROBLEM SOLVING

Crime prevention requires constant vigilance and thorough crime-specific planning. A crime prevention survey provides the basic tool for accomplishing these goals. This tool assists police leaders in identifying hot spots and crime templates. Crime analysis allows police leaders to become proactive. The strategic planning and anticipation of events can produce valuable tactical information. The SARA model can assist law enforcement agencies by focusing on specific problem-solving approaches.

Accurate criminal intelligence remains essential to the process of analysis and the ultimate success of problem-solving policing. Once departments acquire the necessary data, they can develop and implement analyses and tailor-made responses to eliminate the one or all sides of the crime triangle—the offender, the victim, and the location of the crime.

In a time of diminishing resources, the police must learn to do more with less. The cost of crime prevention is minimal; however, the opportunities and rewards are optimal.

CONCLUSION

The strategic planning process requires the support of the chief and the whole department. Critical thinking and strategy planning are essential when developing vision and direction. Participation of all ranks must help secure the successful achievement of a department's goals and objectives.

The plans must be pursued and progress should be evaluated within certain time-frames. When possible, police planning should normally precede the decision-making process. The terms, planning, problem-solving, and decision-making are interconnected and form the foundation of the leadership process.

Finally, excellent strategic and tactical planning does not assure success, but it may increase the probability. Furthermore, if vision is essential to successful leadership and direction, the strategic planning process should: (1) help define the mission, (2) keep the department on track, (3) pursue goals and objectives and (4) evaluate whether the department has been successful. Strategic planning provides the inspiration, vision and path to successful outcomes.

Chapter 11
EVALUATION: HOW DO WE KNOW WHEN WE HAVE ARRIVED?

Effectiveness is doing the right things,
and efficiency is doing things right.
- PETER F. DRUCKER

Evaluation is necessary to redirect the leadership process and to help reorient the planning process. It answers three crucial questions: (1) Have we arrived? (2) Where are we now? (3) Where do we go from here? It provides the map for developing strategic goals and objectives; furthermore, it provides the plans for directing officers to specific tasks.

If police leaders plan their vision and journey well, evaluation will be part of the process. Evaluation research is essential to the measurement of programming effects, goals, and objectives that support the accomplishment of the mission. This chapter seeks to emphasize the need for defining excellence and developing evaluation systems.

Quality is what excellence is about! Without evaluations how can we measure achievement? With the exception of a few studies on patrol and domestic violence, the lack of scientific evaluation constitutes an information gap in policing. The main advantage of implementing community-oriented and problem-solving policing is applied research.

THE PURPOSE OF EVALUATION: WHY EVALUATE?

Evaluation assesses and determines the quality of outcomes. The evaluator obtains information that guides police leaders in the decision-making process. This process reduces uncertainty and assists officers and citizens in the reduction of crime. However, research methods must be accurate; over simplification of issues may misinform decision-makers, obstructing their plans for the future.

As described in **CHAPTER 3**, **SENIOR LEADERSHIP**, the question of "Where are we going?" is designed to define "vision" and clarify the department's goals. Therefore, goals and objectives secure direction toward the completion of the vision. Tasks and objectives are starting points toward the goals. The department's goals are major sub-components of the vision. The evaluation process helps decipher whether we have "arrived," and points the department's vision and goals in new directions.

Evaluation is an indispensable tool when reorienting planning cycles and implementing the new planning process: Where do we go now? The evaluation process is essential when adjusting the vision, mission and values statement. It helps design new goals and objectives and formulates new action plans. The newly defined tasks, conditions, and standards should help guide police leaders. Evaluation research is an applied social science intended to provide valid information for future applications.

THE STARTING POINT: WHERE ARE WE NOW?

Once the assessment of the present state (Where are we now?) is conducted, the future state (Where are we going?) can be projected. Timely evaluations help determine future changes. Assessment and measurement should be taken seriously when conducting evaluation research, which provides feedback in measurable terms.

A comparison of the present state versus future state conditions is essential to successfully evaluating and formulating the problem. In summary, the evaluation process offers several advantages to police leaders. It:

*   Compares the impact of completed goals and objectives

*   Documents the consequences of program objectives

* Compares performance data from present and future situations

* Specifies and provides relevant information for judging future conditions that may impact on the mission

* Describes and interprets action plans in a wider context of the mission and values statement

* Judges program efforts critically

Determining a department's present position will be essential to the selection of a department's goals and objectives. The assessment process must include evaluating the whole picture and identifying what needs to be changed. This may be the most difficult part of the process. One may encounter considerable resistance to analysis and change.

ASSESSING STRENGTHS AND WEAKNESSES

A primary consideration is identifying and improving weaknesses. The strengths of the department tend to proceed as expected. Working on the 20% of the causes of negative outcomes offers the best opportunity for improvement. Identifying the goals, objectives and action plans for changing the 20% should be a top priority.

"As goals and objectives are considered, the Pareto Principle should come into play. The Pareto Principle states that 80% of the problems in any system result from 20% of the causes. Effective leaders pay attention to the 20% and concentrate on improvement in those areas. The percentage is not always 20/80, but it is usually close. Consider the following:

1. 20% of your activities may produce 80% of your accomplishments.

2. 20% of your problem officers may account for 80% of the department's problems.

3. 20% of your outstanding officers may account for 80% of your department's successes." [134]

This does not mean that one should ignore the 80% that is going well. However, the most promising outcomes will be found by concentrating on the 20% that need addressing. There is a natural tendency to avoid what is distasteful and possibly ignore the primary needs of the department.

DEFINING STRATEGIC GOALS

As described in **CHAPTER 3, SENIOR LEADERSHIP**, and **CHAPTER 10, CRITICAL THINKING, PLANNING AND PROBLEM-SOLVING**, defined strategic goals and objectives are essential to plotting the course. A community-oriented and problem-solving philosophy develops the mission and values statements. Broad goals then extrapolate from those documents and serve as the foundation for the objectives. Objectives are then refined into action-programs and relevant tasks, which serve as the building blocks for the evaluation process.

EVALUATION: PERFORMANCE INDICATORS

American policing has recently experienced an interest in evaluation research, not the least reason for which is justification. The evaluation process should identify realistic and measurable performance indicators. If evaluation research is to help identify strengths and weaknesses, it must be relevant.

EVALUATION: POLICE ORGANIZATIONAL STRUCTURE

A lack of faith and trust in police officers results in closer control and supervision. This structure has been quite successful in many aspects. However, it needs to be modified to accommodate the community-oriented and problem-solving policing (COPPS) approach.

The organizational structure of policing has changed little in the modern era of policing. The basis for this structure is paramilitary with power coming from the top, down a tightly organized chain of command. This bureaucratic organization tends to stifle initiative and creativity. The new structure should emphasize flexibility and participatory management. The emphasis would shift from organization by function to organization by area and neighborhoods. The decision-making process would be decentralized from the top management and middle leaders to sergeants and police officers, serving in a line capacity.

The COPPS approach has five central characteristics that distinguish it from the professional model: "(1) workers can have substantive interest in their work; (2) officers' discretion can be encouraged and supported though community engagement, problem solving, and other strategies; (3) decentralization of decision-making to line personnel in neighborhood specific assignments, can be effective; (4) increased participatory management; and (5) more involvement of top executives in strategic planning and implementation. While these are considered defining characteristics of organizations during the current community problem-solving era, we are quick to point out that few if any police organizations have fully implemented this model." [135]

Many community-oriented and problem-solving programs have been established across the nation. Unfortunately, little transformation in organizational structure has followed these philosophical changes. Community-oriented programs have been established without the foundation for change being in place. Therefore, organizational reform has remained static. Organizational structure should move toward reform to implement the movement toward community participation. The starting point for change can be found in the evaluation of a department's command structure.

EVALUATING STAFF AND INFORMATION

The chief must have an excellent staff in order to evaluate. Most successful leaders gain their effectiveness through their staff and support system. Staff personnel and logistical support help determine a leader's success. Excellent leaders understand that they must surround themselves with superior staff members who provide additional support and direction for their officers. Surround yourself with the best, and excellence will take care of itself!

Selecting the right staff personnel means finding independent people who think critically and solve problems. To obtain an excellent staff, senior leaders must evaluate candidates carefully. To avoid "miscommunication" and secure accurate information, police executives must avoid selecting people who tell you what they think you want to hear, rather than the truth.

ESTIMATING AND EVALUATING THE SITUATION

If leadership is not a status but a role, it is to be played by the department's teams and police officers. A clear understanding of the tactical situation is the essential starting point. An explanation of situational analysis can be found in **CHAPTER 10, CRITICAL THINKING, PLANNING AND PROBLEM SOLVING**. The accurate assessment of the present situation is required for a leader to apply the appropriate leadership style and skills. Strategic and tactical planning and operating policies help facilitate a speedy response to rapidly changing environments. Police training remains the foundation for rapid responses. As described in **CHAPTER 3, SENIOR LEADERSHIP**, the mission, values statement, goals, and objectives remain the framework for decision-making. Problem-oriented policing and crime-specific planning serve as basic analytical tools to be applied to each situation.

EVALUATION: COMMUNITY POLICING

Once the community-oriented philosophy is established, the next step is to engage in problem-solving. To implement the problem-solving approach, evaluation must be considered, for it is a necessary part of the strategic and tactical problem-solving strategy of the COPPS philosophy.

EVALUATION: CULTURE AND CHANGE

The analysis and assessment of police organizational structure and cultural dimensions should prove valuable. If the assessment of the community is to be successful, the evaluation process must start within the department. The transition from "chain-of-command" to autonomy and problem-solving is not an easy transition. Assessing internal resistance helps facilitate the community-oriented philosophy.

EVALUATION: PERSONNEL

The evaluation of police personnel includes reaction to the problem-solving approach and measuring the degree of acceptance of the community-oriented philosophy. The assessment of resistance and cooperation is important to the successful implementation of the community-oriented philosophy. Central to this process is the evaluation of police behaviors and performance.

EVALUATION: INTEGRITY AND ETHICS

Police decentralization and the empowering of officers to operate freely in the community may not be without problems. The evaluation and assessment process may dismiss or affirm the notion that corruption and other ethical problems may result because of accountability issues. One must evaluate ethical issues that impact on policing: (1) leadership; (2) departmental values and policies; (3) supervision; (4) disciplinary systems; (5) reward structure; and (6) insufficient training.

EVALUATION OF STRATEGIES

Community-oriented policing must succeed at problem-solving. The ability to measure effectiveness will be found in the evaluation process. Without the accurate information generated by an effective evaluation program, community-oriented policing will remain a philosophy, not an effective problem-solving approach. An effective evaluation process identifies the best components of the problem-solving strategies as well as those that are ineffective and non-productive.

EVALUATION: COMMUNITY

The last and most important phase of evaluation concerns the impact on neighborhoods. This kind of evaluation varies between cities and localities, but some remain consistent: (1) fear of crime; (2) crime and disorder; (3) availability of drugs; (4) police performance and effectiveness; and (5) tension between the police and the community.

FOCUS POINTS: EVALUATION

The evaluation process must be comprehensive and thorough for policing to succeed in the twenty-first century; evaluation is the bridge to successful social change. Police leaders can engage the evaluation process, that is, the scientific identification of departmental personnel and staffing requirements.

Staff with the expertise to participate in extensive evaluations would include staff psychologists, social workers, and professional planners. Police organizational structure will need to accommodate these new staff professionals by initiating an era of scientific policing, professional planning and evaluation.

A partnership needs to develop with outside researchers and evaluators. The trend has been for police administrators and researchers to view each other with suspicion and mistrust. Both groups need to identify roles and responsibilities that will build the foundation for excellent evaluation. Some conflict is likely to remain because of separate roles. However, boundaries can be established and honest dialogue maintained to enhance communication. Police leaders must understand the need for researchers and evaluators to conserve their neutral and objective stances.

CONCLUSION

The characteristics of effective and efficient police organizations are: (1) excellent leadership; (2) superior staff officers; and (3) superb strategic planning and evaluation. How do we achieve these characteristics? The answers are to be found in scientific research and evaluation.

The basic steps in evaluation research include: (1) problem formulation; (2) the identification of goals and objectives; (3) design of instruments; (4) evaluation model; (5) data collection; (6) data analysis; (7) findings; and (8) applications. Evaluation is the primary means for improving decision-making and improving future programming.

Vision defines destination. Strategic planning offers a vehicle for getting there. Evaluation serves as the navigational instrument for the journey. The evaluation process allows police leaders to stay on course.

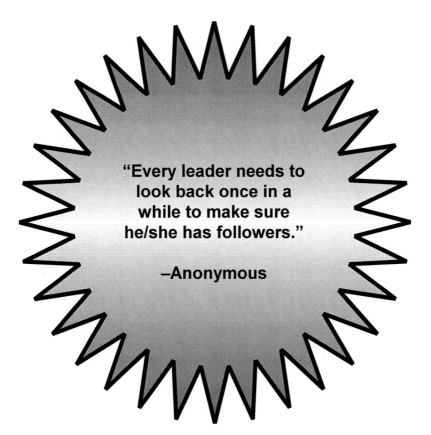

"Every leader needs to
look back once in a
while to make sure
he/she has followers."

–Anonymous

Chapter 12
EFFECTIVE LEADERSHIP:
10 "CAN DO" POINTS

---

*To lead in the 21st Century...You will
be required to have both competence
and character.*
- GENERAL NORMAN SCHWARZKOPF

This chapter summarizes 10 "can do" points for effective leadership. The twenty-first century will require the application and continuous refinement of essential "can do" leadership skills. Successful leaders do more than manage; they communicate and listen. The "can do" leadership fundamentals form the basis for empathetic communication, which emphasizes trust. When leaders provide feedback, communication is accurate and trust is high. This chapter concentrates on what the leader must do to gain followship: (1) communicate vision and high expectations, (2) demonstrate character and competence and (3) show concern for officers and civilians.

"CAN DO" POINT #1:
COMMUNITY-ORIENTED POLICING

We expect too much from police and demand too little from our citizens. The community-oriented philosophy (COP) is focused on neighborhood leadership. The COP + POP = COPPS strategy reinforces a community's ability to create safe neighborhoods. The problem-solving process (POP) is applied block by block to address problems of a particular neighborhood while Neighborhood Watch Programs support the goals of the community-oriented philosophy.

Neighborhood Watch police coordinators are selected for their communication skills and training. Coordinators are trained in Neighborhood Watch and Crime Prevention techniques prior to assignment. Competencies in basic leadership skills and group dynamics will enhance citizen communication and trust.

The most promising candidates are recruited and selected as Block Watch Captains, who need support and training. However, citizen participation is essential to successful outcomes, and is based on collaboration and mutual respect.

Neighborhood Watch Programs require planning and dedication. Coordination, recruitment, and motivated leadership are necessary for success. The most difficult task is to maintain citizen interest and participation, which effective leadership helps to ensure.

"CAN DO" POINT #2:
CHARACTER AND ETHICS

Truthfulness and kept promises indicate character; however, keeping a pledge can be difficult if honesty and conviction are penalized. Telling the truth and keeping promises are essential when communicating and developing relationships with police officers. Leaders who waver on trust issues may be permanently tarnished in the eyes of their officers. Leaders with reputations for competency, truth, and integrity motivate officers to follow and comply because the latter have faith in the leadership. Officers respect and support leaders who demonstrate trustworthiness.

Taking credit for ideas that belong to another police officer destroys morale and damages initiative. More importantly, failure to share recognition results in an information vacuum; conversely, acknowledging creative suggestions produces new ideas. In addition, further cooperation, loyalty, and support benefit the department. Credit police officers for the contributions they make to the department; stealing credit is dishonest. Publicly highlight an officer's personal achievement, ideas, and outstanding accomplishments.

When officers know their leaders are honest, that they refrain from using their leadership positions for personal gain, officers will trust leadership. Officers highly regard police leaders who avoid abusing privileges at the expense of their officers.

A dishonest leader weakens moral authority and may not regain respect amidst ridicule and criticism. Dishonesty undermines leadership influence of officers in the field. Honest police leaders earn respect through the proper uses of power. Leaders who put the needs of their officers first earn cooperation and support.

Police leaders who demonstrate character build a reputation for reliability and credibility. Leaders who fulfill promises and demonstrate moral courage build followership. Excellent leaders stand for what is just, place duty and honor first, and accept responsibility when they are wrong. Leadership demands more than trustworthiness and character; leaders must display competence. Leaders who are incompetent are untrustworthy and unreliable.

"CAN DO" POINT #3:
SENIOR LEADERSHIP

There is a place for orders, even when the department has developed a participatory or empowering climate. Senior leaders may confront a situation where direct orders are appropriate, even mandatory. Be specific about what is expected. If possible, be flexible and allow officers to respond using their own methods for accomplishing the task. Officers may fail to successfully complete tasks because they misunderstood what was expected of them. Vague, conflicting, or unnecessary orders may also result in an officer's failure to comply. Police officers respond to clear, concise, and easy-to-follow orders.

Most importantly, never give an order that is beyond an officer's ability. Ask the officer if he or she knows how to complete the assignment; and, if necessary, repeat the order for clarification. Ask questions to determine if the officer understands the assignment. Evaluate the results for positive outcomes. Empowering officers does not mean relinquishing all the control over results.

Written orders define the objective or outcome but not necessarily the method, which should be left to the officer, along with the proper authority to successfully complete the assignment. Telling officers how to complete assignments decreases motivation, initiative and ingenuity. Officers should develop their own plan of action. However, leadership should remain available for support, questions and progress evaluation.

Establish your authority to issue the order; then determine who needs the information next, follow the chain of command. Direct the orders to a specific line of authority, never passing officers in the chain of command. This circumvents conflict with previous orders and immediate supervisors. Conflicting orders create poor morale, confusion, and lowers motivation. Moreover, officer compliance will be minimal.

A final word of caution: never issue an unenforceable order. Issuing orders that cannot be enforced by leaders is self-destructive. Experienced leaders determine if orders have been executed. If they have not, find out why. Discipline if necessary. However non-compliance may be the leader's fault, and this must be accurately determined. Collaboration may improve performance, and reliable advice may be useful.

"CAN DO" POINT #4:
MIDDLE MANAGERS

Successful middle managers who delegate and empower officers conduct personal inspections. The concepts of empowerment do not preclude inspecting results. Personal accountability for positive outcomes defines police leaders. Inspections guarantee that assignments will be completed, responsibility delegated, and accountability received. The inspection function is often neglected, yet it remains a primary leadership function.

Inspections may be neglected for many reasons. The officer is safe and comfortable, the field full of potential risks. In some cases, fear may be a factor. The fear of committing a mistake or embarrassing oneself or others may be a consideration.

A "can do" leader knows the area and prepares for the inspection in advance. Scheduling and planning for inspections is indispensable. Learn as much as possible about the officer and understand the tasks they perform. "Can do" leaders know how to turn inspections into an opportunity to meet officers and improve relationships. Treat people with respect and dignity during the inspection. Demonstrating a sincere interest in the officer improves morale. However, a hostile inspection affects subordinates adversely.

While leaders always allow officers to explain the logic of their performance, they should never punish all for the mistakes of one. Group punishment only produces low morale. Make every effort to achieve accountability. Target a specific behavior, not specific officers.

One should not show favoritism during inspections, and not engage in popularity contests, which erodes respect. Further, inspection results should specify recommendations that are not vindictive. Criticism should be issued privately. Remember to praise laudable accomplishments.

Generally, officers perform well when inspected because inspections help identify priorities. Even seemingly unimportant things, if neglected, can lead to severe consequences. For example, defective safety equipment can have severe repercussions. The safety belts in the police cruiser can be crucial in an accident situation. Inspect and remember: Never inspected, most likely neglected!

"CAN DO" POINT #5:
SERGEANTS AND POLICE OFFICERS

The sergeant leads through personal and position power. The emphasis should be on the former. Personal power exercises influence in the sergeant's absence. The key to exercising personal power is established in the pacing process, which establishes communication and rapport with the officer. The process includes: sharing experiences, assumptions, and making officers comfortable. The sergeant matches officer range of behavior and develops connecting points. The sergeant assesses officer responses to leadership by pacing officers. Once the sergeant has a relationship with the officers, they will be more likely to follow.

Successful leading motivates officers to keep pace with sergeants by shaping officer behavior and performance. To pace officers, the sergeant must have a range of behavior that parallels the officers. The secret of establishing rapport with the officer remains with the pacing process. To pace the officer, the sergeant matches behavior or gets "in sync" so the follower feels comfortable with the leader. [136]

This means achieving alignment in words, voice characteristics, and non-verbal communication. The primary objective is to establish a rapport that positively influences performance and enables the sergeant to lead. [137]

Communicating and leading encourages officers to keep pace with leaders, thereby motivating officers to consider leader behavior and response. Pacing necessitates listening.

To "synchronize" with an officer, one must attend to his concerns and complaints. [138]

Effective sergeants attend to officer complaints. To discover what officers think, one must listen with an open mind. Allow officers to discuss their personal problems, issues, and concerns. Leaders take care of details; anxiety often causes officers to focus exclusively on concerns and problems.

The act of listening is the highest complement a leader can give an officer, and often all the officer wants or needs. When leaders know and understand each officer better, they more readily discover officer concerns. Sergeants who actively listen to officers effectively build rapport. Listening builds greater officer self-respect and enables them to vent hostility. Listening demonstrates leadership interest in officers.

Treat officers with respect and allow them to speak without interruption. This procedure initiates empathetic listening. After listening to the officer, communicate your understanding, thus disarming an officer positioned adversarily. This technique reduces the pressure an officer may feel and creates a climate of friendship, rather than warfare.

Conflict reduces when officers determine that the leadership is not the enemy. Ask what assistance is needed. In many cases, complaints can be avoided by simply giving officers what they want. When this is possible, both the leadership and the officer can feel good about the outcome.

If a leader fails to listen, morale is destroyed and officers feel rejected. Paying attention makes officers feel good about their leadership. When officers respect their leaders, everyone wins, the department and the citizens.

Make it easy for officers to contact leaders, and explain the grievance procedures to everyone. Do not demonstrate hostility toward the individual who has a grievance. Provide the solution in a timely manner and contact the officer personally concerning the decision.

Concern is what leadership is all about. The only way to completely understand the officer is to give undivided attention. Handling complaints is the responsibility of an effective sergeant. This effort reduces grievances and legal conflicts.

Finally, leaders sometimes equate complaints with trouble, an attitude that can spell disaster when a serious complaint is unwittingly stifled or blocked. Always grant hearings, even to a chronic complainer.

"CAN DO" POINT #6:
MOTIVATION

Police leaders who perform at a minimum level should not expect a maximum effort from their officers. For example, the sergeant who arrives late and fails to follow the department's regulations is a poor role model. Police officers will adopt the same attitudes and mirror their leadership's behaviors.

One cannot expect to inspire others without being motivated and committed to the department's mission and goals. Leaders who set the example through positive and enthusiastic behaviors will motivate officers to respond in kind. Police leaders are in the best position to set high standards and achieve the maximum effort from their officers.

Successful leadership motivates by setting the example, and by identifying and training correct behaviors. Positive field behaviors should be praised, for police officers need recognition and approval, both powerful incentives. Police officers who take pride in their work exert the maximum effort the public demands.

When officers enter police service, they often perform routine tasks without personal goals. Leaders who help officers identify personal goals will be respected and supported. Leadership that cares, supports, and demonstrates concern for the individual officers demands respect.

Helping officers get promoted and setting immediate professional goals can be beneficial to the individual as well as the police agency. Police leaders who support officers and help them develop professionally are remembered. Telling officers they are exceptional is often self-fulfilling, while emphasizing the negative may promote the worst. With professional pride, all things are possible.

"Can do" leadership empowers officers and builds confidence, self-esteem, and ultimately competence. Police leaders gain power by sharing it because their source of power comes from others. When releasing personal power, leaders can achieve significant goals and objectives. These goals and objectives include preventing and solving crimes. The failure to delegate, build teams and listen to officers' needs, destroys motivation.

"CAN DO" POINT #7:
TRAINING

Creative training builds trust and confidence. Training should prepare and build problem-solving skills. Tough training pays off! It brings officers together and builds morale. Repetition builds skills and endurance. Placing officers in difficult circumstances improves performance and understanding. Excellent leaders share the hardships of rugged training with their officers. They don't leave them in the rain, at the range, while seeking their own comfort.

Tough training inoculates officers against stressful encounters because it builds confidence. Training helps officers develop the skills necessary to perform the requirements of the mission. This is best accomplished through realistic training. Over-training transcends the mastery of basic skills.

Over-training produces predictable, reliable performance and teaches officers how to perform under stress. Vigorous training encourages confidence and promotes positive outcomes for real conflicts. It even saves lives!

Men and women training together, working toward common goals, are less susceptible to tension and stress within and outside the department. Well trained officers are likely to cooperate under stressful conditions and perform the mission successfully. Realistic training prepares for hardship and develops the mental and physical toughness needed during difficulty and stress.

"CAN DO" POINT #8:
HUMAN RESOURCES

Human resources management is at the heart of successful police administration and a core leadership responsibility. To plan for the future, police leaders develop today the vision for meeting requirements. Leaders are responsible for developing and establishing a strategic officer recruitment plan. Excellent recruiting is the active pursuit of potential applicants for the purpose of influencing them to apply for positions in the police department.

The most important strategic objective remains recruiting. Without adequate recruiting and selection, other police strategic objectives cannot be accomplished. The recruitment of excellent police officers enhances the human potential of the entire department. The recruitment program must select the most capable officers.

Once the best officers are selected, their leaders should know each officer as an individual. Then it will be possible to match each individual's talents to specific positions. Leaders cannot always tailor the position to the officer, though this would be advantageous.

When a leader makes every officer feel important, morale, efficiency and productivity increase. The importance of treating each officer as a valued member of the department cannot be underestimated. "Can do" leaders recognize each officer by first and last name. The best technique for accomplishing this is to keep a notebook. Each officer should be listed in the notebook, along with the following information: (1) interests, (2) family history, and (3) hobbies. This kind of concern demonstrates leader interest in officers and is essential to effective leadership.

Treating officers as individuals has many benefits. Job performance is enhanced when the leader understands the capabilities of the officer. Many leaders would admit that it is essential to make their officers feel important; however, few take time to communicate that message. Once the police agency hires the best officers, its leaders should take the time to invest in human resources. Then police leaders will have influence and power that can produce positive results.

Certainly, emotional intelligence remains the key ingredient for a successful police officer. What matters is not what is on the outside, but on the inside. This unique quality must be included in the job description and actively recruited for in the labor market.

"CAN DO" POINT #9:
CONFLICT MANAGEMENT

Communication has many channels, both formal and informal. Police leaders are responsible for developing and maintaining effective communications. The best way to avoid conflict is to keep officers informed. Information vacuums are filled with rumor, fear and conflict. Excellent leaders inform officers about what they are going to do and how it will affect them. Without accurate information, many officers will assume the worst and speculate on outcomes.

Keeping officers informed avoids rumors and gossip. Accurate information helps to reduce friction and misunderstanding. The truth prevents dissatisfaction, alienation, and conflict among officers and helps prevent low morale, eroded confidence, and poor performance.

Provide timely information on up-coming events and new developments. Officer statements like, "Why don't they keep us informed?" impact on anxiety and fear. This is the best way to avoid fear and conflict. Explain the why, where, and how it is going to impact. Leaders, who tell the truth, retain officer respect and confidence. They garner loyal support and cooperation.

Conflict often results from the failure to make timely decisions. Occasionally, a leader is frozen into inactivity by fear, which often results from the improper use of authority. Procrastination and hesitation may result in unnecessary conflict due to a power vacuum and lack of information. The leader must demonstrate the strength of character to make a decision, and announce it at the right time and place to achieve desired results. Making sound decisions builds respect and confidence. If leaders reason logically and reach decisions quickly, officers trust their orders, impressed with the leader's good judgment.

The leader who becomes a trouble-shooter and conflict manager will become known as someone who makes things happen, enhancing the leader's value in a crisis situation. Effective conflict management improves esprit de corps and morale throughout the department.

At the heart of conflict management is an effective grievance procedure. Grievances must be handled expeditiously and resolved at the lowest level possible. The collective bargaining agreement guides the process and should be followed without exception. The agreement should be kept handy.

If there is a violation, act immediately to avoid costly legal fees. Put your officers first, if the issues do not violate the rights of management. In addition, refer to local government charters and ordinances. Resourceful officers find issues that favor their position. Numerous administrative issues regarding police personnel will emerge. Be prepared! Police leaders should not be intimidated by these procedures. If the officer has done something wrong, punish the behavior, not the officer. If punishment is indicated for disciplinary reasons, follow through. Carefully research the case before administering punishment. Once the punishment is announced, administer it or face a credibility gap.

Failure to face this responsibility conflicts with effective, functioning leadership. Officers who identify a leader out of control may abuse the responsibility. Leaders cannot abdicate responsibility because they fear police unions and collective bargaining agreements.

However, if the officer is right, the leader must make every attempt to support the grievance. Leaders who ignore the justice issues, lose officer respect. However, do not promise officers anything beyond leadership authority. Never make promises that cannot be kept. This leads to distrust and emotional reactions. Promise support but not outcomes. Finally, handle complaints or grievances at the lowest level before they become major conflicts.

"CAN DO" POINT #10: PLANNING

There is a tendency not to involve officers in the planning process. In the business world, when problems cannot be solved, leaders call on outside consultants and efficiency experts. In recent years, law enforcement has acted similarly. This can be especially beneficial when grants are involved.

However, some of the best advice concerning problems can come from field police officers. They can make a significant contribution to field operations. Officers may offer the best ideas, and for free. When a leader seeks advice from officers, the latter feel valued and needed, not just another badge number, but part of a team. This is the best way to make someone feel connected to the department. More importantly, they will contribute as full-fledged members of the team. They may feel motivated to make additional contributions. Involving officers in planning makes them feel needed, as if sharing ownership. Acknowledge your needs and officers may commit to the problem and the solution.

Encourage officers to think creatively and participate in the problem-solving process. Advocate communication of ideas and acknowledge the possibility that someone else can make a valuable contribution. Follow through on a good idea and evaluate outcomes with an open mind. Implement an acceptable suggestion immediately. Keep the officer informed and communicate that the solution will be taken seriously. Hopefully, additional suggestions will improve the planning process. Do not forget to recognize and reward all contributions.

Evaluation starts with the officer on the beat, not at the management level. Excellent evaluation procedures should be developed at the officer level and include placing full responsibility on police officers for their own work. When they have the authority to make decisions, officers have the responsibility for positive performance.

However, leaders must allow some mistakes, the latter inherent in the early stages of officer development. The leader is always ultimately accountable for officer performance. "Can do" leaders must take risks to encourage the growth and development of their officers.

Evaluation and decision-making at the officer level provides opportunities to gain experience that will have future value. Allowing a margin of error promotes greater officer effectiveness in the long term.

"Can do" leaders develop a sense of responsibility for the mission and hold their officers accountable for the results. The effective leader follows up on the task and tests for the desired results. However, the main advantage of delegating some of the evaluation process is that it saves valuable time. Supervision time is reduced to a minimum.

Moreover, leaders who demonstrate trust build trust. Developing the officer's sense of responsibility for the evaluation of tasks increases their abilities and opportunities to get the job done. In most cases, officers develop pride in their work and develop respect for themselves and their leaders. More importantly, officers will take initiative and work hard for their leaders.

Once an officer assumes responsibility for the evaluation process, they contribute to the benefit of the team and the whole department. The return may be greater imagination, ingenuity, and concern for their professional contributions. Delegating the evaluation process makes evaluation less difficult.

"CAN DO" LEADERSHIP POINTS: AN INTERVIEW SERGEANT RAYMOND T. HAYES

As foundation for this chapter, three basic questions were asked in an interview conducted by Ms. Colleen A. Sexton. The interview was based on the BE, KNOW, DO, leadership approach. [139] The respondent was police Sergeant Raymond T. Hayes.

Sergeant Hayes exemplifies what a leader should BE, KNOW, and DO. The answer to these three fundamental questions is essential to understanding the "can do" leadership process.

WHAT SHOULD A LEADER BE?

I believe the leader's reputation is earned on a daily basis. The competence of a leader is often judged by police officers on the issues of character and trust. Values, beliefs, and ethics are the foundation for this relationship with your police officers and as the foundation for a leader's character. Police officers will know if you have character problems. Adherence to your values and ethics must be consistently demonstrated.

Character and trust are essential leadership issues. However, the leader must also be competent. Trust is established when the leader demonstrates the appropriate competencies. Police officers will not follow an incompetent leader, even if they possess excellent character. The leader must be technically and tactically competent, which forms the basis for trust. Competence and character establish the police leader's right to lead.

Every police leader has the responsibility to maintain an ethical climate. They are the primary guardians of our constitution and together with street officers ensure the civil liberties of the citizenry. Without this coordination, the Constitution will never be realized on the street. The rule of law is not based on personalities. While we represent and enforce the law, we are not the law.

POWER AND DISCRETION

Police officers must have discretion; they must balance their duties with the public's civil liberties. Sometimes officers need guidance and checks. While there is nothing more important than our personal freedom and liberty, these can be severely curtailed by the police. Police officers can take freedom away, which is one reason for the importance of ethics in law enforcement, the only profession that can give a life, save a life, or take a life! This is why it is so important for police officers to keep ethical issues in perspective. Ethical issues are important, and police officers must adhere to a Code of Conduct. "Can do" leaders enforce the Code of Ethics and develop a sense of responsibility.

DEMONSTRATE THE CORRECT BEHAVIORS

I believe excellent role models lead by positive example. I will not assign anything to subordinates I have not or would not be willing to do. I try to set a positive example for subordinates from the beginning, so that they know what I expect them to accomplish–the who, what, when, why, and how of the mission.

Furthermore, officers should know whether you lead out of concern for yourself or for the mission and officers. It doesn't take long for subordinates to assess your motives and true concerns. Leaders who ensure that assignments are in the best interest of the group and mission more easily earn respect from their subordinates. Respect maximizes success and overrides the worst dilemmas.

When officers enter police service, they often perform routine tasks without personal goals. Leaders who help officers identify personal goals will be respected and supported. Leadership that cares, supports and demonstrates concern for the individual officer demands respect. "Can do" leaders help younger officers find the correct path to excellent job performance and career advancement.

"Can do" police leaders help young officers advance their careers. I am always interested in helping officers achieve their potential. Responsible leaders prepare and train their replacements. A few may try to restrict the flow of communication and knowledge to their subordinates. The goal is to make themselves indispensable. This is a mistake because it does a disservice to their subordinates and ultimately their own careers. When a leader restricts information, there can be no trust.

Emphasize the positive and reap the positive. Develop professional pride, and all things are possible. "Can do" leaders praise often and complement officers for excellent work. They always credit outstanding performance. If leaders steal credit from officers, performance dips, officers cease to be motivated and do not bring their best ideas forward. The best way to give credit is publicly in the form of a letter of commendation, or establish a Trooper of the Month program. My program is worth the extra effort by establishing pride in the officer's work.

WHAT SHOULD A LEADER KNOW?

This issue is directly linked to the basic leadership competencies. Gaining basic skills requires a significant amount of education and training. Leaders can possess the correct values and professional ethics but still not lead because they lack basic competencies, that is, essential skills required of police officers and leaders.

A leader should be fully aware of his/her responsibilities before applying for a particular position or rank. I enhanced my knowledge before I applied for my sergeant position. I didn't take outside classes, however I became familiar with the duties of the position by talking to a previous admired sergeant. This is often done in police work. During my sergeant's training sessions I recall thinking, "I wish I could do that job the way my sergeant does it."

The "can do" leader appreciates human relationships and how to establish rapport. Understanding the human dimension remains essential to influencing police officers. I believe the leader must start by understanding himself; then understanding and anticipating the behaviors of others is possible. In addition, understanding the strengths and weaknesses of officers will assist in getting the best performance.

GETTING THE FACTS

Superior leaders need accurate facts before making a decision. It may take some time to assemble the details. Accuracy is important; however, in some instances, speed is paramount. Getting the facts is not a center stage activity and may be monotonous. However, the failure to acquire the facts may jeopardize the mission and the leader. When the leader clearly sees the situation, the mission can be accomplished. Success comes from gathering accurate facts and information.

Identifying appropriate resources to accomplish goals and objectives may require coordination. Excellent leaders ensure that the service and logistical elements are in place and coordinate goals and objectives with diligence. Coordinating resources in a timely manner remains a key leadership responsibility.

Starting a new assignment may be exciting, but finishing it in a timely manner is demanding. After the excitement dies down, tedious details become wearisome; however, the details are important and timing may be everything. Leaders who meet deadlines focus on target dates. Not getting work done on time is an important "can't do" indicator.

Most importantly, communicating facts in a way that builds trust, confidence, and respects leads to elevated morale, cohesion, and discipline. Once leaders develop trust, they can teach team skills necessary for superior performance.

WHAT SHOULD A LEADER DO?

Leadership involves modifying subordinate behaviors to accomplish work and should be distinguished from management. True leadership changes behavior and encourages officers to want to do what you want them to do!

"Can do" leaders provide vision and direction: planning, setting goals, problem solving, and decision making. Leaders implement, communicate, coordinate, supervise and evaluate. These skills help achieve goals. Leadership motivates towards the achievement of goals. In addition, leadership includes teaching, mentoring and counseling. These "can do" leadership skills are necessary in the process of influencing officers.

There has been much discussion recently about delegation and empowerment. Sharing power with officers does not mean relinquishing control, for leaders remain accountable. They do not delegate a task and then forget it. But they must also avoid micro-management, which discourages initiative. However, the leader who does not follow-up and inspect the results may risk disaster. Empowerment involves standards, not indifference. The leader provides communication and feedback.

POSITIVE DISCIPLINE

Managers want to manage in the right way, but their emphasis is not on motivating people. Leaders acknowledge what makes each person an individual and different. Leaders should determine what motivates people, individually, a key leadership responsibility.

Consider positive and negative discipline, two entirely different ways to tell someone to do something. I can ask you to stop by my office because you made a mistake and simply reprimand you for your error, but there are better ways of understanding the underlying circumstances and sources of problems.

Sometimes it is important to discover why a mistake is committed. For instance, was the mistake intentional or honest? If the mistake was mental, then training is in order.

If an officer doesn't know what to do or how, this can easily be repaired through instruction.

If, however, the mistake was made intentionally then that is a different story altogether. An appropriate level of discipline would be in order. So it is important to distinguish between honest and malice mistakes. Before I discipline, I gather the facts and then conclude.

For example, if a police officer doesn't perform a particular duty on a certain day, I gather all pertinent facts before I judge as to why an order was disobeyed. Investigate and get the facts before talking to the officer. Not finding out the circumstances of a situation first turns people against leadership. Rushing to judgment suggests unwarranted criticism and injustice.

For example, I may find out that a member of the officer's family died or the officer was just served divorce papers. I respond too quickly—I neglect the "why" behind the behavior. I think there is a reason behind all of our behaviors and in a leadership position, finding out "why" becomes an essential responsibility.

Skilled leaders discipline officers and leave them thanking the leader for helping them to see something they did not understand. On the other hand, poor leaders discipline subordinates leaving them with only disrespect and dislike. Proper discipline is a talent.

REWARD THE RIGHT BEHAVIORS

Note when officers do something correctly. We tend to notice when someone's behavior does not meet our expectations. However, we often forget that positive reinforcement significantly affects job success. I always praise my officers in public and criticize them in private. The worst mistake a leader can make is publically to humiliate a subordinate.

There is no recognition like public recognition. Reinforce positive actions by informing others of individual or group success. I recognize subordinates for who they are rather then who they have failed to become.

FOCUS POINTS: EFFECTIVE LEADERSHIP

Finally, "can do" police leaders have respect and develop social cohesion and discipline. The leader must possess professional character traits that include: courage, competence, and integrity. Most importantly, the leader must be competent. Ability remains the cornerstone for leadership. The "can do" leader has the ability to communicate in a way that builds mutual respect and confidence.

The "can do" leader applies the principles of motivation, encourages morale and esprit. This is ultimately achieved when the leader teaches, coaches, and counsels police officers. The leader provides direction by setting goals, planning, problem solving and decision-making. "Can do" leaders understand what it takes to BE, KNOW, and DO to succeed at the leadership process. They understand more than basic definitions. They implement, motivate and support the mission.

CONCLUSION

Superior leadership demonstrates a "can do" communication and trust approach. The communication-oriented leader builds trust and pulls the department toward a vision of the future. However, success comes in increments. Leadership is a building process that incorporates success and failure. Hopefully, the leader who has mastered all forms of communication will succeed more often than fail. Remain optimistic and face adversity with persistence and consistency. Don't forget to acknowledge small accomplishments, first. Be bold, not timid; exceed expectations. Wait for the big opportunities and be prepared to seize the moment.

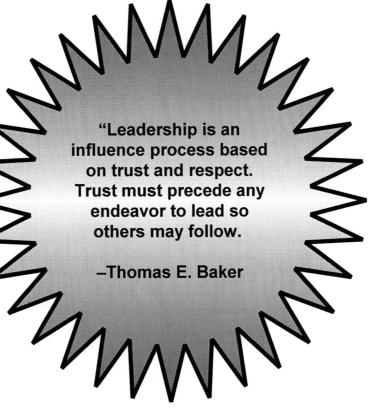

"Leadership is an influence process based on trust and respect. Trust must precede any endeavor to lead so others may follow.

–Thomas E. Baker

Chapter 13
INTELLIGENCE-LED POLICING PULLING IT ALL TOGETHER

First, have a definite, clear, practical ideal; a goal an objective. Second, have the necessary means to achieve your ends, wisdom, money, materials, and methods. Third, adjust all your means to the end.

— ARISTOTLE

Strategic Leadership requires vision and feedback from diverse sources including officers, analysts, stakeholders, and the community. Excellent communication is the primary means of deciphering feedback for developing vision and forecasting the future. The foundation requirements of Intelligence-Led Policing (ILP) strategies have complex organizational requirements in state police organizations and large metropolitan police agencies. This chapter offers strategies and suggestions for minimizing barriers to successful ILP implementation.

OVERVIEW: FUTURE REQUIREMENTS

Terrorism, enterprise crime, and homeland security have changed policing requirements dramatically. The World Trade Center, Pentagon, and global terrorist attacks emphasized the need for actionable intelligence requirements. Therefore, innovative and centralized intelligence gathering systems do not simply focus on street crime. In addition, the multi-dimensional approach to conspiracy crimes became

243

obvious. Enter the new architecture and additional intelligence requirements.

ILP addresses management coordination of raw data, collected at all levels of the law enforcement organization, and serves as the driving component of the police business of intelligence. Intelligence analysis involves collection, analysis, and dissemination. There is a clear delineation of both intelligence definitions, because both differ conceptually, and eventually merge. ILP is an intelligence driven philosophical and management approach to policing at every level of the law enforcement organization.

The ILP management approach offers an information sharing advantage over the former traditional intelligence approach. ILP made its first policing appearance in the United Kingdom. The 1990's UK Intelligence-Led Policing innovation transitioned from business and management theory to policing.

The United Kingdom's National Intelligence Model (NIM) advocates the concept of applying a business management model to law enforcement. The following questions require answers: (1) What is an accurate picture of the business? (2) What is actually happening on the ground or in the environment? (3) What is the nature, and extent of the problem, (4) What are the trends, and (5) What is the main threat. [140]

The NIM approach recommends that intelligence-led policing abide by the following objectives: (1) establish a task and coordination process, (1) develop core intelligence products to drive the operation, and (3) develop systems and protocols to facilitate the intelligence cycle. In addition, ensure successful training protocols for all levels of policing.

American ILP has for the most part, adopted the United Kingdom Intelligence Model; however, local policing strategies persist with some modifications. The UK recommends the emphasis be on a business model and management philosophy that includes the following components: (1) use of core intelligence products and task coordination, (2) the maximum use of the intelligence cycle that incorporates protocols, and (3) training at every level of the organization. [141]

Many police departments in the United States have adopted their own modifications and definitions, however, basic tenants include: (1) targeting career criminals, (2) using offender interviews, (3) analyzing repeat victimization and hotspots, (4) informants, (5) undercover operations, (6) physical and electronic surveillance, (7) targeting criminal organizations, (8) targeting serial crimes, (9) partnerships, and (10) intelligence sharing. ILP derives its power from the logic that supports the philosophy and management of information. [142]

On the state level, the New Jersey State Police's definition of ILP advocates: "Intelligence-led policing is a collaborative philosophy that starts with information, gathered at all levels of the organization that is analyzed to create useful intelligence and an improved understanding of the operational environment. This will assist leadership in making the best possible decisions with respect to crime control strategies, allocation of resources, and tactical operations. The adoption of ILP processes requires a concerted effort by all parties, including analysts, operators, and senior leaders. For analysts, the key components of this process include the creation of tactical, operational, and strategic intelligence products that support immediate needs, promote situational awareness, and provide the foundation for longer-term planning. [143]

According to *Intelligence-Led Policing: Getting Started,* an IALEIA publication, "Intelligence led policing (ILP) is the model that brings intelligence and analysis to the forefront of police operations. It promotes the efficient use of resources, the production of workable crime prevention strategies, and the successful completion of investigations and prosecution. [144]

The ILP management approach has translated into the National Intelligence Model, and into the National Criminal Intelligence Sharing Plan (NCISP) in the United States." The NCISP recommends every law enforcement agency incorporate the minimum standards for policing. The NCISP plan provides guidance for intelligence sharing, and a blueprint for building an intelligence system. In addition, the plan provides a model for intelligence policies. [145]

ILP helps reduce the unknown or information gaps, provides feedback, and enhances effective decision-making. The process of receiving and sharing criminal information offers reciprocal feedback opportunities. Police leaders and ILP managers cannot achieve successful prevention and intervention strategies without critical information, intelligence sharing, and collaboration. Unwillingness to share intelligence is a major barrier to receiving appropriate and timely feedback.

JOHARI WINDOW: LEADERSHIP FEEDBACK

Police leaders may not choose the right course of action in the decision-making process, not because of existing *knowledge,* but from the *unknown.* The unknown is what one cannot see or observe. That which one cannot observe and receive feedback acts as the principal deterrent to effective leadership and decision-making. Enhanced communication allows leaders to see and observe by achieving a proper feedback loop that includes police leaders, analysts, officers, and other customers. [146]

ILP offers opportunities to improve communication among police managers, analysts, and agency members. When police leaders and ILP managers share information, doors to the *unknown,* become accessible through the feedback process. Excellent feedback may assist and encourage sharing information, community partnerships, and building bridges to external law enforcement agencies.

Vision requirements are particularly important in counter terrorism, global enterprise crime and organized drug trafficking operations. Johari opportunities for effective communication and feedback improve criminal information management. Strategic and tactical opportunities result when the *blind spot* and *unknown* panes shrink, creating new vision opportunities.

Why is the Johari Window an excellent intelligence strategic and tactical approach to critical thinking? The answer: communication is the major component of ILP management.

The Johari solution enhances intelligence information strategies and eliminates major communication barriers. Information sharing and feedback provide intelligence concerning the *blind spot* for police leaders, and opens the door to the *unknown.*

The Johari Window Model offers opportunities to examine leadership, and ILP from communication and feedback perspectives. Two psychologists, (Luft and Ingham, 1970), originated the Model as means of giving and receiving information feedback. This Model offers applications in police leadership, and intelligence operations. Refer to Figure 13-1 for examples and Johari Window concepts (Lufts, 1970).

Figure 13-1. Overview of Johari Window

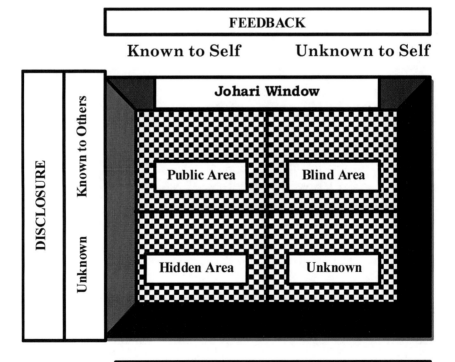

Source: Adapted from: Joseph Luft, Group Process: An Introduction to Group Dynamics (California: National Press Books, 2ed., 1984).

The "Johari Window" encourages the expansion of shared intelligence and achieving accurate feedback, but requires personal risks. The ILP management/ leadership style requires candid leaders who establish trust and mutual respect. Excellent leadership suggests information exchanges, rather than one-way dialogues, not involving feedback.

Feedback provides information concerning how organization members feel about and perceive leadership and ILP management strategies. Open police leaders who are willing to disclose, encourage opportunities to understand how others feel about their leadership. Leaders deny followers opportunities to disclose feelings because of poor approachability, the facade, and the absence of leader feedback.

The Johari Window offers leaders the possibility of expanding personal power. Feedback is the reaction of officers and civilians (feelings and perceptions), thereby informing leaders about how his/her behaviors affect them. Police leaders and ILP managers equipped with crucial feedback are in the best position, to be effective decision-makers. Candid behaviors amplify communication and feedback, enhancing follower information and support.

Police leaders or ILP managers, who hide behind their façade, or remain silent and do not take risks, fail to communicate. Open leaders and analysts, who ask for feedback and disclose information about self, position themselves to influence others. Leadership self-disclosure encourages rapport and trust relationships with individual officers, civilians, informal groups and the police organization. The willingness to self-disclose affects multiple relationships in police organizations.

The goal is to obtain information not known to self, but known to others. The opportunity to gain information from the *blind spot,* and *unknown* portions of the four Johari quadrants, proves essential to successful decision-making. Sharing information from the *hidden area* (sometimes referred to as the façade) of the police leader or ILP manager provides greater understanding for officers and analysts to follow and share feedback.

Peering into the Johari Window allows police leaders or ILP managers to expose the façade or the *hidden area* (the issues others do not know about the leader). The purpose is to gain sufficient knowledge about the *blind spot and unknown* (the issues the leaders do not know about).

The *open space* is the key to personal power, the quadrant, or windowpane where leaders have opportunities to be authentic and open. Openness allows for the exchange of what one knows about self and what others know. This form of personal leadership interaction and risk taking invites the necessary feedback for effective decision-making.

Police Leaders and ILP staff unwilling to share the *hidden* or *façade* windowpane and keep secrets do not receive proper feedback. The returning flow of information or feedback data helps shrink the blind area and unknown. Shrinking the windowpanes or quadrants around the *blind spot* ultimately offers insight into the *unknown area* and related issues. Insight provides opportunities to communicate, seize initiatives, and problems solve with appropriate police strategic and tactical remedies.

In summary, blending of the Johari Window and ILP analytical skills offers a systematic structure to communicate and receive essential feedback. Candid leaders, willing to disclose information, are in the best position to receive adequate feedback. Successful ILP and new ILP leadership requirements include willingness to: (1) self-disclose, (2) avoid the façade, (3) build trust, (4) accept feedback from others, and (4) learn about themselves. The Johari Window serves as the window of opportunity to improve intelligence requirements and implement Intelligence-Led Policing.

HUMAN EQUATION BARRIERS

Eliminating the barriers and synchronization of existing American police strategies requires excellent leadership strategies. American policing encompasses its own unique policing strategies to accommodate Intelligence-Led Policing (ILP) Community-oriented Policing (COP), Problem-oriented Policing (POP), and CompStat tactical operations. The proponents of these strategies have broad support and may present barriers for advancing the "new ILP architecture."[147]

Excellent communication and feedback represent essential ingredients for removing barriers. When examining impediments to successful ILP operations, two obvious factors surface: (1) poor communication and (1) poor feedback. Johari Window analysis remedies both negative communication factors. Positive communication helps resolve barriers and negative issues.

Communication issues evolve from the human component of the ILP equation. The human relations impediment, between police officers and civilian groups, is first on the priority list. The Johari Window, candor, and superior communication, assist police leaders in achieving quality human relations and bonus related positive outcomes. Mutual respect and equality among police officers and civilian analysts serves as a transition point.

The merging intelligence and crime analysis under a unified command will ultimately take place on the reorganizational level. Joining both operations in the same location is the starting point, however, not the absolute solution. Communication, openness, and feedback may provide essential social adjustments. Decentralized analyst access to police patrol operations and investigators, is a logical conclusion when viewed through the Johari Window.

Direct access to the chief and senior commanders by analysts is controversial, but necessary. The manger of the ILP staff should be able to report the commander of the Operations Division. However, it will likely evolve with the assistance of Johari communication analysis. The need to be open and candid with analysts and other members of the department becomes evident when examining the four quadrants of the Johari Window.

Information and power sharing it with others, empowers everyone, and may save lives. However, intelligence protocols restrict criminal intelligence to those who have a need to know. Police leaders assure some flexibility on the flow of internal information, and the allocation of proper security clearances. External sensitive information may require additional privacy and security clearance restrictions.

PLANNING STRATEGIES

Centralized planning forms the foundation for critical thinking, and strategic intelligence analysis. ILP and intelligence analysis can support: (1) problem-oriented policing and SARA planning strategies, (2) CompStat and operations and crime analysis, (3) emergency operations planning, (4) incident action planning, and (5) evaluation. Centralized planning model forms a natural conduit for the consolidation of these mutual planning foundations.

State police and large metropolitan law enforcement agencies require seven points of planning linkage: (1) police decision makers and central strategic planning, (2) intelligence-led policing, (3) intelligence analysis, (4) crime analysis, (5) community-oriented policing, (6) problem-oriented policing and (7) CompStat tactical operations. Staff planners, ILP managers, and analysts serve as central points of coordination to key decision makers.

An overlapping planning relationship supports strategic intelligence analysis, and problem-oriented policing (POP). Problem oriented policing has a long-term view that focuses on community oriented policing (COP) strategies. The long-term considerations are similar to strategic intelligence analysis: (1) capabilities of criminals and organizations, and (2) related community problems.

COP and POP apply statistically incident-based reporting, in the search for broadly based targets. Strategic intelligence involves scanning for broadly based targets. The POP and SARA planning models are similar to the strategic intelligence model. POP differs in the use of citizen strategies: (1) community feedback, (2) partnerships, and (3) Neighborhood Watch participation. CompStat operations require near-term and real-time crime analysis, and tactical planning.

The Criminal Intelligence Cycle prepares leaders to move forward, with a vision for direction, and sharing criminal intelligence with officers and civilians. The intelligence cycle is important as a guiding methodology. When leaders communicate and share information, access to the unknown increases.

The intelligence cycle is the primary means for obtaining and confirming feedback from the criminal world. Three basic steps include: (1) *define the intelligence problem*, (2) *identify the target*, and (3) *define the collection plan*. Refer to Figure 13-2 for an example of the intelligence cycle, planning, and targeting which incorporates a continuing cycle feedback loop.

Figure 13-2:   Targeting Information: Selection and Evaluation

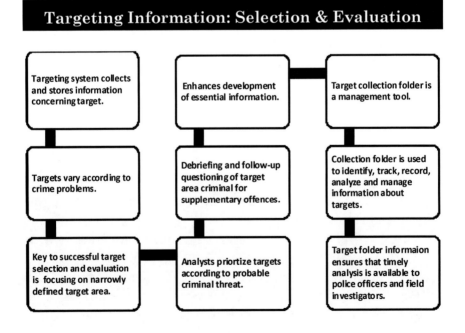

Targeting Information: Selection & Evaluation

Targeting system collects and stores information concerning target.

Enhances development of essential information.

Target collection folder is a management tool.

Targets vary according to crime problems.

Debriefing and follow-up questioning of target area criminal for supplementary offences.

Collection folder is used to identify, track, record, analyze and manage information about targets.

Key to successful target selection and evaluation is focusing on narrowly defined target area.

Analysts priortize targets according to probable criminal threat.

Target folder informaion ensures that timely analysis is available to police officers and field investigators.

Planning and ILP management have mutual goals and objectives; therefore, both are not mutually exclusive. Strategic planning cannot exist in a vacuum, without ILP management of criminal information and mutual feedback. ILP intelligence analysis and feedback permits tactical planning to function effectively. Moreover, quality coordination with tactical planners avoids counter-productive outcomes in high profile strategic cases.

The little things or details in the planning process can make a significant difference in successful tactical outcomes. Skilled execution of tactical operations depends on carefully planned details coming together. Police leaders generate opportunities for superior crime fighting when staff planning is centralized. Moreover, the synchronization of the planning process, promotes opportunities for successful tactical outcomes.

SYNCHRONIZATION STRATEGIES

The philosophy of community-oriented policing is part the fabric of American policing. However, the planning process incorporates POP and SARA strategies to realize COP philosophy goals and objectives. These problem-solving strategies focus on crime generators and hot spots, which anguish communities. CompStat enhances the tactical aspects of the COP and POP models, and when properly coordinated, the tripod can improve police effectiveness.

ILP and successful policing strategies determine much of what transpires. The synchronization of strategies is preferable to competing strategies. Moreover, blending strategies requires cooperation and assimilation into the ILP management philosophy. Refer to Figure 13-3 for the synchronization and integration of law enforcement strategies.

Figure 13-3. ILP, COP, POP and CompStat Integrated Strategies

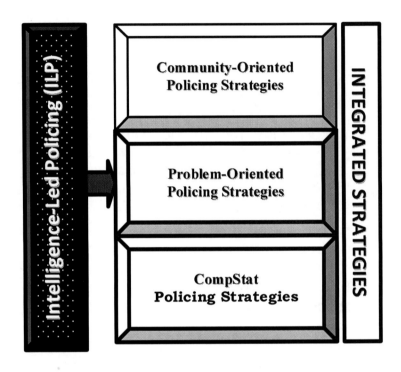

Integration and synchronization requires superior planning to achieve the goal of effective administration. Police leaders must seize opportunities to implement effective strategies. Finally, the new intelligence-led policing *grand strategy* would include ILP + COPPS + CompStat + Quality Leadership = Police Excellence.

A clear sense of vision enables us to understand the importance of diverse strategies, which allow police agencies to "arrive" and achieve improved crime control, prevention and homeland security. The formidable goal becomes possible with proactive ILP strategic and tactical intelligence planning, supported by excellent police strategic leadership.

FOCUS POINTS: INTELLIGENCE REQUIREMENTS. Why is the Johari Window an excellent intelligence strategic and tactical approach to critical thinking? The answer: communication is the very substance of ILP management. The Johari solution enhances intelligence information strategies and eliminates major communication barriers. Information sharing and feedback provide intelligence concerning the *blind spot* for leaders, and opens the door to the *unknown*.

Human interpersonal communication remains the primary facilitator in the *diffusion* and *adoption* of any innovation. Social change impediments may emerge from the: (1) community, (2) civilian staff, and (3) police missions. Related to that problem is the police organizational structure and diverse areas of specialization.

Moreover, intelligence managers and analysts serve as the vanguard change agents for ILP management philosophy. They must advocate and inform police leaders of the need for improved intelligence, and decision-making capabilities. Intelligence personnel serve as tactful facilitators and trusted advisors to law enforcement leaders.

The resistance to change is a powerful force, but the truth will prevail on convincing and actionable intelligence verifications. The Johari Window provides the widow to view intelligence from a unique perspective. It opens communication opportunities, improves information sharing, and eventually opens doors to information sharing.

Johari opportunities for effective communication and feedback improve criminal information management. Strategic and tactical opportunities result when the *blind spot* and *unknown* panes shrink, creating new vision requirements. Vision requirements are particularly important in terrorism, global enterprise crime, organized drug trafficking operations, and street crime offenses. Refer to Johari Window: Intelligence Opportunities in Figure 13-4.

Figure 13-4: Johari Window and Intelligence
Opportunities

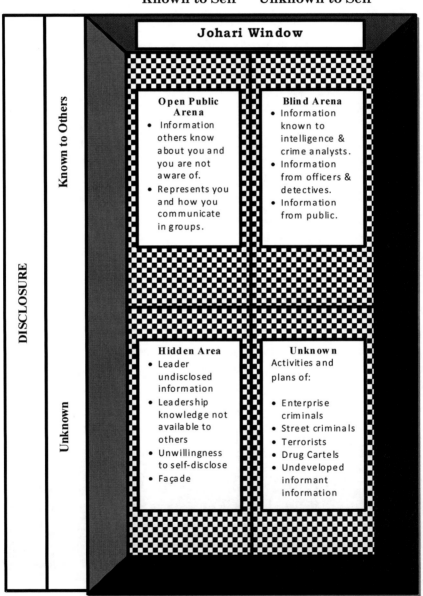

CONCLUSION

"Crime is a national crusade that involves commitment to a grand strategy." Our survival as nation depends on superior strategy implementation. The "grand strategy" is INTELLIGENCE-LED POLICING. Therefore, we should apply ILP, and carefully pick our battles, if we want to win the war. We can afford to lose some battles, but not the war against crime and terrorism. ILP is the leadership and intelligence "grand strategy," and mortal enemy of criminals and terrorists. However, the "grand strategy" calls for excellent intelligence, leadership, and vision." [148]

Chapter 14
EPILOGUE:
FUTURE LEADERSHIP
STRATEGIES

The art of progress is to preserve order amid
change and to preserve change amid order.
- ALFRED NORTH WHITEHEAD

Police career stressors add up over the years, especially with high profile and dangerous assignments. Leadership responsibilities generally preclude traumatic and critical events. However, the vast majority of street officers experience a considerable amount of trauma, critical incidents, and multiple stressors. Some officers have very high rates of trauma exposure, while others serve in low to medium stress environments.

Police agency leadership has a profound impact on officer resilience and ability to cope with trauma. Effective leadership strives to mitigate the adverse affects of trauma and deter the consequences of long-term exposure to trauma and related hazards. The management and organizational milieu can offer a proactive risk management approach, vulnerability assessment, and resilience training.

Planning is essential to managing critical incident stressors effectively. This means that police leaders act proactively with some vision toward the future. The planning process considers career transitions. Risk management planning assumes that some career transitions are in response to changes in the policing environment and can affect the future risk of their officers.

Paton cited several important police organizational changes: (1) the need for a paradigm shift in the conceptualization and management of critical incident stress risk, (2) the need to move beyond the relationship between the officer and event in a single point in time, and (3) to adopt a broader career-length approach. This is difficult to achieve because the counseling focus is on the officer and the critical event. However, the career approach compliments the officer's resiliency and recovery process. [149]

Paton acknowledged that many career transitions offer predicable pathways that respond to negotiation, appropriate programming, and support. However, sudden traumatic events that occur without warning or past experiences create unpredictable consequences that influence officers and their organization. Risk management requires proactive management that responds to the immediate and long-term impact of organizational and environmental changes.[149]

The adaptation of police organizations to critical incidents is an important precursor to organizational resilience. Many of the experiences and transitions police officers encounter are predictable. Police leadership that anticipates the career stage consequences develops policy rules and procedures that enhance the pathway. However, some transitions remain unpredictable, including the impact of catastrophic crisis events.

The "Life Stage Principle" advocates that the way personal experiences and social events affect individual officers influences them by where they are in their career and the time span when events occur. The authors suggest that observers often collapse the officer and critical incident into one single event that begins and ends with clear deliberate moments in time. Critical risk management is an evolving process that accommodates officer integration into the organizational structure and immersion in the police culture.[149, 150]

This Life Stage Principle considers the impact of both prior experiences and experiences learned from the job that influence an officer's interpretation of the fluid and sometimes-unpredictable environment. The ideal broader career-length perspective offers acknowledgment of the residual effects of decades of challenging encounters that affect the lives of police officers as they maneuver through their life/career transitions. Stressful events recur throughout the officer's career; measuring those exposures remains the challenge. Moreover, the trauma may affect the officer's retirement and eventually lead to suicide.[149,150]

Proactive leadership monitors officer trauma exposure. The importance of a career perspective becomes an issue that spans an officer's lifetime of exposure. The Life-Course Theory cites three significant dimensions in a police career that influence traumatic exposure. The three critical elements of trauma exposure are *frequency, seriousness*, and *length of exposure.* [151]

The effort to take full advantage of human potential requires sensitivity and timely intervention. The human developmental needs and capabilities of a particular stage in the life span are extremely relevant. The social, psychological, and biological needs of an individual change from the beginning to the end of life. These needs may intersect, connect, and change one's life social trajectories.[149,150]

Life-Course Theory offers central themes concerning aging and development processes that unfold throughout a lifetime. The life-course model applies to a police career and beyond the multiple dimensions and duration of a "person's existence." History and social conditions that affect personal outcomes influence an officer's human development. Social trajectories in different realms of life are interconnected. Most important, these social paths have reciprocal effects on one another.[149,150]

"Can do" leaders do not fear the future; they challenge and welcome it. Leaders with vision have the ability to foresee trends. Those who understand the leadership process acclimate to rapidly changing environments; they preserve what succeeds and identify needed modifications.

Maintaining stability while initiating change is an essential leadership function. Event-driven leaders miss the opportunity to influence outcomes; however, proactive leaders seize the moment. Successful police leaders can plan for change by implementing twelve effective policing strategies.

STRATEGY 1: COP + POP = COPPS

The winning formula is **COP + POP = COPPS**. Excellent COPPS leadership demonstrates values that support human relationships. The formula for successful COPPS leadership is community-oriented policing (COP) + problem-oriented policing (POP) = COPPS and Quality (Q) + Service (S) = Excellence. "Effective police departments learn from the people they serve. They provide unparalleled quality, service and reliability—things that work, help and last." [152] The COPPS philosophy serves as a basis for empowerment, teamwork and action.

STRATEGY 2: VISION AND COPPS

"Can do" leadership requires courage and vision. Therefore, leaders need character to follow through on the shared vision. This kind of leadership is enhanced by demonstrating analytical and forecasting skills, enhanced by social skills and a sense of timing. Leadership depends on the understanding of how things work.

However, instant decision-making rarely occurs in the leadership environment. The leader's ability to assess the readiness to change often makes the difference between a visionary leader and a manager. "Can do" leaders maximize the forces of change and encourage innovation.

COPPS leaders must have the strength of character and persistence to accomplish the mission. The success of any organization depends on the ability to forecast the future. COPPS leaders envision what needs to be accomplished, and influence subordinates to complete related goals.

STRATEGY 3: TQL = EXCELLENCE

Many police departments are civil service, not customer driven. The bureaucratic model is impersonal; total quality leadership (TQL) is community-oriented. In the future, police departments will adopt TQL because it is quality service-oriented and supports the community-oriented philosophy.

TQL is a leadership process, not just another program which requires minimal commitment. The leadership effort is on continuous improvement, quality teams, and officer participation. [153] Consequently, police leaders develop strategic planning to improve mission performance. "This simple but powerful formula provides the strategic plan. The Q denotes quality of service and S refers to speed of accomplishing the job. The results of Q + S = E, for excellence." [154]

STRATEGY 4: COPPS PLANNING

Conflict often results from the failure to make timely decisions. Procrastination and hesitation may result in unnecessary conflict due to a power vacuum and lack of information. Timely planning helps leaders avoid unnecessary confusion, rumor, and delay.

The leader must demonstrate the strength of character to make a decision, and announce it at the appropriate time and place, to achieve desired results. Making sound decisions builds respect and confidence. Planning allows leaders to reason logically and make effective decisions.

POP analysis is the primary means for identifying crime problems and hot spots. As previously discussed, SARA planning emphasizes *scanning, analysis, response* and *assessment.* The SARA approach and analysis works best as a team strategy involving patrol officers, crime analysts, sergeants and lieutenants, captains and senior leaders.

Analysis is the most important part of the SARA process. "There are several principles of analysis: (1) analysis is based on common sense, (2) there is no one way to do analysis, (3) individual problems require individual analysis, (4) analysis requires creativity and innovation, and finally, (5) analysis does not need to be complex." [155]

Table 14-1
DETERMINING THE
ORDER OF ANALYSIS

❖ What part of the analysis can be strengthened by what is learned in another aspect of the analysis? ❖ What do I know about the problem? ❖ Who should be consulted to gain better understanding of the problem?	❖ What type of assistance and expertise is needed in analyzing the findings from each activity? ❖ Who should implement each activity? ❖ At what point will initiating each activity complement the analysis plan?
❖ What type of analysis activities must be conducted (i.e., surveys, interviews, etc.)? ❖ How time-intensive is each activity? ❖ What type of assistance and expertise is needed in designing, administering, and managing each activity?	❖ What data (police department data or data from external agencies) are available to develop a better understanding of the problem? ❖ How accurate are the data? ❖ Do I need assistance from anyone to gain access to the data and to analyze the data?

Source: Author adapted table from Timothy S. Bynum, U.S. Department of Justice, Office of Community Policing Services. Using Analysis for Problem-Solving: A Guidebook for Law Enforcement (Washington, DC: GPO, 2001) 6.

STRATEGY 5: TRAINING

Successful leaders explain the benefits of police training. Furthermore, they will create the need for accepting the knowledge by focusing on what officers need to understand. The training emphasis will be on community-oriented and problem-solving policing. Persistent and consistent COPPS training will require advanced planning.

New training systems provide methods that produce the required ability levels at the lowest costs. Technology serves as the foundation for interactive learning. Computerized learning simulations individualize training and tailor field performance requirements.

Computers serve as the infrastructure for training programs. Reduced instructor contact and computer evaluation systems are cost effective. Police training managers establish training goals; the trainers provide direct training and support for officers.

Active learning includes various forms of collective inservice training and recruit training. Other forms of training include roll call programs and field training. Most importantly, computerized training will be leadership driven, focusing on systematic goals and objectives.

The most common form of training is decentralized team training, that is, training programs that meet specific team needs. The trend is on continuous training that emphasizes mission requirements.

More often, future leaders take advantage of training and educational opportunities. Some officers hesitate to take time away from recreational pursuits; this is a mistake. Opportunities to train should be exploited, for such sacrifices will be fruitful.

Proactive police leadership and training reduces trauma, stress, and police suicide before it occurs. Police training must offer practical solutions for adjusting expectations of police candidates who enter the field. When the training addresses the field realities, rather than unnecessarily high expectations, the stress levels may be manageable, and this may influence suicide rates.

The academy program should emphasize content information that prepares officers for dealing with stressful issues in the real world. Maddi offered the following solutions for police academy training: (1) developing a meaningful purpose in life, (2) encouraging a belief in one's ability to influence the outcome, (3) encouraging a belief that one can learn and develop as a result of experiences, and most important, (4) the willingness to accept uncontrollable outcomes. These life skills are difficult to address in police academy classrooms. [156]

Police training offers the opportunity to desensitize police recruits to traumatic field experiences. The police academy that provides realistic training and approximates operational requirements serves recruits well. Training simulations impose meaning and coherence for future operational experience that allows real-world applications. [157] Training that approximates critical incidents and simulation-based training exposes officers to challenging situations to practice skill levels.

Simulations encourage the integration of theory and field applications. They provide a broad range of opportunities to apply the officers' knowledge to realistic scenarios. Lessons learned from the critique and reactions of others participating allow the trainee to apply the knowledge from a critical incident perspective. The application of critical thinking skills offers the opportunity to transfer expertise to different field scenarios.

Learning simulations allow officers to develop, review, and rehearse operational skills. The secondary benefit is to anticipate and rehearse stress management skills. The high-pressure training scenarios in a safe, controlled, and supportive environment encourage positive feedback. Simulations instill the understanding and teach variable reactions under replicated standards and conditions. [158] Training goals and related training objectives according to active learning criteria find venues for application and assessment.

STRATEGY 6: TEAM BUILDING

Teams are small groups held together by strong social bonds; they cooperate for the common good. Superior police teams proficiently perform their tasks and possess a high degree of skills that can be applied in stressful circumstances. Strong mutual interaction and cooperative behaviors evidences effective teamwork. Police officers, working together as team members identify with the group, its goals, and objectives.

In the future, leaders who can successfully integrate team members will be in demand. They will have people skills that maximize the potential of men and women. They will emphasize cooperation and diversity.

Teamwork will serve as the central theme for organizational management and the administration of police agencies. Police culture will strive toward creating an environment in which the rewards for working together will outweigh those of working for individual interest. The foundation for teamwork will be based on a reward system that encourages teamwork. This new police culture will improve teamwork and community relationships.

Police leaders should use carefully selected and trained teams for critical situations, not groups or shift-platoons. There is a difference between shift-platoons and police teams. Anyone who has served on a winning team can easily identify the unique differences between a group of officers serving on a shift or a platoon and a winning team.

STRATEGY 7: NEIGHBORHOOD-ORIENTED POLICING

The COPPS philosophy is focused on neighborhood leadership. The COPPS approach reinforces a community's ability to create safe neighborhoods. Problem-solving policing (POP) is applied block-by-block to address problems in a particular neighborhood, while Neighborhood Watch Programs support the goals of community-oriented philosophy. Working with Neighborhood Watch programs requires exceptional leadership skills and a great deal of patience; however, the rewards should prove considerable.

STRATEGY 8: GIS CRIME MAPPING

Why do police officers need to appreciate crime mapping? Military officers have excellent map reading skills. More recently, crime mapping is a prerequisite police leadership skill. Police leaders need to understand the fundamentals concerning Geographic Information System(s) GIS mapping strategies. The new technology replaces old pin maps, making offenses easier to up-date. If asking yourself the following police leadership questions is important: Where are you going? How will you get there? Then reading a map becomes an essential leadership skill.

Why are GIS fundamentals important? Mamalian and La Vigne's research demonstrates the value of crime mapping: "Departments reported that crime mapping improves information dissemination, evaluation, and administration. Specifically, police departments use mapping to: (1) inform officers and investigators of crime locations (94%), (2) make resource allocations (56%), (3) evaluate interventions (49%), (4) inform residents about crime activity and changes in their community (47%), and (5) identify repeat-calls-for service (44%). [159]

Clarke comments on GIS: "A geographic depiction of all or part of a geographical realm in which real world features have been replaced with symbols in their correct spatial location at a reduced scale. A map is composed of a set of basic cartographic elements, including the neat line, scale, border, figure, ground, labels, credits, legend, and title. A map has a visual grammar or structure that must be understood and used if the best map design is desired. The selection of map type is often determined by the geographic properties of the data and the attributes." [160] GIS crime mapping strategies have their own symbols in layered format to include: (1) type of offense, (2) location, and (3) demographic considerations.

Standing before pin maps that cover police headquarters walls can be overwhelming. Computers have replaced old pin maps in most jurisdictions. Moreover, many police leaders may be reluctant to engage computer-mapping technologies. One cannot ignore the importance of crime mapping advancements.

GIS definitions may sound intimidating. Do not become discouraged by the jargon. User-friendly GIS computer programs facilitate understanding and the opportunity to learn. The failure to understand GIS mapping basics may have career implications. Mapping technology enhances crime analysis and provides necessary tools for crime prevention and intervention. For example, implications for offender patterns include: (1) offender evolution, (2) space and time profiles of a series, (2) hunting grounds, (3) spatial distribution and (4) offender travel distance. [161]

More importantly, crime mapping allows police leaders to plan tactical responses and develop crime hot spots, crime hot dots (repeat victims), and hot products (stolen property). [162] Do not miss opportunities to engage GIS mapping technology; attend training sessions and practice your computer/mapping skills. Mapping strategies provide insight and critical thinking leadership opportunities. Police leaders who understand crime-mapping strategies will be in the best position to apply strategic and tactical crime analysis strategies.

STRATEGY 9: CRIME ANALYSIS

Crime mapping and crime analysis strategies are essential to effective police leadership. One cannot lead, unless the destination includes crime-specific planning. Crime analysis allows leaders to plan tactical strategies and allocate resources. The term "crime analysis" refers to street crimes, i.e., burglary, larceny, robbery, rape and stalking. Crime analysts generally focus on PART I, Uniform Crime Reporting Offenses and provide crime bulletins to field officers. In addition, Criminal Investigative Analysis (CIA) provides psychological profiles and investigative leads in serial murder and rape cases.

Defining Crime Analysis:"(1) Crime analysis is defined as a set of systematic, analytical processes directed at providing timely and pertinent information relative to crime patterns. (2) Trend correlations assist operational and administrative personnel in planning the deployment of resources for the prevention and suppression of criminal activities, (3) Thus, crime analysis aids the investigative process, increasing apprehensions and the clearance rate of criminal cases. (4) Furthermore, within this context, crime analysis supports a number of department functions including: patrol deployment, special operations and tactical units, and investigations. (5) Strategic planning and applied research are enhanced through crime analysis, and (6) successful crime prevention strategies offer optimal opportunities when accurate data serves as the basis for action. In addition, administrative services, budgeting, and program planning are connected to successful planning and accurate criminal information." [163]

Successful leaders take advantage of information; the crime or intelligence analyst provides criminal information that ensures successful operations. Take advantage of opportunities to coordinate information gleaned from credible sources. Police leaders coordinate criminal intelligence from crime analysts, and police officers, and then obtain feedback for specific operations.

STRATEGY 10: HOMELAND SECURITY

Terrorist acts require real time intelligence to provide excellent Homeland Security. The role of COPPS and Neighborhood Watch is more important than ever before. The new technology is important; however, citizen support is key to the timely flow of terrorist intelligence. Teaming up law enforcement agencies and citizens is a perquisite to intelligence analysis. Homeland Security, law enforcement and citizen collaboration remain essential leadership requirement tasks.

Intelligence analysis is a subspecialty of criminal analysis. Intelligence analysis focuses on terrorism, criminal organizations and their leadership. Criminal groups may support terrorism through illegal and legitimate businesses, i.e., drug cartels and legitimate charities. Excellent leadership and intelligence analysis remain our best defense against terrorism and criminal organizations.

STRATEGY 11: COMPSTAT
Compstat is a leadership and management-by-objective program. COPPS, Total Quality Leadership and Theory Z adapt well in the program. In addition, crime analysis, statistics, crime mapping and operations analysis have direct applications. Compstat allows leaders to set goals and objectives and evaluate officer achievements.

"Analyzing crime trends and patterns is important because: If you can predict it, you can prevent it. The Four Steps to Crime Reduction have been critical to the New York City Police Department's crime-fighting success:

The Four Steps are:

1. Accurate and Timely Intelligence

2. Rapid Deployment

3. Effective Tactics

4. Relentless Follow-up and Assessment" [164]

Table 14-2
COMPSTAT
LEADERSHIP PROCESS

ACCURATE AND TIMELY INTELLIGENCE

If the police are to respond effectively to crime and to criminal events, officers at all levels of the organization must have accurate knowledge of when particular types of crimes are occurring, how and where the crimes are being committed, and who the criminals are. The likelihood of an effective police response to crime increases proportionally as the accuracy of this criminal intelligence increases.

EFFECTIVE TACTICS

Effective tactics are prudently designed to bring about the desired result of crime reduction, and these are developed after studying and analyzing the information gleaned from our accurate and timely crime intelligence. In order to avoid merely displacing crime and quality of life problems, and in order to bring about permanent change, these tactics must be comprehensive, flexible, and adaptable to the shifting crime trends we identify and monitor.

RAPID DEPLOYMENT OF
PERSONNEL AND RESOURCES

Once a tactical plan has been developed, an array of personnel and other necessary resources are promptly deployed. Although some tactical plans might involve only patrol personnel, experience has proven that the most effective plans require that personnel from several units and enforcement functions work together as a team to address the problem. A viable and comprehensive response to a crime or quality of life problem generally demands that patrol personnel, investigators and support personnel bring their expertise and resources to bear in a coordinated effort.

RELENTLESS FOLLOW-UP AND ASSESSMENT

As in any problem-solving endeavor, an ongoing process of rigorous follow-up and assessment is absolutely essential to ensure that the desired results are actually being achieved. This evaluation component also permits us to assess the viability of particular tactical responses and to incorporate the knowledge we gain in our subsequent tactics development efforts. By knowing how well a specific tactic worked on a particular crime or quality of life problem, and by knowing which specific elements of the tactical response worked most effectively, we are better able to construct and implement effective responses for similar problems in the future. The follow-up and assessment process also permits us to re-deploy resources to meet newly identified challenges once a problem has abated.

Source: http://www.ci.nyc.ny.us/html/nypd/html/chfdept/
          chief-of-department.html

Compstat achieves accountability, and allows leaders to measure progress. Crime statistics, weekly Compstat reports and commander profiles highlight critical crime issues. Commanders, police officers, detectives and staff are encouraged to initiate solutions to crime problems in their area of responsibility. One vital asset involves coordination among different components of the organization and teamwork. The goal is to empower precinct commanders and hold them responsible for reducing crime under their area of authority. This process includes not only quantitative factors, but also quality of life issues.

STRATEGY 12: OPERATIONS ANALYSIS

Operations analysis assists police leaders in the planning process for patrol allocation. Crime analysis provides the best data for decision-making, logistical requirements, deployment of officers, tactical objectives and specific tasking orders.

Taylor and Huxley define operations analysis as: "(1) the analytical study of police delivery problems, (2) which provides commanders and police managers with a scientific basis for decisions, (3) thus improving operations or deployment of resources. It provides essential information to those in the department who exercise authority over planning, direction, and control. The goals, objectives and tasks are directly connected to the functions essential to the conduct of police operations." [165]

Operations analysis allows leaders to apply the sound principles of time management, personnel deployment and demonstrate competencies. Crime analysis provides the basic data for optimal use of resources. Decisive police leadership provides the means to be effective in field operations. Proactive leadership and insightful knowledge when applying police resources are generally superior to unplanned reactive leadership. Armed with crime analysis and operational analysis, police leaders have opportunities to prevail and earn the respect of staff and field officers under stressful circumstances.

FINAL FOCUS POINTS: HOLISTIC POLICING THEORY

When the 12 basic strategies fall into place, they provide a "Holistic Policing Theory" for senior leaders, mid-level managers/leaders, and sergeants. The synchronization of ILP, COPPS, SARA, Compstat, GIS crime mapping, crime analysis and statistics offer the best means to prevent crime and intervene successfully. Synchronization is not the perfect solution; however, it offers another important dimension to reactive policing.

Compstat provides the leadership component that reinforces the department's philosophy, mission and values statements. Moreover, Compstat provides criminal intelligence, goals, objectives, tasks, conditions and standards for effective police leadership. In other words, Compstat provides answers to three basic leadership questions: Where are we going? How will we get there? How will we know when we have arrived? Refer to Figure 14-1 for The Synchronization CompStat and Police Holistic Strategies.

Figure 14-1
Synchronization of Police Holistic Strategies

Intelligence-Led Policing	
CompStat:	How will the department know when it arrives?
SARA Planning:	How will the department get there?
POP Procedures:	Identifying related crime problems
COP Philosophy:	Where is the department going?
Police Holistic Theory and Synchronization	

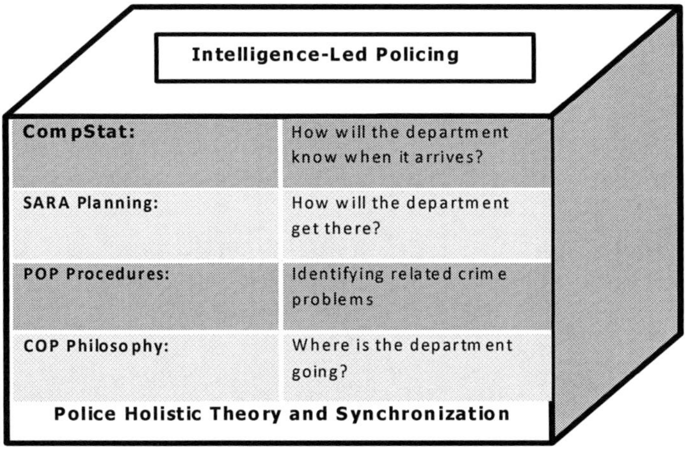

"Perhaps the single most important factor in the whole process is the ability to select specific objectives. The leader must know what he or she wants to achieve, what improvements citizens demand, and what targets will ultimately improve public safety." [166]

Compstat is congruent with "empowerment" and "power-down" objectives of participatory leadership. The importance of delegation of authority and accountability for crime control/suppression is clearly defined. Opportunities for critical thinking and individual contributions and creativity multiply. Patience, coaching, and mentoring all play a vital role in coordinating team participation. The success of any program is dependant on effective police leadership plus the cooperation of civilian staff and officers.

Change can be difficult and may be unwelcome. Effective police leaders consider consequences and unintended consequences when planning. Concealed consequences are the most difficult to anticipate. "Building commitment for change is fundamental to successfully implementing change, but all too often it's a process that is ignored." [167] In the table that follows, Captain Merle Switzer identifies five steps to building commitment for change.

Table 14-3
Five Steps to Building Commitment for Change

STEP ONE: Identify Whose Commitment is Needed	Who are the key people whose commitment would help bolster chances for success?
STEP TWO: Determine Level of Commitment Needed	This is a *two-step* process. First determine how committed they are to the intended change. Second, determine what level of commitment you need from specific people.

STEP THREE: Estimate Critical Mass	Determine how many of those people are needed to implement the change. The number of people committed to make the change happen is called *critical mass*.
STEP FOUR: Get Commitment of Critical Mass	Ask the key people what it would take to get them to a 75% level of commitment.
STEP FIVE: Status Check to Monitor Level of Commitment.	*Status checking* refers to creating a monitoring system to identify progress in gaining commitment.

SOURCE: **Author adapted table from Merle Switzer, "Five Steps to Building Commitment for Change,"** *The Police Chief* **10 (October 2003): 54-56.**

"Policing in the twenty-first century will become more demanding and delicate new issues and problems create challenges for the police."[168] Excellent police leaders understand the need for vision, strategic and tactical planning. Strategy development based on threat analysis reveals cost efficient methods for personnel and logistical deployment. In addition, police planning develops appropriate proactive and reactive responses. Plan validation requires role-training exercises with neighboring agencies. Response plans require active implementation, plus constant review and evaluation.

CONCLUSION

Addressing community crime problems requires synchronization of all existing strategies into a holistic strategic formula: **(ILP) + (COP) + (POP) + COMPSTAT + QUALITY LEADERSHIP = POLICE EXCELLENCE.**

The formula provides the "strategic picture," deriving pathways to tactical solutions. The "Holistic Theory of Policing" allows current strategies to successfully serve communities, neighborhoods and citizens.

Life is full of speculation and risks, some calculated, others forced by the pressure of social change. Leaders who do not embrace social change face stagnation and failure. Those leaders who are able to face and challenge the forces of change, will survive. So much of what happens tomorrow is determined by what one chooses today.

Predicting the future is not without risk. However, a clear sense of vision enables one to understand the importance of "getting there." Aspiring leaders must envision the future to answer the basic question: Where are we going? This question provides leaders the road map for getting there.

Leaders who demonstrate trust are trusted by others. Developing mutual trust is the objective of every leader. Trust must precede any endeavor to lead so others may follow.

Endnotes

1   U.S. Department of Justice, Bureau of Justice Assistance, Understanding
     Community Policing (Washington DC: GPO, 1995), 5.

2   U.S. Department of Justice, Bureau of Justice Assistance, Neighborhood-
     Oriented Policing in Rural Communities: A Program Planning Guide
     (Washington, DC: GPO, 1994), 55.

3   Willard M. Oliver, "Community Policing Defined," Law and Order (August
     1992): 46.

4   Mollie Weatheritt, "Community Policing: Rhetoric or Reality," In
     Community Policing: Rhetoric or Reality, ed., Jack R. Green and Stephen
     D. Mastrofski (New York: Praeger Publishers, 1991), 153-175.

5   Weatheritt, 53-54.

6   Jerome H. Skolnick and David H. Bayley, National Institute of Justice,
     "Community Policing: Issues and Practices Around the World"
     (Washington, DC: GPO, 1988): 37.

7   Lee P. Brown, National Institute of Justice, "Community Policing: A
     Report From The Devil's Advocate" (Washington, DC: GPO, 1985): 1-5.

8   Robert Trojanowicz and Bonnie Bucqueroux, Community Policing: A
     Contemporary Perspective (Cincinnati, Ohio: Anderson Publishing
     Company, 1994).

9   Trojanowicz., 5.

10   Herman Goldstein, Problem Oriented Policing: A Practical Guide for
     Police Officers (New York: McGraw-Hill Publishing Company, 1990).

11   Goldstein, 20.

12   Goldstein, 20.

13   Goldstein, 66.

14   Bureau of Justice Assistance, Understanding Community Policing, 5.

15   D. P. Rosenbaum, "The Theory of Research Behind Neighborhood Watch,"
     Crime and Delinquency (33, 1987): 103-134.

16   National Crime Prevention Institute, Understanding Crime Prevention
     (MA, Butterworth Publisher, 1986), 201.

17   B. W. Tuckman, "Development Sequence in Small Groups," Psychological
     Bulletin (63 June, 1965): 6.

18   Jon P. Howell and Dan Costley, Understanding Behavior for Effective
     Leadership (Upper Saddle River, New Jersey: Prentice Hall, 2001).

     SPECIAL NOTE: Endnotes 17 and 18 have been integrated and
     synthesized. In addition, the author's comments have been included in
     the section on stages of group development.

19   SPECIAL NOTE: The section on the Neighborhood Watch: Leadership
     Challenge was originally written for this book while the author was
     working on a Department of Justice Grant. The article was later

published based upon a grant issued by the Office of Community-Oriented Policing Services (COPPS): Thomas E. Baker, Jane P. Baker, and Ralph Zezza, "Neighborhood Watch: Leadership Challenge," The FBI Law Enforcement Bulletin (February 1999): 12-18.

20   Fred Himelfarb, "Rediscovering Ethics," The Police Chief (February 1995): 24.

21   Nair Keshavan, A Higher Standard of Leadership (San Francisco: Berret-Koehler Publishers, 1994), 1-22.

22   Robert Wasserman and Mark H. Moore, National Institute of Justice, "Values in Policing: Perspectives on Policing." Washington, DC: GPO and John F. Kennedy School of Government, Harvard University. 1998: 1, 3.

23   Keshavan, A Higher Standard of Leadership, 13-34.

24   Saul Gellerman, "Why Good Managers Make Bad Ethical Choices," Harvard Business Review 7 (1986).

25   Arnold Mitchell, The Nine American Lifestyles (New York: Macmillan Publishing, 1983), 33.

26   Paul M. Whiseand and R. Fred Ferguson, The Managing of Police Organizations (Upper Saddle River, New Jersey: Prentice-Hall, 1996), 29.

27   Ronnie Garner,"Leadership in the Nineties," FBI Law Enforcement Bulletin, 12 (Winter, 1993): 2.

28   James M. Kouzes and Barry Z. Posner, The Leadership Challenge: How To Get Extraordinary Things Done in Organizations (San Francisco: Jossey-Bass, 1988), 87.

29   D.J. Van Meter, "Your Agency's Driving Force: Mission and Its Value," Law and Order (August 1991): 65-66.

30   Garner, 2.

31   Garner, 2.

32   Garner, 2.

33   David C. Couper and Sabine H. Lobitz, "Leadership for Change: A National Agenda," The Police Chief (December 1993): 15.

34   Randall Aragon, "A Chief's Survival Kit," Law and Order (November 1993): 67-68.

35   Leonard G. Wood,"What Do City Managers Expect?" The Police Chief (April 1988): 36-38.

36   Ronald G. Lynch, The Police Manager (New York: Random House, 1998), 154-155.

37   J. French and B. H. Raven, "The Bases of Social Power" In Studies of Social Power, ed., D. Cartwright (Ann Arbor: Institute for Social Research, 1959).

38   Richard L. Hughes, Robert C. Ginnett and Gordon J. Curphy, Leadership: Enhancing the Lessons of Experience (Illinois: Richard D. Irwin, Inc., 1993), 116-119.

39   Paul Hersey, Kenneth H. Blanchard and Dewey E. Johnson, <u>Management of Organizational Behavior</u>: Utilizing Human Resources (Upper Saddle River, New Jersey: Prentice-Hall), 2000, 3.

40   Luther Gulick, "Notes on the Theory of Organization," In the papers on The <u>Science of Administration</u>, ed., Luther Gulick and L. Urwick, (New York: August M. Kelly, 1969 reprint of the 1937 edition), 13.

41   Donald C. Withham, "Environmental Scanning Pays Off," <u>The Police Chief</u>, 3 (March 1991): 29-31.

42   Chris Braiden, "Leadership: Not What (or Where) We Think," Law Enforcement News (April 15, 1994): 14-16.

43   Arend Sandbulte, "Lead, Don't Manage," <u>Industry Week</u> (November 1, 1993): 16-18.

44   Thomas Gee, "Are You a Management Cop?," <u>The Police Chief</u>, (April 1990): 151-152.

45   U.S. Department Justice, How Police Supervisory Skills Influence Police Behaviors (Washington DC: GPO, 2003), 1; R. Engel, "Patrol Officer Supervision in the Community Policing Era," <u>Journal of Criminal Justice</u> 30(1) (January/February 2002): 51-64.

46   George L. Kelling and William Bratton, National Institute on Justice, Perspectives on Policing, "Implementing Community Policing: The Administrative Problem" (Washington DC: GPO 1993): 9.

47   Herman Goldstein, National Institute of Justice, <u>Research in Brief</u>, "The New Policing: Confronting Complexity" (Washington DC: GPO December 1993): 5.

48   Alan M. Webber, "Crime and Management: An Interview with New York City Police Commissioner Lee P. Brown," <u>Harvard Business Review</u> (May-June 1991): 32.

49   Keith M. Rippy, "Effective Followership," <u>The Police Chief</u>, 9 (September 1990): 22-24

50   Terrence L. Rock, "On Being an Employee-Oriented Company," <u>Industry Week</u> (November 1, 1993): 35.

51   David C. Couper and Sabine H. Lobitz, "Leadership for Change: A National Agenda," <u>The Police Chief</u>, 12 (December 1993): 15-19.

52   Roger Fulton, "Surrounding Yourself With Confidence," <u>Law Enforcement Technology</u>, 10 (October 1994): 82.

53   William C. Byham and Jeff Cox, <u>Zap! The Lighting of Empowerment: How to Improve Quality Productivity, and Employee Satisfaction</u> (New York, New York: Fawcett Columbine, 1997).

54   Steve Bucholz and Thomas Roth, <u>Creating the High-Performance Team</u> (New York: John Wiley and Sons 1987), 3.

55   M.S. Wadia and Bill Kolender, "Holistic Management: A Behavioral Theory of Successful Leadership," <u>The Police Chief</u>, 3 (April 1988): 86-88.

56   Bucholz and Roth, <u>Creating The High Performance</u> Team, 14.

57   Warren Bennis and Burt Nanus, <u>Leaders: The Strategies for Taking Charge</u> (New York: Harper & Row 1997), 224-225.

58   Braiden, "Leadership: Not What (or Where) We Think," 14-16.

59   William Ouchi, <u>Theory Z: How American Business Can Meet the Japanese Challenge</u> (Reading Mass: Addison-Wesley, 1982).

60   W. Edwards Deming, <u>Out of Crisis</u> (Cambridge, MA: MIT, 2000); Joseph M. Juran, <u>Juran on Planning for Quality</u> (New York: Free Press, 1988).

61   H.P. Hatry and J.M. Greiner, National Institute of Justice, "How Police Departments Can Better Apply Management-by-Objectives and Quality-Circle Programs (Washington, DC: GPO, 1984).

62   L. Griener, "Antecedents of Planned Change," <u>Journal of Applied Behavioral Sciences</u>, 21 (1967): 51-86.

63   Rosebeth Moss Kanter, <u>The Change Masters: Innovation for Productivity</u> (New York: Simon and Schuster, 1983), 101.

64   Wally Bock, "Generals Win Battles But Sergeants Win Wars," <u>Law and Order</u> (May, 1993): 39-40.

65   Mary Ann Wycoff, "Evaluation Report on Training for First-Line Supervisors: A Program Conducted for the City of Minneapolis," <u>The Police Foundation</u> (December, 1992).

66   John Van Maaen, "The Boss: First-Line Supervision in an American Police Agency," <u>In Control in the Police Organization</u>, ed. Maurice Punch, 1983 (Cambridge Mass.: MIT Press.), 275-317.

67   Jim Weaver, "Supervising the Veteran Officer," <u>The Police Chief</u> (February, 1990): 47-49.

68   James M. Burns, <u>Leadership</u> (New York: Harper and Row, 1978), 19-20.

69   Paul Whiseand and George Rush, <u>Supervising Police Personnel</u> (Upper Saddle River, New Jersey: Prentice-Hall, 1988).

70   Paul Hersey and Ken Blanchard, <u>Management of Organizational Behavior: Utilizing Human Resources</u> (Upper Saddle River, New Jersey: Prentice-Hall, 1996), 366-368 and Instructor Manual; Paul Hersey, Ken Blanchard and Dewey E. Johnson, <u>Management of Organizational Behavior: Utilizing Human Resources</u> (Upper Saddle River, New Jersey: Prentice-Hall, 2000).

71   Hersey and Blanchard, 366-368.

72   Hersey and Blanchard, 366-368.

73   Hersey and Blanchard, 366-368.

74   Hersey and Blanchard, 366-368.

75   Hersey and Blanchard, 366-368.

76   Hersey and Blanchard, 366-368.

77   David M. Mozee, "Motivation of Police Personnel: A Different Approach," <u>Law and Order</u> (May 1989): 24-26.

78 Edward A. Thibault, Lawrence M. Lynch and R. Bruce McBride, Proactive Leadership (Upper Saddle River: New Jersey, 2001).

79 J.P. Campell and R. D. Pritchard, "Motivation Theory in Industrial and Organizational Psychology," The Handbook of Industrial and Organizational Psychology, ed. M.D. Dunnettee, (Chicago: Rand McNally, 1976), 60-130.

80 Steven J. Sarver, "Twelve Steps to Getting the Most Out of Your Employees," The Chief of Police, 10 (October 2003): 46-52.

81 John J. Fay, "Setting and Achieving Professional Goals," Security Management (February 1992): 18-19.

82 E. A. Locke and G. P. Latham, "Work Motivation and Satisfaction: Light at the End of the Tunnel," Psychological Science (January 1990): 240-246.

83 Victor H. Vroom, Work and Motivation (New York: Wiley, 1964); Victor H. Vroom, Leadership and Decision-Making," Organizational Dynamics (Spring 2000): 82-94.

84 Shari Caudron, "Motivation? Money's Only No. 2," Industry Week (November 15, 1993): 33.

85 Richard L. Hughes, Robert C. Ginnett and Gordon J. Curphy, Leadership: Enhancing the Lessons of Experience (Illinois: Richard D. Irwin, Inc., 2002), 278.

86 Kenneth Blanchard and Spencer Johnson, The One Minute Manager (New York: Morrow, 1992), 44.

87 Blanchard and Johnson, 59.

88 Robert R. Johnson, "Constructive Corrections Benefits: The Agency and the Officer," Law and Order (September 1993): 125-128.

89 Robert Trojanowicz, Bonnie Bucqueroux, and Ron Sloan, "Making the Transition to Mission Driven Training," The Police Chief (November 1993): 16-25.

90 Tim Jones, Compton Owens, and Melissa Smith, "Police Ethics Training: A Three-Tiered Approach," The FBI Law Enforcement Bulletin (June 1995): 24-26.

91 Ralph Galvin and Bruce Sokolove, "A Strategic Planning Approach to Law Enforcement Training," The Police Chief (November 1989): 18-19.

92 Jack Molden, "Training as a Management Function," Law and Order (September 1992): 17.

93 John Fay, Approaches to Criminal Justice Training (Georgia: Carl Vinson Institute of Government, 1988), 169.

94 Anthony J. Pinizzotto and Edward F. Davis, "Killed in the Line of Duty: Procedural and Training Issues," FBI Law Enforcement Bulletin (March 1995): 3.

95 Thomas S. Staton, How to Instruct Successfully: Modern Teaching Methods in Adult Education (New York: McGraw Hill Book Company, 1960).

96   Jack Molden, "Characteristics of an Effective Trainer: Eight Practices for Excellence," Law and Order (March 1994): 10.

97   Lois Pilant, "High-Tech Training," The Police Chief (July 1994): 29-30.

98   Robert W. Pike, Creative Training Techniques Handbook (Minnesota: Lakewood Books, 2003), 15.

99   O. Glenn Stahl and Richard A. Staufenberger, Police Personnel (Washington, DC: Police Foundation, 1974), 111.

100 David W. Belcher and Thomas Atchison, Compensation Administration (New Jersey: Prentice Hall, 1987), 175.

101 Ralph S. Osborn, "Police Recruitment: Today's Standard–Tomorrow's Challenge," FBI Law Enforcement Bulletin (June 1992): 21-14.

102 Daniel Goleman, Emotional Intelligence: Why It Matters More Than IQ (New York, New York: Bantam Books, 1995), 34.

103 Goleman, 36.

104 Donald H. Weiss, Managing Conflict (New York: AMACOM, 1981): 11.

105 Dan DeStephen, "Mediating Those Office Conflicts," Management Solutions (New York: March, 1988): 5

106 Rensis Likert and Jane Gibson, New Ways of Managing Conflict (New York: McGraw-Hill, 1976), 7-8.

107 Jim Murphy, Managing Conflict at Work (New York: Irwin/Mirror Press, 1994), 15.

108 Mary Parson, "Peer Conflict," Supervisory Management, (May, 1986): 25.

109 Parson, 31.

110 Murphy, "Managing Conflict at Work," 7.

111 Larry Cipolla, "Coping with Personality Clashes," Minnesota Business Journal (December, 1983): 67.

112 Kurt Lewin, "Group Decision and Social Change," Readings in Social Psychology, ed.,. E.E. Maccoby, T.M. Newcomb, and E.C. Hartley (New York: Holt, Rinehart and Winston, 1958), 197-212.

113 Stephen P. Covey, The Seven Habits of Highly Effective People (New York: Simon and Schuster, 1990), 207.

114 Joseph Billy, Jr. and Ronald J. Stupak, "Conflict Management and the Law Enforcement Professional in the 1990's," Law and Order (May, 1994): 39-43.

115 Billy and Stupak, 40.

116 Harry P. Dolan, "Coping with Internal Backlash," The Police Chief (March, 1994): 49-50.

117 Isaac Fulwood, "Community Empowerment Policing," The Police Chief (May, 1990): 49-50.

118 Timothy N. Oettmeier and Lee P. Brown, "Developing A Neighborhood Policing Style," In Community Policing: Rhetoric or Reality, eds. Jack R. Green and Stephen D. Mastrofski (New York: Praeger Publishers, 1991), 126-127.

119 Ottmeier and Brown, 127.

120 Charles M. Mottley, Strategy in Planning: Planning, Programming, Budgeting: A System Approach To Management, ed., J.F. Lyden and E.S. Miller (Chicago, Ill.: Markham, 1972), 1.

121 John M. Bryson, Strategic Planning for Public and Nonprofit Organizations: A Guide To Strengthening and Sustaining Organizational Achievement (San Francisco: Jossey Bass, 1995), 163.

122 Bryson, 48-62.

123 Bryson discussed seven steps of strategic planning. The author comments under each of Bryson's steps. Bryson originally identified eight steps.

124 Robert Cushman, Department of Justice, Criminal Justice Planning for Local Governments (Washington, D.C.: U.S. GPO, 1980): 4.

125 Cushman, 26.

126 Wayne W. Bennett and Karen M. Hess, Management and Supervision in Law Enforcement (St. Paul: West Publishing Company, 1996), 151-185.

127 Herman Goldstein, Problem-Oriented Policing (New York: McGraw-Hill, 1990), 32.

128 U.S. Department of Justice, Bureau of Justice Assistance, Neighborhood-Oriented Policing in Rural Areas: A Program Planning Guide (Washington DC, GPO, August 1994, 44.

129 B. D. Cummings, "Problem-Oriented Policing and Crime-Specific Planning," The Chief of Police, March 1990: 63.

130 W. Spellman and J.E. Eck, "Sitting Ducks, Ravenous Wolves, and Helping Hands: New Approaches to Urban Policing," Public Affairs Comment (Austin, Texas: School of Public Affairs, University of Texas, 1989).

131 Spellman and Eck, 344.

132 Paul J. Brantingham and Patricia L. Brantingham, Patterns in Crime (New York: Macmillian, 1984), 345.

133 Brantingham and Brantingham, 345.

134 Wayne W. Bennett and Karen M. Hess, Management and Supervision in Law Enforcement, 192.

135 George L. Kelling and Mark H. Moore, National Institute of Justice and Harvard University, "The Evolving Strategy of Policing" (Washington DC: GPO, 1988): 11.

136 Hersey, Blanchard and Johnson, Management of Organizational Behaviors, 344-354.

137 Hersey and Blanchard, 1996, 344-354.

138 Hersey and Blanchard, 1999, 344-354.

139 HQ TRADOC, Fm 22-100, Military Leadership (Washington, DC: Department of the Army, 1983), 50.

140 National Criminal Intelligence Service, United Kingdom, The National Intelligence Model (London, England, 2000): 8.

141 United Kingdom Home Office, "Operational Policing: National Intelligence Model," Internet URL, London England, 2006.

142 National Criminal Intelligence Service, United Kingdom, The National Intelligence Model (London, England, 2000).

143 Joseph R. Fuentes, et al., and New Jersey State Police: Practical Guide to Intelligence Led Policing, the Center of Policing Terrorism at the Manhattan Institute, September 2006, 3.

144 International Association of Law Enforcement Intelligence Analysts, Law Enforcement Analytical Standards, November 2004: 3. International Association of Law Enforcement Intelligence Analysts, Booklet Committee, Intelligence-Led Policing: Getting Started, January 2005: 3.

145 Global Intelligence Working Group, National Criminal Intelligence Sharing Plan, October 2003, 2.

146 Joseph Luft, Group Process: An Introduction to Group Dynamics (California: National Press Books.

147 Marilyn Peterson, U.S. Department of Justice, Bureau of Justice Assistance, Intelligence-Led Policing: The New Intelligence Architecture (Washington, DC: GPO, 2005): vii.

148 Thomas E. Baker, Intelligence-Led Policing: Leadership, Strategies, & Tactics (Flushing, New York: Looseleaf Law Publications, Inc.): 297.

149 Douglas Paton, Karena Burke, John M. Violanti, and Anne Gehrke, Traumatic Stress in Police Officers: A Career-Length Assessment from Recruitment to Retirement (Springfield, Illinois: Charles C. Thomas, Publishers, 2009).

150 Glen H. Elder, Perspectives on the Life Course, In ed., G. H. Elder, Life Course Dynamics, (pp. 23-49), (Ithaca, NY., Cornell University Press, 1985).

151 Gerald G.Turkewitz, and Darlynne, A. Devenney, Developmental Time and Timing, (Hillsdale, NJ: Erlbaum, 1993).

152 Thomas Peters, Thriving on Chaos (New York: Alfred A. Knopf, 1997), 22.

153 W. Edwards Deming, The American Who Taught the Japanese About Quality (New York: Simon & Schuster, 1991).

154 Paul M. Whisenand and R. Fred Ferguson, The Managing of Police Organizations (New Jersey: Simon & Schuster Company, 2001), 1.

155 Timothy S. Bynum, U.S. Department of Justice, Office of Community-Oriented Policing, Using Analysis for Problem-Solving: A Guidebook for Law Enforcement (Washington, DC: GPO September, 2001), 11-17.

156 Salvatore R. Maddi, "The Story of Hardiness: Twenty Years of Theorizing, Research, and Practice," Consulting Psychology Journal, 54 (2001): 175-185.

157   Douglas Paton, "Disaster Relief Work: An Assessment of Training Effectiveness," Journal of Traumatic Stress, 7 (1994): 275-288.

158   Douglas Paton, and Rhona Flin, "Disaster Stress: An Emergency Management Perspective," Disaster Prevention and Management, 8 (1999): 261-167.

159   Cynthia Mamalian and Nancy La Vigne, U.S. Department of Justice, National Institute of Justice, "The Use of Computerized Mapping by Law Enforcement Survey Results," Research Review (Washington, DC: GPO, 1999), 2.

160   Keith Clarke, Getting Started with Geographic Information Systems (New Jersey: Prentice-Hall, 2001), 210.

161   Dan Helms, "Trendspotting: Serial Crime Detection with GIS," Crime Mapping News (Spring 2000): 1-4.

162   Ronald V. Clarks, Policing and Reducing Crime Unit, Police, Research Series, Paper 112, "Hot Products: Understanding, Anticipating, and Reducing Demand for Stolen Goods" (London: Home Office, 1999).

163   Career Criminal Apprehension Program: Program Guidelines (Sacramento, CA: Office of Criminal Justice Planning, 1992), 8.

164   Rudolph W. Giuliani and Howard Safir, COMPSTAT: Leadership in Action (New York: New York City Police Department, 1997), 2-7.

165   Philip E. Taylor and Stephen J. Huxley, "A Break from Tradition for the San Francisco Police: Patrol Officer Scheduling Using an Optimization-Based Decision Support System," Interfaces, 19, no. 1 (January – February 1989): 4.

166   Phyllis P. McDonald, "Implementing COMPSTAT: Critical Points To Consider," The Police Chief, 1 (January 2004): 33.

167   Merle Switzer, "Five Steps to Building Commitment for Change," The Police Chief, 10 (October 2003): 54-56.

168   Edwin Meese and P.J. Ortmeier, Leadership, Ethics and Policing (Upper Saddle River, New Jersey: Prentice-Hall, 2004), 276.

Chapter 14

Appendix A
LAW ENFORCEMENT
CODE OF ETHICS

As a law enforcement officer, my fundamental duty is to serve the community; to safeguard lives and property; to protect the innocent from deception, the weak against oppression or intimidation and the peaceful against violence or disorder; and to respect the constitutional rights of all to liberty, equality and justice.

I will keep my private life unsullied as an example to all and will behave in a manner that does not bring discredit to me or my agency. I will maintain courageous calm in the face of danger, scorn or ridicule; develop self-restraint; and be constantly mindful of the welfare of others. Honest in thought and deed both in my personal and official life, I will be exemplary in obeying the law and regulations of my department. Whatever I see or hear of a confidential nature or that is confided to me in my official capacity will be kept ever secret unless revelation is necessary in the performance of my duty.

I will never act officiously or permit personal feelings, prejudices, political beliefs, aspirations, animosities or friendships to influence my decisions. With no compromise for crime and with relentless prosecution of criminals, I will enforce the law courteously and appropriately without fear or favor, malice or will, never employing unnecessary force or violence and never accepting gratuities.

I recognize the badge of my office as a symbol of public faith, and I accept it as a public trust to be held so long as I am true to the ethics of police service. I will never engage in acts of corruption or bribery, nor will I condone such acts by other police officers. I will cooperate with all legally authorized agencies and their representatives in the pursuit of justice.

I know that I alone am responsible for my own standard of professional performance and will take every reasonable opportunity to enhance and improve my level of knowledge and competence.

I will constantly strive to achieve these objectives and ideals, dedicating myself before God to my chosen profession...law enforcement.

SOURCE: The International Association of Chiefs of Police, Originally written 1957, amended 1989.

Appendix B
POLICE CODE OF CONDUCT

All law enforcement officers must be fully aware of the ethical responsibilities of their position and must strive constantly to live up to the highest possible standards of professional policing.

The International Association of Chiefs of Police believes it important that police officers have clear advice and counsel available to assist them in performing their duties consistent with these standards, and has adopted the following ethical mandates as guidelines to meet these ends.

Primary Responsibilities of a Police Officer

A police officer acts as an official representative of government who is required and trusted to work within the law. The officer's powers and duties are conferred by statute. The fundamental duties of a police officer include serving the community, safeguarding lives and property, protecting the innocent, keeping the peace and ensuring the rights of all to liberty, equality and justice.

Performance of the Duties of a Police Officer

A police officer shall perform all duties impartially, without favor or affection or ill will and without regard to status, sex, race, religion, political belief or aspiration. All citizens will be treated equally with courtesy, consideration and dignity.

Officers will never allow personal feelings, animosities or friendships to influence official conduct. Laws will be enforced appropriately and courteously and, in carrying out their responsibilities, officers will strive to obtain maximum cooperation from the public. They will conduct themselves in appearance and deportment in such a manner as to inspire confidence and respect for the position of public trust they hold.

Discretion

A police officer will use responsibly the discretion vested in his position and exercise it within the law. The principle of reasonableness will guide the officer's determinations, and the officer will consider all surrounding circumstances in determining whether any legal action shall be taken.

Consistent and wise use of discretion, based on professional policing competence, will do much to preserve good relationships and retain the confidence of the public. There can be difficulty in choosing between conflicting courses of action. It is important to remember that a timely word of advice rather than arrest—which may be correct in appropriate circumstances—can be a more effective means of achieving a desired end.

Use of Force

A police officer will never employ unnecessary force or violence and will use only such force in the discharge of duty as is reasonable in all circumstances.

The use of force should be used only with the greatest restraint and only after discussion, negotiation and persuasion have been found to be inappropriate or ineffective. While the use of force is occasionally unavoidable, every police officer will refrain from unnecessary infliction of pain or suffering and will never engage in cruel, degrading or inhuman treatment of any person.

Confidentiality

Whatever a police officer sees, hears or learns, that is of a confidential nature, will be kept secret unless the performance of duty or legal provision requires otherwise. Members of the public have a right to security and privacy and information obtained about them must not be improperly divulged.

Integrity

A police officer will not engage in acts of corruption or bribery, nor will an officer condone such acts by other police officers. The public demands that the integrity of police officers be above reproach. Police officers must, therefore, avoid any conduct that might compromise integrity and thus undercut the public confidence in a law enforcement agency. Officers will refuse to accept any gifts, presents, subscriptions, favors, gratuities or promises that could be interpreted as seeking to cause the officer to refrain from performing official responsibilities honestly and within the law. Police officers must not receive private or special advantage from their official status. Respect from the public cannot be bought; it can only be earned and cultivated.

Cooperation with Other Police Officers and Agencies

Police officers will cooperate with all legally authorized agencies and their representatives in the pursuit of justice. An officer or agency may be one among many organizations that may provide law enforcement services to a jurisdiction. It is imperative that a police officer assist colleagues fully and completely with respect and consideration at all times.

Personal-Professional Capabilities

Police officers will be responsible for their own standard of professional performance and will take every reasonable opportunity to enhance and improve their level of knowledge and competence. Through study and experience, a police officer can acquire the high level of knowledge and competence that is essential for the efficient and effective performance of duty. The acquisition of knowledge is a never-ending process of personal and professional development that should be pursued constantly.

Private Life

Police officers will behave in a manner that does not bring discredit to their agencies or themselves. A police officer's character and conduct while off duty must always be exemplary, thus maintaining a position of respect in the community in which he or she lives and serves. The officer's personal behavior must be beyond reproach.

Reprinted with permission of The International Association of Chiefs of Police, adopted by the IACP in 1992.

Appendix C
CANONS OF POLICE ETHICS

INTERNATIONAL ASSOCIATION OF CHIEFS OF POLICE

Article 1. Primary Responsibility of Job

The primary responsibility of the police service, and of the individual officer, is the protection of the people of the United States through the upholding of their laws; chief among these is the Constitution of the United States and its amendments. The law enforcement officer always represents the whole of the community and its legally expressed will and is never the arm of any political party or clique.

Article 2. Limitations of Authority

The first duty of a law enforcement officer, as upholder of the law, is to know its bounds upon him in enforcing it. Because he represents the legal will of the community, be it local, state or federal, he must be aware of the limitations and prescriptions which the people, through law, have placed upon him. He must recognize the genius of the American system of government which gives to no man, groups of men, or institution, absolute power, and he must insure that he, as a prime defender of that system, does not pervert its character.

Article 3. Duty to be Familiar With the Law and with Responsibilities of Self and Other Public Officials

The law enforcement officer shall assiduously apply himself to the study of the principles of the laws which he is sworn to uphold. He will make certain of his responsibilities in the particulars of their enforcement, seeking aid from his superiors in matters of technicality or principle when these are not clear to him; he will make special effort to fully understand his relationship to other public officials, including other law enforcement agencies, particularly on matters of jurisdiction, both geographically and substantively.

Article 4. Utilization of Proper Means To Gain Proper Ends

The law enforcement officer shall be mindful of his responsibility to pay strict heed to the selection of means in discharging the duties of his office. Violations of law or disregard for public safety and property on the part of an officer are intrinsically wrong; they are self-defeating in that they instill in the public mind a like disposition. The employment of illegal means, no matter how worthy the end, is certain to encourage disrespect for the law and its officers. If the law is to be honored, it must first be honored by those who enforce it.

Article 5. Cooperation with Public Officials in the Discharge of their Authorized Duties

The law enforcement officer shall cooperate fully with other public officials in the discharge of authorized duties, regardless of party affiliation or personal prejudice. He shall be meticulous, however, in assuring himself of the propriety, under the law, of such actions and shall guard against the use of his office or person, whether knowingly or unknowingly, in any improper or illegal action. In any situation open to question he shall seek authority from his superior officer, giving him a full report of the proposed service or action.

Article 6. Private Conduct

The law enforcement officer shall be mindful of his special identification by the public as an upholder of the law. Laxity of conduct or manner in private life, expressing either disrespect for the law or seeking to gain special privilege, cannot best reflect upon the police officer and the police service. The community and the service require that the law enforcement officer lead the life of a decent and honorable man. Following the career of a policeman gives no man special perquisites. It does give the satisfaction and pride of following and furthering an unbroken tradition of safeguarding the American republic. The officer who reflects upon this tradition will not degrade it. Rather, he will so conduct his private life that the public will regard him as an example of stability, fidelity and morality.

Article 7. Conduct Toward the Public

The law enforcement officer, mindful of his responsibility to the whole community, shall deal with individuals of the community in a manner calculated to instill respect for its laws and its police service. The law enforcement officer shall conduct his official life in a manner such as will inspire confidence and trust. Thus, he will be neither overbearing nor subservient, as no individual citizen has an obligation to stand in awe of him nor a right to command him. The officer will give service where he can, and require compliance with the law. He will do neither from personal preference or prejudice but rather as a duly appointed officer of the law discharging his sworn obligation.

Article 8. Conduct in Arresting and Dealing with Law Violators

The law enforcement officer shall use his powers of arrest strictly in accordance with the law and with due regard to the rights of the citizen concerned. His office gives him no right to prosecute the violator nor to mete out punishment for the offense. He shall, at all times, have a clear appreciation of his responsibilities and limitations regarding detention of the violator; he shall conduct himself in such a manner as will minimize the possibility of having to use force. To this end he shall cultivate a dedication to the service of the people and the equitable upholding of their laws whether in the handling of law violators or in dealing with the law-abiding.

Article 9. Gifts and Favors

The law enforcement officer, representing government, bears the heavy responsibility of maintaining, in his own conduct, the honor and integrity of all government institutions. He shall, therefore, guard against placing himself in a position in which any person can expect special consideration or in which the public can reasonably assume that special consideration is being given. Thus, he should be firm in refusing gifts, favors, or gratuities, large or small, which can, in the public mind, be interpreted as capable of influencing his judgment in the discharge of his duties.

Article 10. Presentation of Evidence

The law enforcement officer shall be concerned equally in the prosecution of the wrong-doer and the defense of the innocent. He shall ascertain what constitutes evidence and shall present such evidence impartially and without malice. In so doing, he will ignore social, political, and all other distinctions among the persons involved, strengthening the tradition of the reliability and integrity of an officer's word. The law enforcement officer shall take special pains to increase his perception and skill of observation, mindful that in many situations his is the sole impartial testimony to the facts of a case.

Article 11. Attitude Toward Profession

The law enforcement officer shall regard the discharge of his duties as a public trust and recognize his responsibility as a public servant. By diligent study and sincere attention to self-improvement he shall strive to make the best possible application of science to the solution of crime and, in the field of human relationships, strive for effective leadership and public influence in matters affecting public safety. He shall appreciate the importance and responsibility of his office, and hold police work to be an honorable profession rendering valuable service to his community and his country.

SOURCE: The International Association of Chiefs of Police

INDEX

Index 303